FIND THE KEY MAN

Other Putnam books by Hal Higdon

PRO FOOTBALL, U.S.A.

FINDING THE GROOVE

THIRTY DAYS IN MAY

SIX SECONDS TO GLORY

Hal Higdon

FIND THE KEY MAN

G. P. Putnam's Sons, New York

*For my sister-in-law Bea and my
brother-in-law Lou Fabbricatore, even though
he is a New York Knicks fan.*

Contents

Illustrations will be found following page 96

viii

Introduction

Basketball is a game that can be enjoyed on many levels. First of all, it is an art form akin to ballet. If you don't think so, then you have never watched Connie Hawkins make his move to the basket, or Kareem Abdul-Jabbar let fly with his sky hook, or Walt Frazier spin while dribbling the ball. There is a rhythm also to the sport, a pulsating beat. The tattoo sound of a basketball being dribbled downcourt echoes through arenas like the beat of a jazz band. When two running teams like the Boston Celtics and Capital Bullets meet, they blend together to form one pendulum that swings from one end of the court to the other, and the pace is so intense that you wonder how any athlete can endure such stress.

Tom Heinsohn, coach of the Celtics, says: "Basketball is a game that is a combination of ballet and wrestling." Indeed, it is a game more violent, more frightening than professional football, whose competitors are sheathed in medieval-like armor. It is more so even than auto racing, whose moments of physical crisis occur sporadically and often somewhere off in the distance. You don't get the full feel of the tall man's game on television. You get it only partially if you sit in the ordinary seats. To fully appreciate how physical pro basketball is you almost have to sit courtside and watch, listen, and feel the way two NBA centers attack each other for position on the floor. It is like dinosaurs clashing.

While giving the appearance of being totally chaotic (after

all, the players don't go into a huddle before each play), basketball is actually highly structured. It is a game where success depends more on intelligent execution than mere technique. "The average fan doesn't realize the strategy that goes on," says Virginia Squires center Jim Eakins, "the plays you try and run at certain times for certain situations, and the things you try to do out there."

I feel I only recently have come fully to appreciate the sport of basketball. While attending high school games for pleasure, I had been absorbed analytically with several other sports. Soon after my arrival in Michigan City I began work on a book about professional football entitled *Pro Football, U.S.A.* that sought to gain for my readers some insight into how that game is played, how each player operates at his position. I interviewed players such as Joe Namath, Roman Gabriel, Gale Sayers, Buck Buchanan, Nick Buoniconti, a total of forty-six in all. "Even though most players were being interviewed day after day by newspaper reporters and television broadcasters," I wrote in the introduction to that book, "I found many of them eager—and even excited—to consider a subject which, surprisingly, they don't get the opportunity to discuss in depth. Yet it became obvious from their answers that it was a subject that occupied their thoughts almost constantly both during and after the season. The simple question I posed to most of those featured in this book was: How do you play your position? Apparently this topic is broached only rarely during the daily give-and-take between pro players and the press."

Following the success of that book, I moved on to another sport, that of auto racing. In *Finding the Groove*, I sat down with Mario Andretti, Richard Petty, Don Prudhomme, Peter Revson, Bobby Unser, a total of twenty-eight drivers, and this time my basic question was: How do you go fast around a racetrack? Again, their tape-recorded responses provided fascinating reading. I rarely had to ask many secondary questions in these interviews; my technique being to simply sit back, shut up, and let the athlete involved take the discussion in whichever direction he chose.

Finally, in my quest to understand the major sports of our day, I have come to basketball, and while in sheer numbers more people attend high school and college games each year, the obvious fountainhead of knowledge is in the professional ranks. In this book I have spoken with the top professionals —Walt Frazier, George McGinnis, Jim McMillian, Spencer Haywood, Dave Cowens, a total of forty-two—asking them again a single, key question: How do you play your position? Their answers make up the bulk of the text of this book: *Find the Key Man.*

On the surface basketball has only three positions: guard, center, and forward. There are two guards, and they generally bring the ball downcourt. Frequently they will pass first to the center, who stands in the middle, and around whom most plays revolve. He may shoot or pass the ball out to one of the two forwards who on many teams do most of the scoring. These are the basic positions on offense, and since there is insufficient time for platooning after the ball changes hands, each offensive player also must play defense.

But there are subtle variations from position to position in the game of basketball. There are penetrating guards (Nate Archibald), shooting guards (Gail Goodrich), and blocking guards (Jerry Sloan). Some centers play with their backs to the baskets (Nate Thurmond) and others (Dave Cowens) play facing it. The offenses of some teams revolve around a good shooting center (Bob Lanier with Detroit), whereas the offenses of other teams revolve around a center who rarely takes a shot (Clifford Ray of Chicago). You have forwards who play on the inside (Dan Issel, Elvin Hayes) and forwards who play on the outside (Tom Van Arsdale, Lou Hudson). Then there is an almost independent position that might be described as swing forward or swing guard, depending on your point of view. Mike Riordan and Austin Carr play essentially the same position although one is listed at forward and the other as guard. Riordan describes himself as a third guard on his team; Carr considers himself a third forward. Football fans have become educated to the fact that instead of merely having ends, we now have tight ends, split ends, flankers, and defensive ends, not to mention outside linebackers who are really ends. Basketball positions may someday also subdivide.

Yet basketball, more than any other sport, is a game of improvisation. The duties of each player depend less on the letter (G, C, or F) behind his name than they do on his own particular talents, how they blend with the style of his team, and the philosophy of his coach. For this reason, I have not attempted to organize the following interviews by position, but instead have let them fall into place in much the order in which they occurred. My knowledge gained about professional basketball was cumulative, as I moved from player to player. The first person interviewed was Walt Frazier and had he been the last, the talk might have been conducted at an entirely different level.

The key to understanding basketball, however, is not merely to listen to what the pros have to say about the game, but also to see them play it. At the risk of becoming a shill for ticket sales, you cannot see enough of the game on television. There is a very simple reason: The cameras always follow the ball. Too much occurs away from the ball to be easily condensed onto a 21-inch screen. In my interview with George McGinnis, he talks about attending basketball games and focusing his attention on a single player. "When I go to a basketball game I never cheer," he says. "I sit there and try to watch the positions."

I suggest you do the same. Many basketball players, particularly forwards, talk about moving without the ball. By this, they mean the series of fakes and moves that they must make to get open so they can receive a pass and shoot. You can't watch a player moving without the ball if you are watching the ball, because he may be going through his gyrations on the other side of the court. Or he may be merely standing, resting, waiting for the precise moment to make his move. You also can get a better appreciation for the amount of contact present in professional basketball by watching what happens away from the ball, because a lot of the shoving, holding, and elbowing occurs when the attention of everybody—including the referee—is diverted to another part of the court. "If you just sit down and keep your eye on the two centers the whole ball game and try not to watch the ball," says McGinnis, "you'd be surprised how much pushing and shoving go on."

On the other hand, isolating on away-from-the-ball action is a lousy way to enjoy a basketball game, which, as Geoff Petrie explains, "is kind of a collage," meaning something made up of bits and pieces pasted together. At times while researching this book I would become so involved in one-on-one play and individual styles that I would forget which team was winning.

Soon though, I began to understand the game better. I became familiar with the players and their styles and knew what to look for. Don Sparks, whose photographs are included in this book, claims that it's much easier to take great basketball photos at professional games than at college or high school games because the players are so much more predictable. "They have refined their games to the point where they know what works and what doesn't," he claims, "so once you know the players' moves you can position yourself and your camera to get certain shots."

After you learn to analyze the game by its parts, you will find it easier to see it as a whole. "When I had aspirations to play professional basketball," Lucius Allen told me, "I would go to see my favorite ball players and watch them all through the game. But my favorites would be a guard this game, a forward the next game, and a center the game after that. As I continued to watch them I began getting an eye, so to speak, where I could watch everything happening on the floor at one time. I would know what to look for. The more you get into the game and the more you watch it, the more you can see."

Unlike football or baseball, basketball is a very elementary sport. It can be understood by a person attending his first game within minutes after he sits down. The object of the game is to put the ball in the basket; all else is frills. Rules vary from year to year and league to league, of course. In the

National Basketball Association, the offensive team has 24 seconds to shoot the basketball, whereas the American Basketball Association allows its teams 30 seconds, and the colleges and high schools permit an unlimited amount of time. After a year of attending dozens of professional contests I'm not certain that even I completely comprehend the sport's many rules. Total comprehension is not necessary to enjoy the sport. Basketball, however, has spawned its own interesting assortment of terms such as dunk, dribble, and back door. A glossary is included in the back of this book.

In my introduction to *Pro Football, U.S.A.,* I made the comment: "In basketball the action occurs so rapidly that the senses are not titillated; they are overwhelmed." I plead guilty to that statement, although now that I am writing a book extolling the virtues of pro basketball I feel a little bit embarrassed by it. The fact is that basketball is a game that seems very simple, if patternless, when you first approach it. You learn it is complex only after you have watched the game, intelligently, over a long period. You begin to realize that certain talents and skills must be brought to bear in an organized manner if one team expects to win consistently. Once you comprehend this, you can relax and enjoy because frequently basketball can best be enjoyed on an emotional level. As the reader follows me through this book, in my talks with the players, he too, I hope, will begin to understand how to find the key man.

—Hal Higdon

Michigan City, Indiana

1. *Walt Frazier*

"For three quarters, everybody is great"

When you think of Walt Frazier, the picture that comes to mind is of the spin: Frazier with the ball moving under control down the court, dribbling the basketball with his right hand, then the pirouette—he turns as gracefully as a figure skater and suddenly is going the other way, dribbling left-handed with a half-step on his defender. It is the characteristic Frazier movement.

Or the Frazier shot: a slow, lazy shot. Left open by his defender twenty feet from the basket, Clyde (as his teammates call him) floats off his feet, locks in position, and releases the ball. It is not a spectacular shot, not a mind-blowing shot like some of those made by his companion guard on the New York Knicks, Earl Monroe, but it is an extremely effective and artistic shot. Walt Frazier is the Rembrandt of the basketball court.

Frazier does not move fast. When the Knicks have the ball on offense, and do not fast break, he trots down the court at an easy pace as though measuring himself, discharging his battery ever so gradually, so that he will be at full charge when he is needed. Another picture: that of Frazier with seconds left on the clock, suddenly finding the basketball in his hands, and Zap! like a bolt of lightning striking a tree, he throws a move on his man that makes you wonder why you thought him slow earlier. Rip-flick! The ball is through the hoop winning the game for the Knicks. It is what Clyde does best: hit the winning shot.

On defense: Frazier again moving loosely, arms dangling from his side, ho-hum, here I am again, folks, seemingly in another world, until his man has the ball, then he surrounds him, appears

Playing guard, you have to be very observant. You have to be aware of everything that's happening on the court. By that I mean, if you're dribbling the ball, you can't have your head down. You have to see the other four guys on your team, because at any moment one of them might break to the basket. It's a split second between completing the pass and not completing it, so in that split second I should be able to stop my dribble and hit my man with a pass.

That's what I teach kids to do: Watch what's happening on the court, learn to dribble while keeping your head up. Don't watch the ball, because guys are coming open and if your head is down you can't see them. That's one of the basic fundamentals for anybody who's learning to play basketball.

It helps if you're familiar with your teammates' moves, knowing what they will do in any given situation. The only way to get that is from experience. Playing together three or four years makes a big difference. It's similar to football if you bring a second-string quarterback in to play with the first team. He thinks the receiver is going inside and the guy goes outside, so the pass is thrown away. In basketball, the forward might fake to go backdoor, and when I release the pass he's going the other way. But if it's Dave DeBusschere, I'll know that move. He's just setting a man up. Now when someone like Harthorne Wingo comes into the game, I'm not used to playing with him because he's not on the first team, so we are going to have problems offensively making passes. Dick Garrett is a new player, and when he comes in we make mistakes on defense because I'm not familiar with what he's going to do and the same thing is true for him with me. The only way to overcome that is through experience and playing together.

Every player has a different style. On our team, most guys like to shoot from outside. For instance, if I'm coming out on a fast break and Bill Bradley and DeBusschere are on the wings, I know they are not going in for the layup. They'll probably pull up for the jump shot, whereas if it's Dean Meminger, he likes to go all the way to the basket. Those things you have to know. And if it's Willis Reed on the fast break I don't want to give the ball to Reed, because he's a big man and he's not going to handle it. All he can do is give the ball right back to me. The only time you want to give the ball to the center on the fast break is when he can shoot it, because you don't want him to handle the ball. All of these things come with experience. You always try to pick your best shooter in a situation like that too.

How many times do you come down the court with a set play, as opposed to just running and shooting?

I would say that 60 percent of the time we come down and set up, but our best offense is our defense, because when you're stealing the ball and running the fast break, you don't need any plays. You get a good percentage shot every time and you have guys in motion, so if you do miss the shot they're going to the basket to get the rebound. If you come down and run a set play guys are standing around, and the defense is able to adjust.

I like to come down and ad-lib, get movement, pass the

ball, go away, which is basic basketball. But there are certain times when we like to call a play. Like the last twenty-four seconds of a period, we call a set play to use up time.

How many plays do the Knicks have?

(*Frazier smiles as he replies*) We have twenty-five or thirty plays, but not all of them work. That's the trick. Only about five or six plays work for us, and it's no military secret in the league what they are. Everybody in the league knows our plays, so it's just a matter of execution. Every play has a different option, so if they overplay the first option we run the second option. If we call a play the other team may know it and make an adjustment, so we have to ad-lib, play give-and-go basketball.

Sometimes we call a play so the other team won't hear it, like when the other team is shooting a free throw. Then we change the names of plays. We have a play that originally was called B-F, so we called it "beef." Sometimes we call it "turkey" or "chicken," just to give it a different name so the other team won't recognize it. Then we use plays from other teams if they work well. Like we have a "San Francisco." We run a "Buffalo," a "Portland." We copy plays from other teams because they work well against us. A lot of teams run the same plays.

Do you try to recognize plays when other teams call them against you?

No, I try not to get into that. I just play defense the way it should be played. If the other player passes the ball and goes away, I stay between my man and the ball whether I think I know the play or not. Otherwise you make yourself vulnerable to backdoor plays. If you think you know the play and react to it, the team may run the second option which you haven't seen. You're caught flat-footed. The main thing on defense is to stay alert, see the man, and see the ball at the same time. Defense should always be played that way.

18

Defense is all hustle. Anybody can play it if they want to, but it's only recently that defense has become the "in" word. Everybody now shouts: "Defense! Defense!" It's a proven fact that if you have a good defensive team you're going to win a lot of games. You can check the records: The teams winning now in the NBA are the ones playing good defense. That's a fact. So the coaches all stress defense, but if a player hasn't played defense most of his career it's going to be difficult for him to do it now. He'll go through the motions for a while, but then he'll revert to his old form. Then too, defense is a team thing, especially on the Knicks. Individually we don't have that many great defensive players, but as a unit we are very tough. The same thing on offense: We have very few players who can go one-on-one, but playing as a team, setting picks, we are very effective.

If the ball is off to the right and my man goes left, I'll stay on the inside playing what we call the passing lane. Kids on defense if their man goes left they want to turn left to follow him, then they can't see the ball. The other team can make a bounce pass behind them and get an easy shot.

A lot of defense is very fundamental. The footwork is very important. On defense, you never want to cross your feet. Once you cross your feet, you're beaten.

I coach kids in the summer and they find it very difficult to play defense. So did I when I first started, but I've been lucky in that I've always had coaches that stressed defense, in high school and in college. After a while it came pretty easy to me. Kids get bored with defense. Getting over a pick, for instance. They say it's impossible. I said the same thing in college: the coach is crazy. There is no way you can do that, but if you work at it hard enough you can.

What's the secret of getting through a pick?

Get up tight. Talking helps too. If I'm guarding my man and one of his teammates sets a pick on me, my job is to say "screen left" if he's coming left, or "screen right," whichever it might be. So my teammate knows he has to get up tight so I can get over that pick. But there's another catch. If I try to get over too soon, the player with the ball might reverse his dribble and go straight to the basket, so you have to make sure he's really going over the pick, and this is where kids get confused.

It's just a matter of teamwork, but there are some picks you can't get over. Then you have to switch. When you see a pick coming, you let the man go and one of your teammates covers him while you take his man. To me, switching is a lazy man's defense, but there are times when it is very effective. The Celtics like to play a switching defense. They switch on every play even if Dave Cowens winds up guarding a guard. They don't care. They apply a lot of pressure and it's very effective for them. It makes it tough to get a shot off, but the Knicks like to stick with our men. We don't switch unless it's absolutely necessary.

We're not a strong rebounding team, so again we have to have a team effort on the rebounding. We have to send five men to the boards to rebound on defense, whereas with other teams the guards always leave for the fast break. At the other end of the court, if our guards are caught going to the offensive boards, nine times out of ten the other team will get an easy fast break going the other way. We can't do that because we are not assured we're going to get that rebound. We have to send everybody to the boards.

How much of rebounding is sheer height, and how much of it is positioning?

I'd say that positioning is the big part. I'm not considered a good rebounder. I can jump adequately, but I'm not great. My success comes from timing. I can see a shot going up and pretty much tell which way it's coming off the board. I can pretty much tell if that ball is going right or left, if it's short or long just by watching the flight of it. I have a knack for that. You see a lot of guys going up when the ball is coming down, so it's a matter of timing which I don't think you can coach.

Also positioning, blocking out, which they very seldom do in the pros. In college we blocked out all the time, but in the pros people have so much ability they rely on their jumping too much. When I say block out, if you take an offensive shot I should put my body into you and keep you from going to the boards. In the pros, you watch: A guy will shoot and the defender will turn around and leave him to wait for the rebound. Very few teams block out.

The Celtics put a lot of pressure on teams to block out because they crash the boards. Silas. Cowens. Chaney. Havlicek. All those guys are great rebounders, and they converge on the offensive boards so it's almost a must that you block them out. You have to concentrate on keeping them off the boards. Dave Bing with Detroit is a great jumper and you have to keep him off the boards. On our team Meminger is the same. I find the big men don't care about blocking out, so that's why I'm able to get a lot of rebounds: a combination of timing and guys not paying me any attention.

It doesn't matter if a guy is eight feet tall, if you block him out he can't get the rebound, because the only way he can get it is by going over your back, and that should be a foul. When I say "block out" that means you have to at least keep him six or seven feet away from the basket otherwise he can get a hand on the ball and keep it alive. A lot of guys block a man out but they're standing under the basket, which is ridiculous because the only rebound they are going to get is the one that comes through the net.

But blocking out is tough and there is a technique to it. What happens with a lot of guys is someone will take a shot and his defender will run under or past him trying to get a piece of the ball. Even if the shooter misses, he has a straight path to the rebound because his man ran past him. So they have an extra man on the offensive boards. Sometimes even the Knicks get in the habit of doing that. But all these things are just desire and taking personal pride in your game, just working at it. These are things you can't coach. It's up to the player.

I'd rather have a guy who gives me one hundred percent than have someone with a lot of talent who doesn't put out. I like a hard worker and I respect him. Like Mike Riordan. He doesn't have a lot of talent, but nobody ever outhustles him. As a result he's a starter with the Bullets now and playing good ball, but all on desire. Mike would work out two or three times a day, even during the season, because he wanted to be good.

But in basketball the difference between a star and a superstar is the ability to take over in the last five minutes. For three quarters everybody is great. You would be a great player if you played. If you started a game and played for three quarters you could make some baskets and get some rebounds simply because you were out there. That's a fact. Now when the game is on the line, that's when you can tell the true players in the NBA: the last five minutes of that game.

After the game I want to be able to say: Even if I missed a shot, I know I shot it with confidence. When I coach kids I keep reverting back to that. I say to them, if I'm on the free throw line with only one second left in the game, behind by one point, and if I concentrate and shoot that shot the best I know how, and miss it, I won't feel bad because I know I did my best. I didn't choke. As long as you do that you are going to make more than you'll miss. But if I go to the line and I'm nervous and afraid to take the shot, then I know I've choked. I couldn't live with myself doing that.

A lot of times I'm asked, what do you look at when you shoot the ball. I don't know. I know you either shoot for the front or the back of the rim, but the only time I revert back to that principle is when I'm in a slump. Then I'll start with the basic shot: looking at the rim, shoot, follow through, body facing the basket. And I watch films to see what I might be doing wrong. A lot of times I find I'm shooting across my body. When I'm playing good I can make shots like that, but there are times when you get into a slump and you have to reevaluate your shot.

Same thing on defense. Guys will start going around me. I ask myself: What's going on? Then I might look at the films and see that I'm crossing my feet, or I'm not in a good stance. I'm standing up too high. All these things are basic fundamentals, but they're very important. Trying to get this across to kids though is really tough. They think: One day I walked on the court and I was Walt Frazier, and I could shoot, and I could pass, I could dribble, and I didn't have to practice like them.

I tell kids that they should always try to take good shots and not force the ball. They say: Well, Earl Monroe did this or Pete Maravich did that. I tell them: When you're a pro maybe you can do that too, but right now we want you to do basic things. Like I see guys that can go behind their backs, but they can't dribble straight ahead. Kids get caught up in the fancy shots that the crowds like. I say: Hey, why don't you pattern yourself after a guy like Oscar Robertson? He's just straight, nothing fancy. Jerry West—just straight, nothing fancy. If you make a mistake on defense they capitalize on it. Just basic fundamental basketball, but they've mastered those techniques.

And if you go behind your back, make it to your advantage. If you go behind your back, you should get a step on the defender in order to be able to go to the basket. If you go between your legs, same thing. Or if you use the spin move. All of these moves should enable you to get open. If you're not getting open, you're just wasting time. I tell them to watch me on the court: I have no wasted motion.

Lots of times if I'm coming downcourt and a defender lunges at me, it's an easy move to spin around, or go behind my back. But if the defender is in front of me, it's tough to get anything. If he's to one side, I can spin and I've got a step on him. But these kids, a man is in front of them and they spin and they look around and the man is still there, so they've wasted a motion. I tell them to set the man up so he overplays them, then you can go the other way.

Once the season is over I don't touch a basketball for about two or three months because I get bored with it. I'm not like Bradley who can go shoot a hundred shots. I get tired shooting. A lot of my game is mental.

Off-season I run, I lift weights. Some days I might feel like playing one-on-one but as far as organized games, no. I know my weaknesses. I work on my legs. This summer I could tell my legs were weak. It took them longer this year than last to get in shape. Next summer I'll start lifting weights and they will be ready. Even my jump shot: I could tell my arms were weak. Guys were pushing me around on court. Next summer I have to strengthen my arms, strengthen my legs. That's the only way to stay ahead of the game: to know your own weaknesses and work on them.

The "Mr. Cool" title: like in high school I was always the catcher in baseball, the quarterback in football, the guard in basketball. In all these positions you have the role of leadership, so I showed no emotion, because in a tight game when people looked to me for leadership I couldn't be cracking up. I always had to keep a calm disposition. That's carried over, and now even in life few things bother me. The worst thing that's happened to me is when my jump shot isn't going in.

I try to excel when the pressure is on because I know a lot of guys are depending on me so I try and fulfill their faith. Our coach Red Holzman, when the game is tight, says, "Give Clyde the ball." That builds my confidence. They want me to have the ball, look for the key shot or find the key man. To me that's the name of the game: coming through when the pressure is on. You've got a lot of guys who for three quarters are tough, but when the game is hanging on the line they don't want to take the shot. That's the difference between the pros , the stars, and the superstars.

2. *George McGinnis*

"There is going to be pushing, shoving, blocking, and elbows thrown"

The word that comes to mind when you watch George McGinnis play forward for the Indiana Pacers is: Crunch! McGinnis led his

24

high school team, Indianapolis Washington, to the state title in 1969 then came to the Pacers after two years at the University of Indiana. He stands 6 feet 8 inches tall and weighs 235 pounds. A half dozen players will collide under the backboard and Crunch! McGinnis will explode from the crowd with the ball, shrugging players from his shoulders as though they were drops of water. At the other end of the court George muscles into position near the side of the key, reaches for a floating pass, and Crunch! The ball is stuffed through the net.

During the 1972–73 season, George McGinnis led his team both in minutes played (40.8 minutes average for all 82 games) and in fouling out of those games (nine times). He also led the Pacers in scoring (27.6 points average), field goal percentage (50 percent), and in one game against Dallas collected 58 points. All that in what would have been his senior year in college.

"I am a physical player," McGinnis admits, but he also is an unusually swift and graceful big man, who occasionally will dribble the length of the court leading his team on the fast break or who at times will come out with the ball so near mid-court, directing traffic, running the offense like a guard. The characteristic McGinnis move, however, is one-handed, floating toward the top of the key, the ball cradled overhead in one enormous hand and then sent, with an almost disdainful motion, spinning toward the hoop. Or McGinnis reaching up and, again with one hand, sweeping the ball off the boards as though it were a piece of dust and he a vacuum cleaner. But the McGinnis trademark is Crunch! and you suspect that his opponents log a lot of time in the whirlpool bath the day after playing him. I spoke with George McGinnis one afternoon in the Pacers office after a morning-of-the-game practice session.

Different players have different philosophies toward the game. I am big and I am strong and I go to my strength. I try to be very, very physical. The man I'm playing knows before the game that there is going to be pushing, shoving, blocking, and elbows thrown, because that's the kind of ball player I am.

There are other players who are very smooth. Like Roger Brown on our team never gets in too much contact. He relies on his quickness and his moves to get open. I rely on my ability to go in and overpower my man. When I play this kind of game I'm effective. When Roger plays his type ball game, he's effective. He's not effective in there pushing and shoving, because he doesn't like it and he's not big enough to dish it out. There are different philosophies for different players.

If I had to play a guy like Dave DeBusschere for a whole ball game, it would be difficult. He'd be pushing and shoving me, and I'd be pushing and shoving him. Forty-eight minutes of that gets you down. You feel it after the ball game. You feel muscles hurting that you never realized you had. Sometimes you end up with more injuries than the normal ballplayer because of the contact. It's more difficult to go out and play a guy who attacks you rather than just attacking your man and having him not retaliating.

The way I play is the way the referees call the game here in professional ball. From high school to college, it wasn't that great a transition, because any time you touch a guy in a high school it's a foul. Any time you touch a guy in college, it's a foul. It wasn't a big difference. They were bigger and better players, but it wasn't hard to adjust. If you ran into a guy and he fell down they were going to call a charging foul where in this game if a guy steps in front of you and falls down, the referee just looks at him. That gives you a feeling of security knowing that the referee knows this guy is faking.

Pro ball is a totally different game. The atmosphere is different. I remember when I was in college, I'd watch a professional game every now and then and I'd say, "Oh wow, that doesn't look rough. I could play right now." Then when I signed with the Pacers I can remember my first game. This has got to be one of my greatest experiences. Just the whole atmosphere. Just so much different. To look at it from a spectator standpoint, I don't think you really get the full impact of it, but to be actually out there in the midst of battle it's totally different. It takes some time to get used to.

The average basketball fan, 90 percent of the crowd, just watches the ball. They see who shoots it. They never watch the guys in there battling for position, or what goes on over here when the ball is over there, when a guy is trying to cut for the ball, the defenders knocking him or pushing him. This is the interesting thing to me. When I go watch a basketball game I never cheer. I sit there and try to watch the positions. A lot of people come out and let off a lot of emotions and drink a little beer and it's fun, but I like to watch different things that go on. If you just sit down and keep your eye on the two centers the whole ball game and try not to watch the ball, you'd be surprised how much pushing and shoving goes on.

Until I became a professional I couldn't function this way. In high school or college, I'd find myself in the first quarter with three or four fouls and it hurt my game. This was one of my reasons for quitting college, because I felt I couldn't play the game I wanted to play. And in pro ball you get to know each player on the other teams, because you play that team eight or ten times a year. And he gets to know you. Also the referees get to know the different players and how they operate. The referees in this league recognize that I am a big and physical ball player and they let me play that way. They don't let it get out of hand, but they let me come out and play my game. I don't feel I have to watch myself, or be overcautious, because I might get a foul. This is something I couldn't do before.

Are the rules that much different from college to professional basketball, or is it the interpretation that referees place on the rules?

I think it's the interpretation. No question about it. People who come to a professional game and pay five, six, or seven dollars for a 48-minute game deserve to see the top players. In college you find referees who are homers: they blow the whistle in favor of the home team all the time. In professional ball this doesn't happen, because the referees go out with the attitude of being consistent. Once you get that attitude you work at that level all the time.

Anything that's not called a foul is being physical. I've constantly got my hands on the player I'm guarding. When the ball goes up on the boards I'm going right up after him. I'm not going for the rebound, I'm going after my man. Just keeping my hands on him, pushing and shoving, keeping him away, keeping him out of position, keeping him a step off stride, anything. Ball players don't like that. I don't like it to be done to me. Once you can get a guy frustrated and off his game, then you have a step on him. That's what I try to do.

I'm not noted for great defensive play, but I am physical. If you can go out and keep your man off stride and stay a step in front of him, you're going to be in pretty good shape. Once you go out and let a guy come at you, let him establish his game and get his confidence up, it's difficult. Sometimes the player guarding me will let me shoot a jump shot or two, and I'll hit a couple and get the adrenalin flowing, get starting to feel pretty good, and before you know it, I've scored a dozen points. I don't want my man to do that to me. I want to attack him. Every time that ball goes up in the air I'm going to be leaning on him. He'll go: "Damn it! There's that damn McGinnis." That's the attitude I like to have. I go out and play the game just as hard as it can be played, with reckless abandon, you know, getting away with all you can.

Some players get irritated. They start hollering at the referees and even get kicked out of games. Sometimes I'll have someone take a swing at me. When that happens, you know you have the upper hand. They've lost some of their cool. But the good ball players, the DeBusscheres, the Julius Ervings, the Billy Cunninghams, they might be frustrated but they will never let you know it. They wouldn't give you that kind of benefit.

I get kicked out of two or three ball games a year, although sometimes that can be healthy. Sometimes I enjoy getting technical fouls, because it gives the team a lift. We'll be lugging up and down the court, not getting any offensive or defensive movement, no teamwork. We'll blame it on the referee, get a technical foul, get everybody pissed off, and we start playing better.

Red Auerbach was one of the best coaches for pulling that. I've seen him get kicked out of so many games and 90 percent of the time, Boston was behind, wasn't playing their game, yet they wound up winning. When you're a coach you've got to do anything in the world to get your players to play, and that sometimes includes getting technical fouls called on yourself. Good coaches like Slick Leonard, or Dick Motta, or Red Auerbach. These are the guys who do a little extra to make you want to play. These are the ones who stand out in the crowd.

You can get a technical called for a lot of reasons. Bad language usually. Once you go up and cuss the referee he'll usually give you a technical foul. But the main thing is after something happens a lot of guys have a tendency to run at a referee, get right in his face, and holler at him. When you say that bad word, that just promotes it. Keep it up and you end up getting kicked out of the ball game

Sometimes you don't have to cuss. It could be the way you are acting, your attitude. I remember very vividly that I stole the ball from my man two years ago. We were playing the Dallas Chapparals.* It was a close game. We were going down the stretch. I was guarding my man. I stole the ball from him and thought it was a good steal. The referee called a foul and I had the ball in my hand so I threw it up in the air, just like that.

The referee will let you go as long as you don't get out of hand and embarrass him. If you go up and talk to the refs 90 percent will talk to you and explain why they called a foul. There are even a couple in this league who have come up and said, "Well, that was a bad call. I'm sorry."

People forget that these guys are human, just like we are. Hell, I go out and make mistakes too. Everybody on this

*Before the 1973–74 season, the Chapparals moved west, becoming the San Antonio Spurs.

team makes mistakes and the referees are no better than we are. But it's hard on the referees, because they don't have a home court. We have our own fans that yell and cheer for us and buy our shirts and shoes, but everywhere they go, they get booed. They have things thrown at them. They get attacked by fans. You have to be a special-type person to be a professional referee.

The coach today was putting you through a series of set plays. How much of the time do you run off a set play rather than run and gun?

Professional ball is more of a free-lance game. We will take one or two basic plays and run them ten or fifteen times a ball game. We rely on our front line getting the ball off the boards to the guards. Our front line—myself, Mel Daniels Darnell Hillman or Roger Brown—filling the lanes on the fast break, getting the ball quick and getting the easy ten to fifteen foot jump shots. When we don't do that we try to set up. But basically we play rebounding, running, taking the shots, and I think it's the easier way because as long as you're running and getting the ball down the court, you keep your man off balance. But once you get down there and have to set up, it gives their defense time to set up too. But it's good sometimes to slow down. It works both ways. Sometimes we get to walking up the court and it hurts us. So we try to mix it up and use both styles depending on the opportunity.

Sometimes we'll get in a ball game where a team runs off five or six shots in a row on us and are up ten or twelve points. We don't try to come back right away and run and gun and try to catch up as fast as we can. It depends on how much time you have on the clock, of course. If it's the second quarter and we have the whole second half to play, too much running will tire you out. In the last few minutes you don't have anything left if the game gets down to where you have to exert yourself. We try and slow it down at that point and run the good play, get the good pick, get the good shot, just chip, chip, chip away at the lead, and when we get close

30

enough then get running and hit the boards hard. We run. We gun. We've had a lot of success that way.

Professional ball is definitely a tall man's game. You have to have the tall man in the middle to be real successful. You can go right down the line and name the great teams. Boston had Bill Russell. New York with Willis Reed. Kentucky has Artis Gilmore. We have Mel Daniels who is a fairly small center, but he's been doing a job for us. You have to have the tall man.

Our basic strength is our inside game. It's what we try and do: set up and get the good pick and the good play. Then after we get our inside play going, that gets the opposite team to thinking, "Hey, we know where the ball is going. They're going inside. Let's stay on them." When we have three or four guys sagging on us, then we just pop it out to Bill Keller and Freddie Lewis and they hit the nice 15- and 20-foot jump shots. We have a good mixture. You need good guards to go along with your good big men.

In an evening game against San Diego after we had spoken, I saw George McGinnis collect 14 rebounds (one short of the ABA record held by his teammate Mel Daniels) in a single quarter. He also scored 29 points in leading his team to a 129 to 117 win. He had one technical foul assessed against him. A typical George McGinnis performance. Crunch!

3. *Dick Motta*

"You win with people"

Dick Motta, coach of the Chicago Bulls, serves as an example of the Jekyll-and-Hyde nature of most basketball coaches. Quiet, soft-spoken, almost diffident in person, he has been known to explode with the fury of a tornado on the sidelines, particularly when he sees a call go against his team. "When the game is going on, you are totally involved," he claims. "Streakers could go running by, and you wouldn't notice. People yell and they think we hear them. I see myself in movies afterward and I can't believe some of the things I did. It's not cornballing. It's not hotdogging. It's not playing to the crowd or anything else. It's just as though you're in a trance."

Seen from the stands, Dick Motta looks like a midget, as though he barely stood five feet. When you stand next to him off court, however, you realize he is merely a normal-sized mortal living in a world of giants. Unlike many professional coaches, he didn't play professional basketball but, instead, coached successfully at Weber State University before being hired by the Chicago Bulls. With Motta as coach, the Bulls—relying on tight discipline and strong defense—have made the playoffs each season.

Basketball is a game of passing, dribbling, shooting, and defense. There are certain fundamental parts of the game where the coach can make a great contribution. We try to work on defense as much as we can.

As a coach I consider myself a teacher. We try to approach practice sessions the same as we would a classroom situation. If I were teaching biology or sociology classes in high school, it would be exactly the same way. We have a lesson plan. When we have practice, we break it down by the minute and work on basketball skills.

Eventually it comes down to the final selection of people. You have to mold five people together to become your starters and also pick the first players off the bench at each of the three positions. These are decisions you make through experience.

I've been coaching now for twenty years. I majored in physical education for another four. I spend must of my year converning myself with basketball. Through experience, I make my decisions on who to keep, who to start, and who to play.

Putting together a basketball team is a very delicate

32

situation. I call it the three D's. It's delicate, it's difficult, and it takes discipline. It also takes a great deal of cooperation. It's like a marriage partnership. You basically have eight people who contribute to a team. You mostly need the three or four others for practice.

It's great when the players know who is going to start and who is going to sit. It's not always easy to accept if you're sitting. We expect problems from the people on the bench, our sitters. They are the most malcontent. Any substitute who is worth his salt shouldn't be happy with his coach or the situation if he doesn't get a chance to play. So basically, we are sitting on a keg of dynamite with a short fuse, and the fuse has been lit. Staying ahead of problems is probably the main challenge of coaching.

Coaching is a problem of human relationships. Particularly on the professional level, you have great egos. Each of our players have been all-Americans, and some of them are called on to contribute in a way that has been different from their past experience. The players have to adapt to our team and to our team situation. Some are able to and some are not.

All the players are great in this league. There are simply degrees of greatness. On the more mature teams some of the players have played together longer. The Bulls have that going now. Our players have had five years together. It takes teamwork to win.

See, you have five men and one ball. The people who are selfish and put themselves above team probably won't be successful. I tell people who are that way to go play tennis, go play golf, go play handball, because those are individual sports. But if you play basketball, you have to be a team player. You win in basketball by putting the ball in the hole, and you do that by helping. You do that by setting screens, throwing passes, not shooting when you aren't hot, and when the other team has the ball working to get it back, and all that takes teamwork. All the action is focused on that one ball, and there are ten people that want it. So I tell people who are selfish and egotistical and can't give of themselves to go play golf where you've got one ball and one player.

The easiest way to solve a problem is to cut it. If a problem arises, then you can get rid of it, or you can try to solve it. There comes a time with each problem, if it can't be solved, to get rid of it. Get the bad apple out of the barrel, so to speak. And knowing when to do that comes through experience, because a problem can spread through teams the same as cancer through a healthy body.

I tell my players that playing basketball for a living is better than working. It's easier to sell some people on it than others. For instance, if you really cut open the top of my Bobby Weiss' head and looked down inside, you would find he would rather start than come off the bench. But he's very mature and has accepted his role as third guard. You need people who can come off the bench, and if you are lucky to find a person willing to do that, who can cultivate the type of attitude necessary to be a third man, then you are fortunate.

It's a selling job. You have to remind this person continually how important he is and how vital is the role he plays. Then when it comes contract time, you have to reward him. The reward in our league right now is money. That's about the only yardstick that we use.

You talk about teaching, but what can you teach someone at this level that he probably hasn't already learned?

That question probably riles me more than any other question I'm asked. I've yet to meet a perfect player. When a player really believes he's reached the maximum of his talent, then he becomes complacent and he's not worth a damn. If he feels he can't grow with every practice, learn, absorb, and perfect his skills, then he doesn't belong on the Bulls. I'm talking about basic skills. I get that question thrown at me more than any other.

There are so many facets to basketball, and when you accomplish one skill and become very proficient at it, there is always another skill you've neglected somewhere along the line. The good coach will find these deficiencies and through the student-teacher relationship sell the player on curing his deficiencies.

My players are aware that I'm probably never going to be completely satisfied with their game. There probably are many times when they say to themselves: "What would it take to please the guy?" I'm never satisfied. Each player should become a little better every day. He shouldn't become stagnant. Every day, I imagine, a lawyer gets a little better. Doctors have to keep up with new discoveries. We challenge our players the same way. Work on the things you are good at, but concentrate on areas where you need improvement.

Most of the players who come into this league are quite good offensively. Most of our teaching is on defense, rebounding, blocking out, doing the things that the all-American glamor player probably never had to do. Down in the trenches, we call it. No one likes to go down in the trenches, dive for the loose ball, take the charging foul, block out, play the good, tough, aggressive defense. These are the skill areas where most players are most deficient.

Colleges play zone. In the NBA the rules require us to play man-for-man. Communications, recognizing switch situations, when to switch and when not to switch, by far takes up most of our teaching time. There are very few players who come out of college who are ready to play NBA defense. Very few. In fact, I haven't had any come to the Bulls who were capable of playing even adequate defense.

Utilization of time is critical. Why does one company make it in the economic field and another doesn't? Some coaches are winners no matter where they go. Vince Lombardi. Bill Sharman. Bear Bryant. Woody Hayes. Some people win, and others don't. If you were to study the successful people in any field—whether it is business or athletics or even teachers—you would find that they are people who (1) have discipline and (2) are able to organize their time and become as efficient as possible. There are the people who are successful.

How do you organize your team in practice, for example? When do you find time during an 82-game season where you're playing four and five times a week and traveling constantly to teach these skills you talk of?

There are many circumstances that dictate what you do in practice. For example, if I'm playing my fifth game in five cities in five nights and I have a day off, then four more games in a row, practice on that off day will probably be very lax. It might be just shooting practice. I may just want to get the team together.

Most of our teaching is done in training camp. We have two-hour practices in the morning and repeat the procedure in the evening, which gives us four hours. We charge our players with the responsibility of being in shape. We tell them you can do two things in practice! Condition yourself or learn. We don't have time for conditioning. We play our first exhibition game within a week, so we don't want to waste time getting in shape. We devote all our time to learning offense and defense. After the season gets going, we practice almost every day, and the practice sessions may be just as intense, but they don't last more than an hour and a half.

How much time will you devote during practice to the teams you will be playing next? For instance, if the Boston Celtics are coming to town, will you have your second team run their plays in practice the way most pro football teams do?

No, I'm different from most people. I practice with *my* team. We try to perfect the things that *we* do well, and we want to do them just a little better every day. When we do the things we do well, we are going to win ball games. I don't worry too much about what the other team does; I worry about us.

There are two ways to do things: the right way and the wrong way. We want to be prepared to execute the way we are supposed to execute. If the other team forces us out of our pattern and makes us do things we are not prepared to do, that's a bad coaching job on my part.

We don't scout other teams. If we meet a team from our division in the playoffs, we'll play them fourteen times in that one season. We know what they're going to do, and they

36

know what we're going to do, so it comes down to a matter of execution and desire. It's that simple. When you get to a certain level, there are very few surprises.

We think we're ready any time we go into a game. We try to make our scouting report of the other team the first five minutes of the game, so I don't spend a great deal of time telling my team we are going to play Boston in five days, let's get ready now. Boston should worry about us, not us about them. I want a team that has confidence in their ability, know what they can do, what they are supposed to do, and have the maturity to stay within those limits and not try to be something they are not. If you do that, you are going to be fairly successful.

Yet a team can play within its own limits and have some hot shooter beat them by hitting nine out of ten long shots in the fourth quarter.

Yes, that's the beautiful part about basketball. Our defense is geared to prevent inside penetration, stop the inside attack, not let the ball get to high-percentage areas. If we've got to give up something, it will be the outside shot. And sometimes we will lose games against a hot hand when we are playing our game plan and doing as well as expected. We'll get beat. But we'll get beat in single games. We won't get beat in series that way or in league championships.

You win games with people, not players. Think of the magnitude of that. That's still the first question my scout is asked when he comes back from a scouting trip to college campuses: "What kind of kid is he?" That doesn't mean we run a monastery or a choir. They don't have to wear white, and they are not pure. But do they play basketball? Will they make the sacrifice to win a basketball game? Will they do anything within the rules to protect the team from losing? Are they team-oriented? Have they been properly coached? Have they been yelled at, and how do they take it? Have they played tough man-to-man defense? It all goes back to the selection process. You win with people.

What do you tell your players in those secret little moments during time-outs when there are no microphones or tape recorders nearby to record your words?

There are three or four places where the fan would like to be. One of them is watching the team ready itself for a game in the dressing room. Another is to be in the dressing room at half time. They would like to be there for the postgame interview, talk to the warriors, so to speak, as they come off the floor and be able to watch the agony or the ecstasy. And they would like to be on the bench during time-outs.

Every time-out is different. Sometimes the players need to rest, get a blow. Sometimes they need to be yelled at. Many times the other team will call a time-out when we're playing well, and there's not much to be said. Sometimes we'll sit through the whole minute and a half, and I won't say much other than "just keep it up." I become a cheerleader. Other times you are a teacher. Or I chew people out for mistakes. You call it out because you see your team is not running its patterns well. You may want to run certain plays. Time-outs are chameleons, because every one is different.

Sometimes you call a time-out in the last two minutes just to advance the ball. The other team scores and while the ball is dead and the clock is stopped, we call a time-out to get the ball out at the 10-second line.

According to the league rules, we also have to call time-outs for TV commercials, so once in a while both teams will be functioning normally and we'll be approaching the 6:00 mark. The home team is responsible for the time-out in the first six minutes. I've seen many times when the time-out will kill the momentum of both teams. It'll be a nice game going up and down the court, the fans are enjoying it, and we'll look up and see 5:50 elapsed in the first quarter. I'll have possession of the ball, and I like to call time-out while I have possession so I can set up the play. And I've seen both teams go flat right after that.

What causes a team to go flat?

I don't know.

If you knew. . . .

Then I could write a book and become a millionaire. Not only teams go flat, but people go flat. There are times in business, or in your own writing, when you get up and feel you've really got it, and when you start to put it down, it doesn't come. Other times you may have a headache, backache, yet everything clicks. It's the same with a basketball team. It's the old cliché about peaks and valleys. Some days we are just clicking and going like crazy, and we'll do it five or six games in a row; then all of a sudden: boom! We are in a slump. We just have to work our way out of that slump. I have a saying on my office wall: "The penalty for being good is you have to be good every night." In other words, you need to be consistent.

I have one responsibility with the Bulls, and that's to win games. Basketball is an intense situation with a lot of pressure. Most people in their lifetime won't go through the amount of pressure that a coach goes through in one game. That's your family. That's your whole life out there on the floor. It may sound corny to some people, but the coaches that don't become involved emotionally don't make it. When you see things go wrong with your team, with your family, with your life, you react. When I see a coach not reacting, I think one of two things. He doesn't give a damn, or he's so secure he's not frightened.

4.   *Gail Goldrich*

"You try to play intelligent basketball"

Gail Goodrich leaned forward while sitting on a courtside chair following a practice session at the Forum in Los Angeles and spoke

What you have out there, hopefully, is five guys working together for a common cause, which is winning the basketball game. So you have to look at how you best can fit into the club and contribute most to this unit.

From an offensive standpoint, I can best help the Lakers by scoring. The Lakers look to me to put the ball in the basket. Playing with Jerry West, I try to complement myself to him. He's one of the two greatest guards to play the game. Oscar Robertson is the other. He likes to have the basketball a lot. He *should* have the basketball a lot. We play better basketball when he handles the ball, so if he's going to handle the ball, you have to ask yourself what can you do?

What I try to do is move well without the ball, and attempt to get myself open so that when I do receive the ball I can do something productive offensively: see another teammate open, or put the ball in the basket.

I'm probably a better guard going without the ball than with the ball. That's something John Wooden at UCLA taught me very well. If I play a 48-minute game, I may have possession of the ball four minutes tops.

When Jerry is not in the lineup, sitting on the bench or hurt, or when I was in Phoenix for two years and handled the ball, the situation was the reverse. I was in the middle of the fast break. You're looking to hit the wings and create the

40

play, to penetrate to the basket. Defensive men come and switch off and then you try to hit the open man. I've played two roles as a guard.

Defense is probably not the strong suit of my game. Yet I think I'm a better defensive player than a lot of people give me credit for. I have to be conscious of my size because players in this league are such good shooters. If I let them penetrate to the point where they can just turn around and shoot over me, then I'm in trouble. So I have to play good position defense and not let them get in on me.

Now here at Los Angeles, we play a team-concept defense where we try to help each other. The Knicks have been successful this way, and so have the Milwaukee Bucks. When the offensive players are talented, it's very difficult for just one man to guard another man, to hold him down, so we look to each other for help defensively. We force players to certain areas knowing that we are going to get help over there. Or you overplay his strength, forcing him to play away from the direction he would like to go. Some players, for instance, shoot better on the base line than they do around the top of the key. Other players are better to the right or the left, so you want to tempt them to move away from their strength.

We like to force players to the base line, keep them out of the middle. Particularly the guards in this league like to go down the middle. When they do, they have a lot of options. They can pass the ball either way, or shoot. Whereas if you force them to the base line, they either have to shoot, or the ball has to come out toward the middle. The guard can go only one direction, so you are using that base line as another defensive man.

When you have a big man you want to utilize him. With Elmore Smith, or earlier with Wilt Chamberlain, we had big centers who could block shots. So lots of time you shade players, or overplay them, to force them to go in toward your center. A lot of people who watch the game would say you are out of position, that you're getting beat, but you are really shading the player to make him go a certain way. You encourage him to drive, or force him into traffic where you are going to get help. If you don't get help, then you look very, very bad.

You want to make a player that shoots the ball well drive to traffic, so he will have to get rid of the ball. You would rather have other players shoot than him. You are out there working as a team, both offensively and defensively.

You try to play intelligent basketball. A number of teams in this league have talented players who don't play intelligently. They don't play under control. Maybe they are young players who don't have the experience. In the past two years the Lakers have been one of the oldest teams in the league, yet we also went the farthest. You have to realize what teams are trying to do and then counteract.

We like to run a lot, so that opens the game. If you can open the game then you don't have to fight that pressure defense where there's a bump, or a hand on you. That makes it easier, particularly for a guard my size. I'm not a physical player. I rely a great deal on my quickness and getting down the court. It's much tougher to guard me if I've got two or three steps coming at you full speed, where if you make one mistake I'm by you. Spectators, of course, like to see a running, wide-open game. Basketball is a game of quickness.

In a wide-open game you have to run a bit more, but it's easier on you physically. You probably end up playing longer. The last few years with Wilt, he'd get the rebound out to us and he wouldn't even have to come over to half court. These are times when he could pace himself, rest, and it wouldn't hurt the ball club. So even though we do a lot of running, we don't burn ourselves out.

What about the pure act of shooting?

I believe there are reasons why the ball goes in the basket. I've always been a good shooter. That's probably one phase of my game that I practice more than any other. Most young players growing up probably do the same.

One of the most important parts of shooting is to be in

balance. In other words, have control of your body. Now being in balance for some players is different than for others, but primarily you should go up straight when you shoot the ball, have your shoulders squared off to the basket, not falling away. Now there are times when, because of my experience, I will fade a bit, or what you might say fall back. But I'm really under control. Some young players may not be able to do that. Elgin Baylor, when he was playing, could hang in the air and shoot, but he was in control of his body and had good balance.

A jump shot, you get squared away and go off straight. Even before you release the ball. Get your foot work getting set up for the shot. There are other things. Follow through. Release. Things like that. But I think foot work and the gathering yourself up for the shot, if done correctly, allow you the chance to get the ball in the basket. You are going to have some hot days and cold days, but what you aim for is a consistent level.

5. *Frank O'Neil*

"They say basketball is a noncontact sport"

Frank O'Neil waited in a room off the dressing room surrounded by the tools of his trade: jars of hot, sticky stuff, rolls of white adhesive tape. O'Neil is trainer for the Lakers, a position he has occupied since that team moved from Minneapolis to Los Angeles in 1960. Prior to that he had worked for the Los Angeles Rams, Philadelphia Eagles, and the University of Southern California.

Injuries in football are more traumatic than those in basketball. The individuals are larger and they're moving faster when they hit, so more damage is done. But football players only play once a week, whereas we play an average of four and a half games a week. If a player is injured in football on Sunday, he has Monday off. They start running on Tuesday, continue on Wednesday, Thursday, and Friday. Travel on Saturday. Sunday they play again. So football players don't have to get out and punish themselves every day. In basketball if someone is hurt and out of the lineup, he misses four games before he can turn around. Also, basketball players don't wear pads.

Jerry West has had an injury which we see a great deal in professional basketball, and it's difficult to deal with. It's a strain to the abdominal muscles. Players get it high in the abdomen or down in the groin area. This injury seems to hit players who have played professional basketball for quite a few years, namely an Oscar Robertson or a Jerry West. The injury is caused by the type of game they play.

Oscar Robertson, with his strength and ball control ability, will physically back his man down underneath the basket where he can shoot a turn-around jumper. This motion of twisting and shooting places severe strain on the abdominal wall. The injury affected Oscar's play. As long as he went straight ahead he was all right, but he lost all his lateral movement.

This also happened to Jerry West. Jerry's game is similar to Oscar's in that they play great defense. They always position themselves on the man with the ball, so consequently there's a great deal of strain put on the abdominal muscles as they try to anticipate the person's move and get better position.

When they get this kind of injury, there's only one way of treating it: Sit the guy down and wait. With Jerry, it would get to the point where he would begin to feel better, so he would go out and try to shoot or run, and the next day he would be sore again. I mean sore to the extent that he couldn't even sit up straight in bed. He would have to roll over on his side to get up. Finally Dr. Kerlan said, "If you don't quit, I'll put you in the hospital and make you stay in bed, because rest is what you need."

When a player comes off his injury and has to start working out again, the problem then is he's out of shape and hasn't been doing anything for ten days, or longer, so he can't practice hard or he'll aggravate the injury. It's a long process and the only thing you can do to help the situation is use the whirlpool to take away some of the soreness and relax the muscle spasms, and keep him warmed-up before he goes out to practice. Then we wrap him with heavy abdominal wraps to give support to his muscles.

Every night before Jerry goes to play we have to make sure he's thoroughly wrapped, then we cross our fingers when he makes a quick move. If he does come out of the game, which he will eventually to rest, we put hot packs on the injured area. We also keep a heavy blanket on the bench, because most of the arenas where we play are cold. They play ice hockey too and the basketball court is put down over the ice.

If you take a player with an injury out of the game—particularly a groin injury or a hamstring pull—and sit him down too long he'll stiffen up and won't be able to move when he gets back in. So with Jerry I'll ask him how he feels, to find out if he's rested sufficiently. If he says he's ready, I'll turn to the coach and let him know.

Groin strain predominantly bothers guards, or some of the smaller more active forwards. The other most common problem we face is knee injuries. Players strain the ligaments or tear a cartilage. But most common in knee injuries is tendonitis. It comes from years and years and years of basketball, where guys have played since they were ten or eleven years old. Particularly blacks who used to play on hard cement or blacktop basketball courts in the middle of the city where they would just play for hours and hours, all day, go eat, then come back and play at night because it was their thing. By the time they get to the professional basketball level they have created a situation which can't be cured. You can only alleviate the problem by quitting basketball, so guys just have to live with it.

They get it young. Here's Jimmy Price, who is only a second-year man in this league, and he has tendonitis in both knees. Elmore Smith has the same problem. Wilt Chamberlain had it. Elgin Baylor had it. It's something that is just part of the game. The constant pounding, jumping, pushing.

The majority of floors in the league are portable, laid down on ice so there is some give, but when we go to play the Capital Bullets, they have a permanent floor. The next day we have complaints. The Houston Rockets have a Tartan floor. On wood your foot will slip, but on Tartan you stop, twist, and there is no give whatsoever. This puts undue strain on ligaments and tendons.

They say basketball is a noncontact sport, but it's ridiculous the amount of physical contact that goes on. When a blind pick is set and the guy coming across is not aware of it, he can get hurt pretty severely. I've seen guys knocked out just by hitting so hard. You take a guard who weighs 175 pounds and run him into some of these big corner men who may weigh 230 or 235, and are planted, it's just like running into the side of a wall. Dave DeBusschere always has had hip injuries and this may be predominant to the corner men in the league because they're the ones who are setting those picks. The defensive guard will run into that big corner man and he'll hit him right about the hip level, so you get hip pointers, bruised hips, or bruised thighs.

Injuries depend a lot on the team's offense. A lot of teams run their offense off their center who comes out high and sets a big pick, so consequently players are banging into him. Willis Reed with his knee injuries. Some guys in this league, Jerry Sloan, are on the floor all the time because that's their game.

Players, the doctor, the trainer all have to work together. Particularly the trainer and the player. You have to be cognizant of what is bothering the guy the most and what kind of support you can give him. West comes to mind. He hates to have any kind of taping. For years he would not tape his ankles. It bothered him, but over the years with injuries he has come around to the point where he tapes all the time.

6. *Charlie Scott*

Charlie Scott can almost be described as a player without a style. You can spend 48 minutes watching the Phoenix Suns, during which time Charlie has handled the ball most of the time his team has been on offense, and not remember seeing him. Then you realize he scored 27 points, six of which came in the last minute of a game the Suns won by six.

Before coming to Phoenix in 1972, Scott played two years with the Virginia Squires of the ABA, leading that league in scoring during the 1971–72 season with a 34.6 average. The following season with the Suns he averaged 25.3 points, sixth in the NBA. He is quick enough to outmaneuver most defenders and tall enough (6 feet 6 inches) to shoot over the others. The morning after the game mentioned above, the Suns practiced at a high school gymnasium near downtown Phoenix. When practice ended I followed Scott, who was dressed in a gray anonymous sweatsuit, back to the dressing room at Vets Memorial Coliseum where we talked.

I'm the quarterback. I set the plays up. My main duty is to generate offense, to get the patterns flowing, to get the continuity going. I have to get the other guys the ball when they are open, set up the offense according to how the other team is playing defense.

Each night before a game I go through the scouting reports to find out who will be guarding me so I can decide what I can do to cause the other team to change their defense. I'm trying to set up what we do best offensively against what they do worst defensively. I approach each game from that respect.

I'm a 6-6 guard, and if I have someone smaller than me, then it's a mismatch. The other team will have to give him help, therefore we should have someone open. I try to get the ball to that man. You have to approach each game according to who you are playing against and decide what you are going to do. And that's how I play.

The sporting public has been educated so they know that pro football players watch films of their opponents before each game. Do pro basketball players do the same?

We watch films sometimes, but most of the time we go by scouting reports. Also, in basketball you have a chance to play a team more than once, so the first time you play them, you feel out what they do. The second time you play them, you know what they're going to do because you've played them before. They make changes, but not drastic ones, because their basic style is what makes them successful.

Different teams have different styles. When we play a team like the Knicks, my job is to keep us running. In other words, they want to slow the ball down, and we want to run. If we run, we're a better team against them than if we slow to their speed. When we play Boston, I try to control the tempo, because I feel that if we control the tempo against them we will have a much better chance of winning. They're a much better running team than a control team.

Now when we play Chicago I'm usually matched up with Norm Van Lier, who is 6–1, therefore I shouldn't have to worry about him blocking shots. So I should position myself for good shots. He's just as quick as I am so I'm not going to try to out-quick him; just take good shots and use judgment on where to move for the ball.

Van Lier is a tough defensive guard though. He'll make you go all out. The guard position is one spot in pro basketball where you do have an abundance of good talent. There are a very limited number of good forwards and centers, but a lot of good guards. Every team has two good guards, therefore I have to prepare myself every night. You can't slack up. If I do, I won't be able to control our offense.

My biggest asset is quickness, being able to beat my man. If I beat my man it forces somebody else to pick me up. In other words, I force a change in the defense. If they're aware of my beating my man, they're looking to help out. If I'm going off the pick and roll, it's forcing them to come out, then I hit the open man and we get the easy shot inside. Even when I'm headed for the basket, it staggers the defense so they don't know whether I'm going to drive, or stop and shoot, therefore it gives our team a better chance to get the ball, because in that one second the defense is standing still trying to anticipate my moves.

Every good basketball player feels like he wants to have the ball in a key situation. What I like to do is make the right play. Usually the other team looks for me to take the last shot; therefore, I try to force them to leave a man open on our team, stagnate their defense, so I can get somebody else in a better position. Everybody in pro basketball can shoot, but I like to have the ball, because I feel I can set things up a lot better than anybody else. That's my responsibility too.

Sometimes we'll use a pressing defense, particularly against a team that likes to set up. That forces the other team to run. If you press them they have to worry about getting the ball up court. Maybe it takes them longer to do so, and from then on they're rushing. We want them to rush their offense more and not take their time. You take each team one at a time and see what their biggest weakness is. Now you wouldn't press a team like Los Angeles because they like to run. So with them we sit back and play a much tighter defense. We force them to take the outside shot. Golden State wants to take the outside shot, so we try to force them to run. A team like the Bullets wants to go inside, so we try to keep them out. We make them do what we want them to do, rather than what they do well, therefore we get the upper hand. We can force them to play our game. When it's the other way around, you find yourself in trouble, because you are reacting to what they make you do. The team that takes the initiative can win, because they will dictate the game.

Pressing takes a lot out of you. Forty-eight minutes of basketball is a lot of time on the court. Guards have the whole court to work on. If you press, you feel it a lot more after the game. But if you're in good shape, it shouldn't bother you that much.

You played in the ABA. Is the style in that league any different from the NBA?

The style is a lot different in the NBA because of the sophistication of the league, the coaching techniques, and the more experienced ballplayers. When you have more players to pick from you're going to have a more sophisticated league. That's the big difference between the NBA and the ABA. When you have ten- and twelve-year veterans, they bring not only ability but insight into the game from playing it so long. That's the big advantage the NBA has. The only thing that makes winners, apart from ability, is insight in the game. The NBA has that insight from experience.

7. *Swen Nater*

"All of a sudden I'm playing"

The most famous player in college basketball during the early seventies was Bill Walton of UCLA, whose team set an NCAA record of 88 consecutive victories. The backup center who had the frustrating job of sitting on the bench and watching Walton play was Swen Nater, a dark-haired, raw-boned giant, who was born in Holland and didn't begin playing the game until junior college. Nater is the greatest testimonial to the fantastic depth of that UCLA team, since midway through the 1973–74 season, the financially troubled Virginia Squires were able to trade Swen (still in his rookie year) to the San Antonio Spurs for $300,000 and a first-round draft choice. Nater helped convert the Spurs (formerly the Dallas Chapparals) from a last-place team to a playoff contender.

I spoke with Swen Nater one afternoon in Louisville before an evening game with the Kentucky Colonels, in which he was able to dominate that team's ABA All-Star center Artis Gilmore.

*Watching basketball players from a seat above the court, it is difficult
to appreciate just how big the tall men are. They are tall, very tall.
After I knocked on his motel room door, Swen opened it and ushered
me in. There was a lattice decoration on the ceiling in the hallway of
his room. It's not that his head would have struck it had he not
ducked; his shoulders would have struck it. The program listed
Swen Nater as 6 feet 11 inches, but when he played that night he
looked the same height as Gilmore, who is listed at 7 feet 2 inches.*

*I confessed to Swen that since I don't follow college basketball too
closely, I hadn't heard much about him until he surfaced as starting
center on the United States AAU squad that played eight games
(winning six) against a touring Russian team in the spring of
1973. "A lot of people who do follow college basketball closely had
never heard of me either," he admitted.*

While I was at UCLA I never got into the game much, but
I learned an amazing amount of basketball. I learned
probably even more than if I were playing, because I could
sit back and observe from the bench. Then I would practice
the things that I saw during the games. It was hard to keep
my head straight and keep saying that next year I'll be
playing, but I've made the adjustment now. Realizing that all
of a sudden I'm playing is really fantastic. I'm finally getting
to put into use some of those things I learned. Coach
Wooden probably knows more basketball than anyone in the
world, and I probably learned only one-hundredth of what
he knows. But even that can get you by.

My main duty with the Spurs on offense is handling the
ball. I have my hook shot which I can shoot from either hand
from either side of the key. At San Antonio when we hit the
posts, we have a splitting action, or a weak-side splitting
action. There's a lot of movement. Most other teams when
they hit the center stand around and wait for the center to
make a move and shoot. But I don't shoot all the time.

What do you mean by a splitting action?

Say I'm in a low post and there are a guard and a forward
on my side, which would be the strong side. When they hit

the post, one of them screens for the other who breaks away so there's an open man for me to hand the ball to. If I don't pass to either one of them they clear out to the weak side or back up and give me room to shoot.

The strong side is a term that relates to which side of the court the ball is on. The weak side is the side without the ball. Weakside forward is a very common term. It's the forward opposite the forward near the ball. Ninety-nine percent of the people at a basketball game look at the side with the ball. They watch the players making the passes or taking the shots. I went to a game once and watched the weak side all the time, and it's really amazing what goes on.

The guards, as they come downcourt, determine what play we're going to run. They'll shout a number, which will designate a certain lineup with different jobs. Like we have one play where I come to the high post and the strongside guard passes the ball to the strongside forward. The weakside guard will cut me off and go down to the baseline. Then I'll get the ball and pass it to the weakside guard who will have cut around the weakside forward. When you can swing the ball quickly from the strong side to the weak side, the play really works, because the weakside defenders usually slough off their men. On the strong side they will play right on their man and be very aggressive in guarding him, but on the weak side a lot of players relax on defense. If you can swing the ball real fast to the weak side you can create situations.

San Antonio has about 30 plays. A number of them are designed for special situations. Say, our forwards are being overplayed, so our guards can't get the ball into them. We have a backdoor play where the guard passes the ball to the center coming up high and if that forward who is overplayed cuts to the basket quickly he may beat his man and get a layup. But against a team that doesn't overplay its forwards, we never use that. It's just like football: If you see a hole in the defense you call a play to take advantage of it.

Before the start of a game, the coach might write on the board: 27, 27 high-post, 3, 4, 1, in that order. We have to remember that, and the first five times we come down the floor we'll run those plays. After that, we go on our own. We adjust to situations. If the forwards are overplaying our men, the guards might come down the court and hold up a fist. That signals the backdoor play. We have to run downcourt looking for a sign. Or they might shout that out, or call a number.

Eighty percent of the time on offense I'll handle the ball. We have a couple of plays where the ball won't come in to me. The guard may go one-on-one and I'll just set a screen. But everybody plays a vital role on every play. That's really the best way to do it, because if you only use two players for a play, you're playing two-on-five basketball and it's tough. You want to take advantage of all five men.

We have other plays designed just to get the ball to me to shoot. Or we may be running another play and I see that the pick didn't work, or something went wrong, and the guy didn't get open. I may just cut right into the key, take a pass, and shoot from there.

But we always run a set play. We hardly ever fast break. We never come down the court and free-lance. Setting plays is the best way to win consistently. UCLA has proved that way to be effective. They're more methodical than any team I've ever seen. They don't have more than three or four plays, but even their fast break is a pattern. It all depends on which side the ball is rebounded on.

Defensively I block shots and clog up the middle to prevent people from shooting. I help out if one of our men gets beat. I'm more or less the leader. Defensively I talk. I tell the guards if they are by themselves or if there's a pick to the right or a pick to the left.

On defense we function on the same principle used by the Lakers when they had Wilt Chamberlain. We funnel guys into the middle and try to force them into me. It's worked well. We're the leading defensive team in the league.

I'll position myself according to where my man is. It's a man-for-man defense and you have to stay with your man, otherwise the referees will call you for using a zone. If he's in the high post I have to help out coming from high. If it's low, I have to help out from there. The name of our defense is helping out, trying to get the guy with the ball into an area where two men can guard him. Two men guarding one man is a lot easier than if one man has him. You get a lot of stolen balls and throwaway passes that way.

Blocking shots is just timing. You jump and you block it. Or if you can't hit the ball, you make him miss which a lot of times is just as good as blocking it. When Bill Russell was playing, he wouldn't block all the shots. He would block maybe five shots a game, but nobody knew which five. Every time somebody shot there was a hand up. Like Bill Walton of UCLA. Every time somebody shoots inside, he's up there, and there's no exception, and you can count on that, so it forces a lot of mistakes. A center who only plays hard some of the time is going to have a lot of baskets scored on him, because people are going to think maybe he won't jump this time. If he doesn't, it's two points. So the main thing is to keep jumping in there and intimidating them. You can't win a championship in professional basketball without having a big center. You need a dominating center who can intimidate people like Wilt, or Russell, or Jabbar, or Thurmond.

When you play against a dominating center, do you have to adjust your game to him?

I have to adjust my play to him. He has to adjust his play to me. We both do adjusting. Like last night I played against Billy Paultz of the New York Nets, and he's a much different kind of ball player than Artis Gilmore is. Now against Paultz I might put up a turn-around jump shot, but against Artis I better not try it because he might jam it down my throat. So I have to shoot my hook, or try to move him around the best I can. If Artis were playing against Paultz, he might be able to get off a turn-around jump, or something, without jumping too high. Against me he would have to jump a little higher. Against different players you have to play a different way. You can't play the same every night.

We have a lot of plays where I go up to the high post and

the forwards post down low. Let's say Rich Jones has a small forward on him. He can post down low and shoot over him from the inside. It's a better percentage shot, so I'll move high, throw the ball to Rich, and he can make his move. Well, if I couldn't shoot from the outside my man would sag off and intercept the pass and our whole offense would break down. But if I can shoot from the outside he has to stay on me. It allows us to create situations.

Speaking of creating situations, the guy who creates more situations than anyone else is Julius Erving. The guy is amazing. He'll drive to the basket with his eyes wide open and people will be cutting all around him and he'll find the open man for a pass. He had eight assists against us last night. That's the kind of player who is really valuable to a team.

I'm doing pretty well for my rookie year, but it's not over yet. I've got to keep improving. I think I'm getting better every game. I'm adjusting more to the different type of basketball in the pros. Here you can block out and not have to worry about knocking someone down. The referees will let most of that go, unless it's intentional. The physical game is better for me because I'm two-hundred-fifty pounds and in college it is almost a disadvantage to weigh that much. The referees like to stick up for the little and skinny guys a lot. That's true to some extent in the pros too. If I get hit they'll say, I can take it, but if I hit some little guy they'll blow the whistle fast.

The future looks good. I'll be all right if I don't break a leg or something. I've got to keep working, keep plugging away. Keeping that competitive edge is important, because you have to have something to fight for. I go into every game and my statistics have to be better than the guy I'm playing against. Rebounding more than scoring, because I really don't care how many points I get in a game. If I can be the leading rebounder in the game then I feel happy.

During the 1973 U.S.-Russian basketball series, the Russian coach had complained about Nater's rough tactics, calling him a hatchet man. Guilty or not guilty?

Guilty, I suppose. We beat them in the first game and I had a giant knot on my head. Some guy hit me. Under the international rules, it's a completely different kind of basketball. The Russians play a very rugged, physical game. Their talent isn't anywhere close to ours; they just go out and beat people up. The whole idea was to create better relationships between the two countries, and I don't think the series did that. There were several fights.

The second game at San Diego they beat us and I got roughed up again, so I said if they're going to do it I'm going to do it too. So the rest of the tour I just went out and killed people. I just ran over them, ripping this and that, elbowing, shoving, pulling jerseys off, doing exactly what they did. And that's one of the reasons why we beat them, because I realized if we were going to win I couldn't be out there finessing while they were pounding lumps on my head. But I don't think that's what Dr. Naismith had in mind when he invented the game of basketball.*

Later during the season, Swen Nater played in the ABA All-Star game, leading both teams in scoring (29 points) and rebounding (22). He averaged 14.5 points per game for the season, led the league in field-goal shooting percentage (55.3 percent), and was fourth in rebounding (12.6 per game). He was named the ABA's rookie of the year.

*In 1891 Dr. James A. Naismith, a physical education instructor at what is now Springfield College, in Massachusetts, nailed two old peach baskets to the gymnasium balcony to give his students a game to play during the winter. Nine-man teams shot with a soccer ball.

8. *Artis Gilmore*

Probably no other player in professional basketball looks taller than Artis Gilmore, center for the Kentucky Colonels. Perhaps some are taller than Artis' listed 7 feet 2 inches, but none look taller. His luxuriant Afro haircut adds several inches to his apparent height but even more, it is because of the way Artis Gilmore carries himself. Some tall people slouch attempting to disguise their height, but Gilmore, rail-thin anyway, stands straight. With his carefully trimmed pointed beard and imperious look, Artis Gilmore is a truly regal personage.

Certainly he is king of the ABA centers, having been named to the all-league team each of his three years as a professional. I spoke to Artis in the dressing room following a Colonels game against the San Antonio Spurs. The battle between Gilmore and Spurs center Swen Nater had been rough, bruising, and one in which, I thought, Nater, with his weight advantage, had come close to dominating the ABA's dominant center. Yet the game had turned on two key moments in the last minute when San Antonio players had seemingly easy close-in shots. Artis had not blocked either shot, but the mere fact of his presence had intimidated the players into missing them, and the Colonels had won.

I'm a pretty good shooter. I have a couple of moves. I like to go straight up with the hook shot, or take a swing: try going to the middle then bring it back. I've been working on my outside jump shot for quite a while, ever since I started playing basketball. I learned to handle the ball outside and shoot the jump shot and as I grew taller this was another advantage I had.

You weren't always 7 feet 2 inches tall?

Definitely not. I played against Boo Kennedy, who is now with the Spurs, in junior college. He's 6 feet 6, and at the time I was only a few inches taller than him. All of a sudden, during the summer before I left to go to Jacksonville State, I grew about five or six inches. I don't know why. Probably the food I ate, or just naturally in the genes.

What about the pounding and shoving that goes on under the basket? Does this bother you?

No, it doesn't bother me. Ever since I came into the league, I've been measured against contact. Most of the players I've played against are probably physically much stronger than I am, and bigger. I may be taller, but they're bigger. Swen Nater is probably the strongest center in the league.

Do you make an attempt to block every shot when they challenge you, or do you pick out certain ones?

Usually I pick out certain ones. Now toward the end of the game, that was in a crucial situation. I believe if I hadn't challenged the player at that time, he probably would have made the shot. So I think my presence distorted him a little bit and changed his shot.

Usually we try to play a sagging position on defense where I can get off my center a bit and try to block a shot if somebody drives in. But most of the centers I play against have very good shots from the outside. The guard driving to the basket may pass the ball back to the center and if I'm not close to him he can hit that jump shot. I try to be in a position where I can make a quick retreat and be back on him.

During the game San Antonio would come down court with the ball and one of the guards would call a play: "27!" Then somebody on your squad would shout "Watch for the backdoor." What is the backdoor?

The backdoor is usually when one of the defensive players has overplayed his man and he gives him a fake and goes straight to the basket, and that's what they usually call a backdoor. You'd have to set up a play for me to explain

58

exactly what I'm talking about, but usually one player will set a pick for another guy and he'll go straight to the basket. Usually the center standing up around the top of the key will throw him a pass and he has an easy layup. That's what you call a backdoor play.

How about rebounding?

There is no secret. Most of the time I just jump straight up and I get the rebound. Sometimes when the ball goes to the other player I can tip the ball away in my direction and get possession. Positioning is more important than jumping. I used to be able to jump up and touch the top of the backboard, but I found out that it was wearing my knees out, and I wasn't gaining that much.

There's a story behind the reason I'm wearing a beard right now, because I had jumped, and was up above the backboard, and a guy was driving in, and my foot got caught on his shoulder, and I fell. I split my chin and put several stitches there and after it healed there was still a scar. So I grew a beard, because most of the time when people are looking up to my face they're looking right at my chin, and it's hard to hide that scar.

Do you find that being left-handed gives you an edge?

Yes, definitely. It's to my advantage. In many situations when the guy comes up with the layup, I'm going right over his left hand which is over his right and that always puts me in a measuring position. Also on offense I think I have the advantage going to my right. I remember one incident when I was in college. The other coach kept saying: "Play him on his left. Overplay his left hand." And every time I went to my right, which means I'm hooking with my left. They didn't catch onto me until the end of the game. It was not that they were stupid or anything, but they didn't realize that I preferred going to my left hand.

Players with the most experience have the advantage, because they have knowledge of the game. You have a younger generation of ballplayers coming in with natural talent, but the veteran ballplayers have the advantage. But then you have this young center who's a rookie this year: Swen Nater, who has been doing a tremendous job on offense. He has a good hook shot and it's hard to stop anybody's hook shot. Mel Daniels, Billy Paultz, every one of the centers I play against, are tough, anybody who I think is physically in the same category as I am. The only center I think I have an advantage over from a physical point of view is the Virginia center. I can't think of his name.

Gilmore called to one of his teammates: "Hey, who is the Virginia center? I can't think of his name." Somebody eventually said: "Eakins."

Most of the other centers try to defense me differently. Swen Nater tries to use physical strength against me. Paultz outweighs me and does the same. Mel Daniels tries to go up and block my shots.

You seem to block a few shots yourself.

I think I hold the record in the ABA. Matter of fact, I do have the record. I think that it's a task for me to help my teammates and be ready whenever it's necessary to block the shot and make whatever contribution I can to the team.

9.   *Jerry Sloan*

"I just consider myself a post"

Chicago Bulls guard Jerry Sloan stands 6 feet 5 inches tall, and all of his height is from the waist up. If his legs were in proportion to his torso, he would be over 7 feet; if his torso matched his legs he probably would be under 6. It is the ideal build for a guard, because he is closer to the ground while dribbling, and his long arms permit him many steals denied better-proportioned players of equal size.

Sloan has straight, coal-black, neatly parted hair. His craggy features include a brow and nose that might have been sculpted by Michelangelo. He is not what you would call a finesse player. He is a hustler, a scrambler, a brawler, a diver for loose balls, an intimidator of opponents. He seems at times awkward, bumbling, always in the enemy's way and when a collision occurs, he does not absorb the blow but, feet planted on the floor, topples statue-like, an advertisement to the referee that a wrong has been committed. Referees who fail to detect infractions, real or imagined, are given dark, scorching glances, the kind that could melt glass backboards.

Jerry Sloan, on offense, is not the player from whom you would expect a behind-the-back dribble. He lurches from pick to post, and when he throws up his one-hand jumper, it is the kind of shot you might describe artistically as: Pretty Fair. Yet when he is in the ball game for the Bulls, things happen. It is a magic that some players possess that seems to transcend their apparent ability. At one game where I watched Sloan play against the Atlanta Hawks, he matched up with Pete Maravich, who outscored him 30 points to 8. Yet I honestly felt Jerry outplayed Pete that night in a game Chicago won. "He is the franchise," says Bulls coach Dick Motta.

"Basketball players often have characteristic moves," I suggested to Jerry Sloan when we talked one afternoon following a Bulls practice session at De Paul University gym. "Kareem with his sky-hook. Frazier spinning with the ball." (Sloan began to smile, anticipating what I was about to say.)"When I think of Jerry Sloan, I visualize you lying flat on your back."

"It's a trait of mine," he admitted. "I was taught that in college: If I can gain possession of the ball for our club by causing an offensive foul, that's as important as getting a rebound."

*"Frazier said your whole team played that way."**

*Walt Frazier had attended Southern Illinois University at the same time Sloan played for Evansville University. With Sloan their top play maker, Evansville won the NCAA small college championships in 1964 and 1965. In the latter, Jerry's senior year, the team went undefeated, winning twenty-nine games. Sloan had one so-so season with the Baltimore Bullets, then came to the Bulls in the expansion draft the following year.

Drawing offensive fouls wasn't anything I started when I came into this league. You're right, it's the way we played in college. And I know the Southern Illinois coach got very upset by the way we used to fall down and draw fouls. I remember him telling my coach, "Why don't you guys start playing basketball?" Well, we weren't doing anything illegal. There's no rule in the book that says you're not supposed to attempt to draw fouls. The offensive player has the right to go around me. If he doesn't then he's just given me the ball. And I want the basketball. I'm selfish enough to think that our team needs that basketball more than they do. If I can help my team get it by stopping and letting somebody run me down, that's what I'll do.

There are a lot of great players in pro basketball. Frazier, by the way, as far as I'm concerned, is at this stage of his game probably the best guard in the league. Look at him. You see all the things he can do. Take a kid who doesn't have those abilities, and he's going to get very frustrated trying to go out and play like Walt Frazier. But even if he is limited in ability, he can help his team if he works hard. It doesn't take a lot of ability to stand straight up and let a guy run over you. It really doesn't. But it's one way you can help your team without being a great player. And if you can dive on the floor for a loose ball, that's another way you can help your team. All those things add up as far as your total performance.

I really don't think I have to score baskets to help our team. Here's the way I try to analyze my game. A lot of guys look at stat sheets, but I'm not really stat conscious. I figure if I can get 8 rebounds a game, and draw 4 offensive fouls and get 3 loose balls, that's 15 times I've given our team possession of the basketball. Now if you keep track of what possession of the basketball means, just having the ball, it's worth approximately one point. Actually, it's worth a little more, but just to round it off, it's worth one point. So if I can get that ball 15 times I'm very definitely making a contribution and I'm not even scoring. Plus, if I can make the guy I'm guarding work a bit harder for shots I'm doing my job. So the way I play may not be glamorous, but maybe some other kid will come along who can get some small enjoyment by knowing he doesn't have to score 50 points a game, or be the fastest person in the world, to play.

I do get upset when I see players who have all the ability in the world and they don't take advantage of it. They get to a point where scoring is so important to them that that's all they want to do.

I'm not what you would call a natural guard. When I came into this league people told me I was too big to play guard and too small to play forward. I've played both positions, and the things I do as a guard make it difficult for the players who have to defense me. They're not accustomed to playing against someone who goes to the boards as hard as I do. I get a lot of rebounds. That's probably the only thing that's different about the way I play.

I don't handle the ball much, by design. Coach likes to have one guy run our offense, and that's Norm Van Lier, so it makes it much much easier on me knowing I don't have the pressure of handling the ball. Some other guards probably are more oriented to working one-on-one with the ball, whereas I go without the ball and hope that I can create something by setting a pick. I set an awful lot of picks because we like to put the big guard down to screen our forwards.

What exactly is a pick? How do you set it? Is it just a matter of moving into position and setting your feet in place?

Well, there's the hard pick, then there's the average pick, and finally there's the pick that doesn't look like a pick, consequently you don't pick anybody. The secret in setting the pick is to make sure that you get meat on someone, get your body into position so the defender has to run through you. And it takes a certain amount of guts to put yourself where some 235- or 240-pounder will run into you, but that's part of our job. Our offense is designed so that our guards set picks to help free the forwards.

Once you've stationed your body into position where it

won't be called a blocking foul, then it's just up to your teammate to make sure he runs the man into you. It's just like setting a post out there in the middle of the floor, and the offensive man tries to shake off the defensive man by making him bump into that post. If it were an actual post, would a guy run over it all night? A lot of times I just consider myself a post. I don't know a lot about football, but I see this happen on TV once in a while. The quarterback will throw at that end zone and try to use the goal post as an advantage for his receiver. If the cornerback runs into the goal post, he's taken out of the play.

What is the fine line between a block and a pick?

Well, I'll tell you, I've played nine years and it's been awfully difficult for me to decide what's a block and what's a pick. What is an offensive foul? That should be a question that I could answer after nine years in this league. I think if you went around the league and asked every player, you wouldn't find one who would give you the same answer. That's the one area where I have trouble as a player, trying to determine what one official will call an offensive foul.

I get upset, although I try to control myself as much as possible. I think I've done a better job this last year in staying calm, although basketball is an emotional game. You get keyed up. If you spend a good deal of your life preparing and hoping for the opportunity to play, once you get that opportunity you're not going to sit down and say, it's not emotional. You stay that way, if that's what got you where you are.

My idea of my own play is that if I don't give the very best I have to offer, if I don't push and work and punish myself as hard as I can, then I'm going to have a hard time playing because I have as much desire as anybody who plays. I'm not going to say I have more, but I have as much. That's what has allowed me to play, not ability. Because I'm a very slow player. I'm probably the slowest player on our team, and that includes everybody. So what I have going is desire, and that sometimes gets me in trouble.

64

As for defense, there's no secret to playing defense. A lot of teams think there must be a secret, because they don't want to play it. It's nothing but hard work. If I were as quick as some of the guys who play, I really believe I could stay so close to the man I was guarding that I could just about eliminate his scoring. I could make him work so hard that he would be completely frustrated. I've been able to do well without much speed, but I've seen young players who are so quick it scares me.

I compare basketball to football. The theory in football is that if you knock a guy down and that guy gets up and makes a tackle then you haven't done your job. That's what we were always taught in high school. So as far as defense goes in basketball, if you move to a position and think you've got your job done, and quit, and that guy gets an easy bucket off you, you didn't do your job. Your total concentration has to be on trying to shut your man out, eliminate him from the scoring. But you need a dedicated team, because no one person can really go out and stop another person. You have to help each other. Basketball is a team game.

There are certain players you have to play tight and others who you stay off. You look and see what they're accustomed to doing. With some players, if I give them three feet they won't shoot as well as if I were right on top of them. They shoot better when you're all over them than if you backed off and gave them a lot of time. I could give you their names, but I wouldn't want you to print it.

You have to watch the particular habits of certain players, and habits of teams. This is another thing we concentrated very hard on in college. If our scout was paid $50 or $60 to go scout another team, we figured he went to find out something to help us win. So we would go into that scouting meeting with the idea that we were going to find something that would help us win.

Some teams don't bother to look at scouting reports. They figure, we're going to go out and do our thing and forget what that other team is going to do. A certain amount of that is good, but there often comes a time when you want to know what a player will do in a crucial situation. If I know that, I may not challenge him until we get to that situation. There are two players in this league who will dribble the ball on the right side of the floor and as soon as they get to a half court they'll switch and dribble with their left hand. Well, over the years I've been able to draw roughly one offensive foul a game off each one of those players.

On some teams a guard will pass the ball to the forward and go to the other side and set a screen. Our college coach would say, why should we back out of that guy's way and give him a free cut to let him help give his teammate an open shot? If I can put my body between him and the man he's going to set a screen on, I may be able to interrupt the timing of that play. Football, baseball, and basketball players sometimes complain that their timing was off tonight, that they didn't execute as well. Well, what causes them to not execute well? Maybe somebody got in their way. That's what defense is all about. That's why scouting reports are valuable, because if I know my man is going to throw the ball to the center and go set a screen, I might as well be there before he gets there and take that spot away from him. It may break their rhythm enough to make them miss a basket and we'll win the ball game.

A lot of this stuff may sound corny, but I was spoiled in college. We won 29 games my senior year and didn't lose one. We were undefeated, and we won a lot of those games because we did things like that. Concentrate on minor points and they pay off for you. Over a season they will net you that extra game. If you were 20 and 5 they may make you 21 and 4. In our case, they made us 29 and 0.

Although he operates most of the time at guard, on occasions Jerry Sloan will move to forward. I asked him if shifting positions mid-game caused him problems?

The biggest thing I have to adjust to is the weight difference. I weigh 190 pounds and am probably one of the smallest forwards that plays. It's not much of a mental adjustment, but it's a physical adjustment trying to keep a

220-pound opponent off the boards. You know who's at the disadvantage. But I'm able to hold my own when I go down there.

10. *Lou Hudson*

"It's up to me to get open"

At 6 feet 5 inches and 200 pounds, Lou Hudson of the Atlanta Hawks is roughly the same size as the Bulls' Jerry Sloan. But whereas Sloan plays guard and moves occasionally to forward, Hudson plays forward and plays a small portion of each game at guard.

Hudson is a scorer, regularly ranking at the top of the NBA in that department. He wears a Fu Manchu mustache and has a smooth one-hand jump shot from outside. He gets open to use it frequently by running in tight, controlled circles until the usually taller and heavier defender falls behind. Then Hudson moves to an empty spot on the court, accepts the pass, shoots, and scores. I spoke with him in the lobby of his hotel in Chicago shortly before his team's game against the Bulls.

Forward is a natural position for me, because I started out playing there, and my size is more suited to that position, especially in the pros. I'm not big enough to play center, and not quick enough to play guard. Basically, I play without the ball, setting picks, going to the basket, being aware of what your man is doing on defense, and filling the lanes for the fast break. If you stay fundamental it's not a very difficult position to play.

When I go into a game, I don't have a set plan as to how I'm going to play, or what kind of shots I'm going to take. I just go out and look at my man and let him determine what I'm going to do. I don't advocate having your mind made up before going into a game.

We don't call many set plays with Atlanta, but we like to keep some sort of order in our offense. Which means the guard passes the ball to the forward, and if one pass is taken away you go to the next option immediately, because once the forward gets the ball, he has options. Everybody else is reading the defense which determines what he will do with the ball.

If he plays me close then I go to the basket. If he plays off me, I take the jump shot. Some guys play that in-between distance where they're going to bump you, drop off, and keep you guessing. But I like to keep the defensive man wondering what I'm going to do, and he's going to have to react to me instead of me reacting to him. That makes me more effective, because you're playing him.

It's up to me to get open, depending on how he plays me. I've found the best way to do that is to lure him into one position, then go to another. Like lure him into the lane when I see the ball is getting ready to come, then you release and pop out for the weakside pass.

Do you deliberately set up on the weak side?

I usually find my way to the weak side. Even if I start the play from forward, I have to pass the ball to the center or guards and they're going to want me to go away from the ball. One way or another, I wind up on the weak side.

Pete Maravich has the ball a lot which means he pretty much controls things. But that doesn't stop me from getting open. It doesn't stop me from filling the lanes on the fast break because that's fundamental basketball. You pass the ball. You set picks. You cut when you want the ball. You play the game. It's only complicated when you make it complicated, although other people can make it complicated for you.

Big quick forwards or small forwards that are aggressive can give me problems. But you're playing under the team concept and that's the time when you should give the ball to somebody else.

We like to run, but we like to control the run, because there are some teams that run better than we do. For instance, Boston runs better because they have better control of the boards. That's the key to running. If you don't get the rebound, you can't run. We have a short team when it comes to rebounding and getting it out.

We have the speed to fast break and the ability to do it, but we don't always succeed against the good teams. We don't even try to go out and rip and run against some teams, because they'll outrun you. Boston is one. Los Angeles is another.

How does your team run the fast break?

Usually the man who gets the ball first passes it to the sidelines. Then the ball goes into the middle, and the next two people take one side or the other of the guy who has the ball. You go down the court staying wide, and the guy keeps the ball in the middle until he passes.

You can see it developing whenever the opposition loses the ball and you get a good release out. Or you have a semibreak where you're going to hit the trailer. I usually look down and see what my role is going to be. You can tell just by taking a quick glance at the situation.

The mechanics of shooting the ball vary from person to person. Different people have different releases and they concentrate on different things. I try to keep the ball in front of me and shoot the ball with a slow backspin on it, which means cocking your wrist and actually shooting the ball rather than throwing the ball. There's a fine line between the two.

The thrower will also make good shots. And the shooter is going to miss some. It all depends on how well he shoots the ball compared to how the other guy throws it. But a lot of times you find that if you shoot the ball you don't have to be as accurate as when you throw it.

You don't need to be 7 feet tall to play good basketball.

How tall is Ernie DiGregorio? How tall is Calvin Murphy? It's a matter of ability. If you have the ability you can make it. If you don't have the ability, sometimes you still might get a shot at making it. It's a matter of being prepared if the chance comes.

If you set your goal as being a professional athlete, you are likely to have it shattered. When you weigh the percentages, they are against you. Thousands and thousands, maybe millions of kids, have the same idea. And teams have a broad age range to pick from. Some guys in this league have been playing fifteen years and that means you have a fifteen-year span of players to compete against. That just increases the odds of your not making it. You have to be good to decrease those odds.

Like most people, when I watch other sports I look at the ball. For instance, I find it very difficult to concentrate on the interior linemen at a football game. But I know what they mean to the running backs, and the same pattern holds true in basketball. The guys who are out there playing hard on both ends mean just as much as the scorer when it comes to the overall result. If they don't set their picks, it's hard to get open. You can still score. A guy can score without other people's picks and he can always score without people moving and passing the ball to him, because he can always take the ball and go one-on-one, but it takes away from the flow of the game and it's a lot more difficult to do. Some people can do it better than others.

Is it difficult to switch from forward to guard?

Not really. I think it's much easier to go from guard to forward than from forward to guard, because you're involved in a situation where you have to go from not being actively involved in handling the ball and running the team to doing just that. It takes a little more concentration to play guard, especially when you're out there and expected to run the plays and keep the offense balanced and keep the floor balanced and other things that a guard is responsible for.

70

Is the Lou Hudson of today a better basketball player than when he joined the league?

I'm a much better basketball player today than I was even three years ago. It's a combination of things: the exposure, the experience. I'm familiar with what I have to do. At times you go through periods where you really don't have any idea what you're supposed to do in relation to what the game is all about. But the guys you read about are the ones who go out and accomplish things consistently. It's a matter of attitude. I realize that I'm going to have good games and I'm going to have bad games. I have just to go out and work hard enough so that my good games outnumber my bad ones.

11.   *Tom Van Arsdale*

"It has to be instinctive"

It was still January, but Tom Van Arsdale admitted shamefacedly that he already had made plans to leave Philadelphia the day after the Seventy-Sixers' final home game of the season. He and his wife would be heading back to Phonix where they live during the off season and where he works for Moerkerke Realty with his twin brother Dick, who plays for the Phoenix Suns. Tom Van Arsdale never has to worry about post-season travel plans because it is a sad fact of life that during nine years in the NBA, not one team he played with has made the playoffs. He has played for Detroit and Cincinnati (which became Kansas City–Omaha), then was traded to Philadelphia toward the end of a year when that team was capable of winning only 9 out of 84 games.
Yet this unfortunate record hardly seems Tom Van Arsdale's fault since he has played well enough to be named to three All-Star

teams while compiling a 16.1-point scoring average. His twin brother Dick, who is a half inch shorter and 15 minutes younger, also has made three All-Star game appearances. One year when Dick made the team and Tom did not, they were going to each play a half, confident that not even their teammates would know the difference. At the last minute Tom chickened out.

Tom Van Arsdale is a pleasant, soft-spoken individual who was smoking a pipe when he greeted me in the doorway of his Philadelphia apartment. He admitted that his string of nonchampionship years also extends back through college at Indiana University where even the presence of he and his brother wasn't enough to assure a Big Ten title. The closest Tom has come to a moment of team glory was in high school when he and Dick led Indianapolis Manual into the finals of the Indiana state high school finals only to lose by a basket in the last minute of play. After talking with him for more than an hour I wished that a Bill Walton could be bequeathed to the Sixers to make that team competitive, or that the next trade would find Tom Van Arsdale on his way to a Milwaukee or a Boston.

I'm a small forward. Usually I can take care of myself physically with somebody the size of Bill Bradley. Those nights I don't mind, because I don't have to worry about him coming over my back to rebound. I have more difficulty when I have to play against the bigger forwards. Like when we play Chicago and I have to guard Chet Walker. He can get the ball in deep and use his weight to go over me, as can most forwards who are an inch or two taller. The big forwards will try to take advantage of a 6-5 forward as much as they can. I have fewer problems on offense. I don't have any difficulty scoring on anybody.

My brother and I played forward in high school and college, and he played forward his first three years as a pro. As it happened he went in the expansion draft to Phoenix and they needed a guard, so he has played guard ever since. I played guard my first three years in the league with Detroit, then after I got traded to Cincinnati I switched back to forward.

Neither one of us is what you would call a good ball

handler. In other words, when we bring the ball up the court it's kind of a struggle. If we get picked up at the ten-second line, instead of being able to keep our heads up and watch what's taking place, we have to worry about the ball. A natural guard like Walt Frazier can be pressed and he still will remain at ease and be able to see what's happening on other parts of the floor. It's important that the guard do that, because that's his responsibility. I know Dick would score a lot more points if he played forward, because he wouldn't have to worry about the responsibility of creating plays.

If we have to dribble too much before shooting, we're not going to be as effective. That's the way Dick and I are. Our forte in college was driving to the basket, but it's extremely more difficult to drive to the basket from the guard position if you're not a good ball handler. That's five or six dribbles to get to the hoop. If you're playing forward, you can take one or two dribbles and be at the basket.

Even though I played three years at guard I feel very ill at ease in the back court. I've talked to John Havlicek about that and he feels the same way. Of course, it's easier if you're playing on a team that runs a lot because then you're not playing set-up basketball like New York. If I had to play guard for New York without getting in on a fast break I'd be in trouble. That's why I mentioned Havlicek. He doesn't have to worry much about handling the ball when he shifts to guard at Boston because most of their offense is generated off the fast break.

I was playing forward when I was at Kansas City, which was fortunate because I could never have played guard for Bob Cousy. Cousy expected his guards to be the ultimate in creating situations—like he did when he played. In a lot of cases, he was too much of a perfectionist. For example, if you have a play where you try to create a backdoor situation, it was very important for him to have his players do it exactly the way he wanted: a bounce pass to the center, then a bounce pass to the guy going backdoor. If it's done another way and the basket is scored he's still not happy because he wants it done properly no matter what the result.

He was on TV last night. He's a man of principle and

integrity, and he said that one thing wrong with this society is that too many people feel it doesn't matter how you do something, as long as you get results. That's not the way he feels. He wants it done the right way. I found it very difficult to play for him because he was such a perfectionist.

Gene Shue, my current coach, also is a perfectionist, but he cares more about results than whether you do it the right way or not. In other words, if you win a basketball game even though you played badly, he's happy. With Cousy, if you played badly yet won, he was still unhappy.

My advantage as an athlete has been that it never has been a problem for me to get open for a jump shot. I'm not a one-on-one player. I have to rely on the offense to get me open, but I feel I'm good in going to an open area.

When I came into this league I wasn't considered a scorer or a shooter. I've been forced to shoot mostly because most of the teams I've played with have needed that.

I became good in moving to an open area when I played with Oscar Robertson at Cincinnati. I started with Oscar in the back court, but didn't have to handle the ball. So I would just move to open areas and Oscar was just great at getting the ball to me at the right time. I began looking for open areas and got confidence in my 15- and 20-foot jump shots. I changed the style of my game. Instead of driving to the hoop all the time, I would take the jump shot, and that's when I started to score points.

I have learned over the years how to shoot off a pick. And I mean *right* off a pick, not dribble one step past. There are guys in this league who have to get one more dribble to shoot off the pick. It's an easy shot only when you shoot immediately over the pick. You don't want to wait, or go on past, because that gives the defense the opportunity to catch up with you.

I used to believe that it was very important to jump high on a jump shot, but if you look at the good scorers in this league you realize they don't jump high, they just have quick and smooth releases. Jerry West releases the ball very fast. He almost lets it go on the way up. It's so quick that even if the defensive man is right with him, he doesn't have time to block the shot. It catches everybody off guard except the person who's shooting.

If you were coaching somebody on how to shoot the jump shot, what would you tell him to do?

Most of us know what to do. It's just a matter of doing it. At the start of the season I find myself missing a lot of shots because as I'm going up I'm not really looking at the rim. In other words it's important, just a half a second before you go up, to have your eye on the rim. You have your head up. You've already stopped dribbling. You're bringing the ball up to get it into position to shoot, and you still might not be looking there, but it's important. I find that sometimes when I don't have my timing together—like at training camp—I'm in the air and ready to release the ball and all of a sudden I'm finally looking at the rim. I have no idea of where I am, or who is on me, or where anybody else is.

Learning to shoot just takes repetition. When my brother and I were growing up we were out every day. We never missed a day, because we knew if we missed practicing, somebody else was going to be out there getting better than us. But we liked it. If you like it and you want to be good, you'll be out there. Nobody has to tell you.

Anybody can be an adequate defensive player if he wants to be. It's just a matter of moving your feet. We played New York the other night and a guy got around me for a layup. It was just a matter of my losing my concentration. I didn't move my feet and he went around me very easily. So playing adequate defense means just thinking about it and moving your feet.

Now to become an *outstanding* defensive player, a certain amount of art is involved. Like Dave DeBusschere. I marvel at the way he plays defense. Even if they wanted to, I don't think everybody could play defense the way he does. I can give him a fake and try to drive on him, think I have him beat, pull up and shoot, and he's still on me. He'll have a hand up in the air trying to block the shot. Now that's tough to do.

When I'm on defense I can be right with a player going up on a jump shot and I'm like a half-second after. Well, that doesn't do any good. But DeBusschere has the knack, call it an art or whatever, to go up as the shooter goes up. There's a certain technique involved. Maybe that's what separates the great ones from the merely adequate defensive players.

Some people have the philosophy that to know what their man is going to do they watch the guy's waist. If his waist moves then he's going to have to move. That's fine, but I don't think you can keep someone from shooting a jump shot by watching his waist. You might be able to keep him from moving laterally, but if you're watching his waist and he goes up in the air he's already up. DeBusschere has said that he watches the ball, and if the ball goes up he goes up. He knows then he'll have a chance to block the shot.

What do you watch?

I don't watch the ball. I watch the guy's chest, his upper torso. I'm not a good defensive player in that I can keep someone from shooting a jump shot. First of all, I've got short arms. I don't block many shots. I do think I can keep a guy from driving on me, but in this game it's important that you keep your man from shooting a jump shot. That's where most of the points are made.

It's interesting to watch the players play defense who are quickest in this league. I don't think they are good defensive players. They are so quick that they overdefense and are more susceptible to fakes. If the guy gives them a fake, they go one way and are so far over that when he comes back the other way, they don't have enough time to recover and get back.

It may appear that there is a lot of technique involved in baseball, but actually there is just as much in basketball. It's harder to recognize unless you know where to look. I try to explain certain things to my wife, but it's hard to tell somebody why it's hard to run a pick and roll. It sounds easy, but executing it is difficult.

Executing plays is very important if you want to become a winner. Plays are not easy to do. They are something that you just have to practice over and over and over again until everybody knows what they are supposed to do.

What is so difficult about running plays?

It's executing all the individual responsibilities. First of all, each individual has to know what he's supposed to do, then he has to do it. It's typical of younger players, particularly, to try to take the easy way out and not do all the moves. If you watch a team that executes well, when a player is going to go one way, before he goes there he will take a fake step the other way and then make his move. That's often the difference between good execution and bad execution. You do something extra to throw your defensive player off so he won't know where you are going to go.

When you have a pick set up, don't just go up to the man and brush him. I mean if you're supposed to pick somebody you go out of your way to pick him. If he's not where you expect him, you go find him. Players on teams that don't execute well see the man they're supposed to pick and just trot after him. These are small things, but if everybody follows his assignment the play will run properly.

Many players in this league think they are so good they don't have to run plays out. But I don't care how good you are, eventually you are going to reach that point in your development where you'll have to face other guys just as good. Then it's important to execute properly.

Lou Hudson talked to me about being able to read the defense and know when to change your options. How easy is it for a basketball player to read and react?

You can do it, but it's important that the other four members of your team read the defense too. In football the quarterback can read the defense and shout instructions in the huddle so everybody knows what to do. Or the flanker will come back and say they're playing me tight, so they adjust their offense. In basketball it has to be instinctive. You have to know what they're doing right now and know how to beat it. If I'm on the base line and I make a move to come back, the man with the ball must know what the defense will do. On a backdoor play, it involves the man with the ball, the pivot man, and me. So there are three men who have to read the defense, and that's hard to do. It takes a smart team.

We've had times this season when our coach Gene Shue has successfully called plays during a time out. He can see where we're being overplayed and tell us about it. Many times we have executed great plays out of the huddle because everybody knew what he was supposed to do. It's amazing, but this year perhaps 90 percent of the plays we have called coming out of a huddle to combat a certain defense have worked. Last Friday Boston was pressing so we called time out, said we were going to throw a lob pass, and I got an easy layup. We had time to do that. But when you're on the floor and all five players have to read the defense it's tough. If you had five Oscar Robertsons out there who knew what was going on you could do it, but we don't have five Oscars.

I found it pleasant to play with Oscar at Cincinnati because he would create situations. He was the kind of guy who on his good days would try to help everybody else score. He was known for the way he would play the first quarter and not look for a shot. He'd try to get everybody else going, then look for himself. Later I played with Nate Archibald at Kansas City. Tiny always was going for his points, so I found it much more difficult playing with him. If you went down on a three-for-one fast break, nine times out of ten he was going to take the shot himself.

But if I were his coach, I don't know what I would have done. Let's face it, he has a great amount of ability. You could give most guys in the league the ball and tell them to shoot as many shots as they wanted and most of them couldn't average 30 points a game. He is uncanny in the way

78

that he can score points. I'm sure his coach became so frustrated with our team that he just said, "Take the ball, Tiny, and score some points," which was what happened. It certainly wasn't conducive to winning games.

At Philadelphia we also have problems. We don't run the fast break well. It's basically because we're not a good rebounding team. A good fast break depends on that, and we don't react fast enough turning over from defense to offense. We don't have three guys saying: BOOM! We got to get down to the other end of the floor! One guy might run and the other two might jog down.

But this year at least we have improved to the point where when we go on the floor, we think we can win. Last year it wasn't that way. We have played well against some of the better teams. We beat Chicago. We beat New York twice. We've beaten everybody except the four divisional leaders. That's what the coach tried to achieve this year. Last year it was just embarrassing.

12. *Dan Issel*

"You have to be willing"

Dan Issel, walking through a hotel lobby in Norfolk, Virginia, the morning of the ABA All-Star game, was stopped by a fan who thrust a program in his way. "My brother is one of your heroes," said the fan. "Would you give me an autograph for him?" With a twinkle in his eye, Dan signed.

As we walked into the coffee shop I commented to him: "I didn't know that his brother was one of your heroes."

"I didn't either," Dan said with a broad grin.

Dan Issel seems to genuinely enjoy the sport he plays. "I think basketball has got to be fun," he says. At the previous evening's practice session, the forward for the Louisville Colonels had run up and down court, all 6 foot 9 inches, 240 pounds of him, practicing fast breaks, smiling and laughing and acting as though nothing in the world could be more fun. "I don't see how you could stand all the travel and being away from your family eight months of the year if you didn't enjoy playing the game. It would be too great a burden mentally and physically. When I don't enjoy the game anymore I'll stop playing it." You notice Dan Issel when he smiles because he displays the same mouth to the world as does hockey player Bobby Hull. He has no front teeth. It is a reminder that although basketball is a game is fun, it also can be rough.

Dan Issel, fair-skinned, straight blond hair, the raw-boned look of a lumberjack, can muscle his way close to the basket, a prerequisite for playing the inside forward position. His heavily muscular legs, like those of a heavyweight boxer, however, combine with the slender torso of a long distance runner, so he can move. He has that quick first step that permits him to drive to the basket, so defenders can't afford to play him too tight. If he is played loose, however, Issel will throw short, accurate jump shots all night. That is one reason why Dan Issel was able to score 10,000 points in only four years as a professional. He played center under coach Adolph Rupp at the University of Kentucky and as a rookie with the Colonels, but after the acquisition by that team of 7-foot-2 Artis Gilmore, Issel moved to forward. "I don't feel as comfortable at forward facing the basket as when I have my back to it," he admits.

Being a converted center, I still play a lot of low post. It works out well with our team because Artis is left-handed and he normally sets up on the right side of the lane.* That way he can come to the middle with his left-handed hook. Or if he turns the other way he has his left hand on the strong side. Since I'm right handed, it's easier for me to turn into the middle from the left side of the lane.

There are plays in our offense designed to get me open for a 15-foot jump shot, but having played center all my life until

*Right, as viewed by the guards bringing the ball downcourt.

my second year of professional basketball, one thing I never learned to do very well was put the ball on the floor. So there is nothing in our offense designed for me to go one-on-one a la Roger Brown or Billy Cunningham. My forward position is almost like a double low post. There's quite a difference on our team between me and the other forward. He has to be able to shoot well from the outside and handle the ball.

Probably two thirds of my field goals are scored from the inside position. Of course, it depends on what you can get. Now when I play against somebody like Julius Keye of Denver or Gerald Govan with Utah, they're both 6 feet 10 and jump real well. They're quick and not bolted to the floor. You can't move around them. It would be foolish for me to go inside and try to beat them all the time. But they're probably not used to guarding someone who can make 15-foot jump shots. On the other hand, when I go against somebody smaller than I am, it's advantageous for me to take them inside and try to post them, because a number of teams in the league don't have a 6-10 forward.

When you get the ball inside, what do you do to score?

Basically, it's just one or two things. If I've got the man behind me, I can turn outside for the bank shot, or the jump-away shot, or turn inside for my hook. In the past I haven't shot a hook very much, but a lot of teams now are playing me strictly to turn outside, so I've started to hook a little bit more. I feel that if I can get the ball on the low post with the defensive man behind me, I should score 75–80 percent of the time, because I definitely have the advantage in that position.

Of course, teams just aren't letting us get that close to the basket, either on my side or on Artis' side. They stop us by fronting the low post position on the ball side and dropping the off-side forward's man in behind to stop the lob.

To combat that we have to move the basketball around. If they're going to front us with one man and drop another man behind, with Artis most of the time and with me on some occasions, we just try to get the ball to the open man. If by moving the ball, you also move the defensive player, somebody is going to make a mistake. Somebody will be open, even if only for a 20-foot jump shot.

For instance, if my man is fronting me and the off-side man is behind me, if we move the ball quickly to the high post, or to the other side, then the defensive man behind me has to go to his man. If I can keep my man outside then I'm open to the inside. But when they start using people to help out, you sometimes have to cross that option out of your offense. Maybe they won't let you have the ball inside, so you have to depend on your outside shooters.

Our offense is designed so that if the ball comes down Artis' side, then I'll go to the high post. Or vice versa. If we both stay in the low post position it clutters things up a little bit.

Once I go to the high post, I'll look to Artis. If my man has dropped off behind Artis with his man in front of him, the guards will dump it out to me at the free throw line. I either have a shot, or if my man comes back I just dump it down to Artis and he has an easy layup. It works the same way on the other side with Artis taking the high post.

Nobody has ever accused me of being a very good defensive player. I usually get the weak forward defensively. Artis makes it a lot easier for me, because he's like what they used to call Bill Russell: the Eraser. Any defensive mistake the Celtics made on the court Russell most of the time erased it as the guy went to the basket. Artis does the same. Having Artis back there in the middle to block shots and intimidate people has made it a lot easier for me.

What about rebounding? Is there any secret to doing it?

I don't think there are any secrets to rebounding. It's just a matter of hard work and following solid fundamentals, especially in my case because I don't have the natural talent that a lot of people have in this league. I don't jump very high. I don't run very fast. It just takes a little extra effort and you have to be willing.

82

My coach told me when I was a sophomore in high school, if you want to play the game you have to be willing to put in the hard work. This is true if anybody wants to excel in any sport. You have to be willing to put in the time.

Of course, you need some God-given talent. Yet, I've seen a lot of people who had all the talent in the world yet weren't willing to work on it. There are others in this league without the talent, but they come out on the court every time and give it their all. That's important.

Shooting doesn't depend on natural ability. It just takes practice. You get the fundamentals down on how to shoot. That's easy: you keep your elbow in and follow through, and release the ball straight. The fundamentals of shooting the basketball are simple. It's the half hour or hour you put in every day from the time you were in grade school that makes you a good shooter.

We practice around an hour and a half a day and the first half hour of that practice is nothing but shooting. Everybody gets a basketball and you put in your half hour. The same thing in college with Coach Rupp. If we practiced only 35 minutes, everybody for the first 30 minutes had a basketball and was shooting.

13. *Marty Blake*

"I never want to measure him"

There was this man smoking a cigar sitting in the stands behind me at an afternoon practice session before the ABA All-Star game in Norfolk, Virginia, and everybody seemed to know him but me. Anecdotes about old days in the NBA, how he once almost had sold Cliff Hagan for $100, how Harrison in Rochester gave away Bill Russell, rattled off his tongue like acorns from an oak tree. Later we *happened to walk back to the hotel together and he gave me his business card. It said* Marty Blake & Associates, Sports Consultants. *At one time in his career Marty Blake was general manager of the St. Louis Hawks. "I'm unique" he said, "in the sense that in this age when there is a war between the two leagues, I work for twenty-five of the twenty-seven pro basketball teams. They employ me to give them information. The only two teams that don't use me are Golden State, who have not signed a player in three years, and Los Angeles, who have lost enough money on their last two draft choices to hire me for seventy-seven years."*

What do you look for in a basketball player?

Size is one thing, but we try to find that certain type of ball player to fit the needs of a club. Too often a team will have four shooting guards and will draft a shooting guard. You can't win with five shooters; the San Diego team is proving that. The old Boston Celtics, until the time they got Bill Russell, had some of the greatest offensive ball players of all time. They had Macauley and Cousy and Sharman, yet when they came to play the Milwaukee Hawks—the team I started with and subsequently took to St. Louis—he used to beat them 130 to 109 with a club that on paper wasn't their equal.

I try to sit down with each team and find out what their needs are. Let's take the New York Nets. They are looking for a strong rebounding forward or a backup center. Now there aren't enough starting centers coming out of college ball, so you have to find some guy who is around 6 feet 8 who can play bigger.

But the basic thing we look for is size and speed, depending on position. There once was a fallacy that guys couldn't play unless they were well over 6 feet, then along came Nate Archibald. And I once had a guy named Slater Martin, and everybody would ask how tall he was. I would answer: "I never want to measure him, because I might find out he's only 5 feet 9, and that's too small to play."

I think the essence of this game is quickness. The Celtics

are a paramount example of that. The running team. The easy basket, which is easier to get than the tough basket. To play a pattern game you better have superior depth. I can't think of any pattern teams that have won a professional basketball championship. The Boston Celtics, my St. Louis Hawks who won in 1957–58, the Philadelphia Warriors, the Los Angeles Lakers, the New York Knicks all have been running teams. The Knicks run with a pattern.

You take a forward. You want a forward anywhere from 6 foot 5 to 6 foot 9 who has agility, who can handle the ball, put the ball on the floor, who can shoot, and play defense—or at least be quick enough to play defense. One of the people I dug up years ago, and people ridiculed me for it, was Paul Silas. He weighed 265 pounds, weight he had acquired working in an ice cream factory his two years at Creighton. He would attempt to crash the boards even at that weight. And today he's probably the key to the Boston Celtics' success. Certainly one of the keys. He'll play defense and probably hustle himself 10 to 12 points a ball game and he can rebound and get the ball on the break.

In 1962 I took Zelmo Beaty. He was the third pick in the country, but nobody had heard of Zelmo Beaty, let alone Prairie View A&M. Zelmo was a zero shooter. Today Zelmo is noted as one of the great outside shooters among big men in the game. I didn't make Zelmo Beaty into a great shooter. Zelmo Beaty made Zelmo Beaty into a great shooter by working on his shot eight hours a day.

And you look at guards. There's a number of kinds of guards. There's the defensive guard, the shooting guard, and the totally well-rounded guard that we all search for. You have owners call you up: "I'd like a penetrating guard." There may be five penetrating guards in all of pro basketball: a guy who can bring the ball up the middle and either shoot or dish it off. Maybe DiGregorio. Possibly Van Lier. Nate Archibald. Mack Calvin. Frazier is a shooter, he's not a penetrator. Frazier will jockey into position. He has quick hands and he will steal the ball. He's a good defensive player, but Frazier is basically a scoring guard. Earl Monroe has transfixed his game from scorer to passer to scorer. Monroe can dish the ball up, but he's not a penetrator. There aren't that many. He has refined his game, however, from the showboat-type ballplayer he once was.

Certainly Pete Maravich is considered one of the great ball handlers, but he is one of the problems that the Hawks have. They have too many offensive ballplayers. They see Maravich shooting so the other guard wants to shoot. A person whose range is 10 feet cannot overnight become a 20-foot shooter.

The line of demarcation between college and pro basketball is wide. Even the worst pro basketball team is way above the best college team. College players come into the pros with a total lack of background. For example, Rick Barry. He is an all-around player now, but if I had Rick Barry in college the last thing I would do is have Rick Barry guard anybody. I wouldn't want him to foul out. So Rick Barry came into pro basketball without a basic knowledge of defense. He's become a pretty good defensive player—adequate, not great. A great passer. He was a quick passer before. But he had agility.

You're able to teach defense. I've thought that anybody who has quickness can be taught to play defense. I've been proven wrong on a couple of occasions when the player didn't want to make the sacrifice. But basketball is a relatively simple game which is compounded sometimes by guys who want to overcoach.

I once asked Bob Cousy: "Who would you pick if you had your choice between yourself and Bill Russell to start a ball club with?" And Cousy responded: "You don't pick a flea over a giant." That's the big thing. Think of the successful franchises, the great ones. Chamberlain with a number of ball clubs. Russell. Reed in the years New York was successful. Jabbar. I mean, you have a number of eras. You had the Russell era, the Chamberlain era, the Jabbar era. Possibly we're coming into the Walton era, or perhaps even the Marvin Webster era, an unknown ballplayer from Morgan State who only the people in the trade have heard about. As good a shot rejector as I have seen in many years.

Scouting is a complex business. There was a team that once took a kid in the first round and didn't realize that he refused to fly on airplanes. We do a real good job of checking. There's a great element of luck. We make mistakes. What we try to do is narrow it down. A lot of times I've used the analogy that I would rather be lucky than skilled. Branch Rickey* once said that luck is the residue of design, and I think if you work hard enough you'll get lucky.

Bill Russell wound up in Boston because he decided to play in the Olympics, and Lester Harrison didn't want to wait five or six months to sign him. Consequently at the last moment he drafted Sihugo Green as his first-round choice. We had made a deal to exchange draft choices with Boston figuring Russell would not be available. Boston actually wanted Sy Green, but Rochester claimed him. Then what happened is Sy Green went into the Army and they couldn't use him for three years. If Russell had played with Rochester I honestly believe there would be no professional basketball today. Boston would have folded. They always say I'm the one who gave Bill Russell to Boston. Maybe so, but I can reply that I have an owner living in St. Louis retired with $8 million he earned because he traded and got Hagan and Macauley. But if Ben Kerner would have gotten Bill Russell, we might now still have basketball in St. Louis. Whatever happens happens for the best.

*A former baseball executive with the Cardinals and the Dodgers.

14. *Mack Calvin*

"I have a book"

The day before the ABA All-Star game Mack Calvin relaxed in his room. Calvin, a graduate of the University of Southern California, plays guard for the Carolina Cougars and made the all-star team for the fourth time in five years in the league, even though he stands only a half inch taller than six feet. He averaged 18 points a game during the 1973–74 season, better than anyone else on the squad except Bill Cunningham, who missed most of the season.

I have the ability. The talent is there. It's just a matter of being mentally ready for every game. I try to put myself in a position where I go out each night and play the best I can. You hear a lot of guys complain that they can't stay "up" for an 84-game schedule. Well, I'm mentally ready to play each night and this is the greatest advantage that I have over my opponents.

I do this even if the games don't seem that serious. When you come to play one of the bottom clubs like Memphis, a lot of players aren't really ready to play. I'm ready to play each game.

This means eliminating from your mind all the outside pressures and things that bother you, such as air travel. Suppose we have to play in Virginia one night and San Diego the next. That's going to present a mental and physical strain for the normal person, but I think you have to get it out of your mind and go play the best you can. So many ballplayers get hung up on these intangible things, but you can't worry about it because it's something you can't stop. You have to travel. And you sometimes have to play three or four ball games in a row. I don't believe in getting hung up on small things. This is what separates your better ballplayers from your fringe players.

It's a matter of concentration. Being emotionally and mentally ready to play is about 75 percent of the game. I might get some arguments from Don Shula or the Maimi Dolphins, who claim they don't get emotionally up, but I cannot buy that. I think each player has got to be psyched up and have that intense feeling that goes on inside a ballplayer, which only an athlete can describe. If you don't have it, then you are going to be an also-ran. You may have great ability but you won't be able to produce, because you are not emotionally ready.

Every ballplayer has their own way of getting ready for a game. Spencer Haywood likes jazz, and he gets ready by listening to music. Bill Russell used to get nauseated. I get in arguments with my wife. I'm crabby around the house, especially if it's a big ball game. But that's just me.

With Carolina I do a lot of ball handling, starting the fast break, and trying to be aware of the game situation. Now I say game situation because this is what a guard has to do. He has to be aware of what player is in foul trouble, be aware of how much time is left on the clock, be aware who has the hot hand and continue to go with him, know where on the floor a certain fellow likes the ball, know which referees you can talk to and which ones you can't.

I'm fortunate in that I have another guard with me, Ted McClain, who plays basically the same role. He's more or less quarterback too. So we both run the club, and two heads are better than one. Larry Brown is a helluva coach and he knows the game too, so he gives us good instructions. But a guard has to know what's going on at all times.

I consider myself a student of the game. I work hard at being the best. Being the best is not just going out and using your ability, because so many ball players have outstanding ability. They have more talent, yet they haven't been as successful as I have because they aren't students of the game.

You have certain ballplayers that like to do certain things. Joe Caldwell and Billy Cunningham, for example. Joe moves very well without the ball. And Billy likes to spot up for his open jump shot. So you have to be aware of these things. If

Billy's in position for his jump shot, you have to give him the ball. And the same with Joe: If he's cutting and moving around the basket, this is where he likes the ball. Sometimes you will have a pigeon on you, who just cannot guard you. If I have a guard I can score on, I might let Ted handle the ball, set up the plays, so I can get open. To be successful you have to do these things consistently night in and night out.

It took me about 15 or 20 games last year to get adjusted to Billy Cunningham and where he likes the ball, where to give the ball to him on the fast break so he can make his move. Don't get the ball to him maybe too far out where he can't do anything, but give the ball close enough to the basket so he can penetrate and score.

The first thing you do is to get your big man going. The old cliché is that if you can get your big men involved in the game earlier, they are going to play better basketball. Because your tall men, your centers and forwards, have a tendency to get lazy if they are not getting the ball. They like to score early and if you can get the ball to them early and let them score, the next thing you know they are blocking shots and rebounding. That starts the small man's game going, running down the court on the fast break.

So many teams have outstanding big men who are denied the ball. If they don't get the ball early in the game, they get a negative attitude. I like to let them be happy and let them start doing their thing. Then my game is going to come to me because I have the ball 75 to 80 percent of the time. I can make my move anytime. I can get my shot. But they are the ones who have to get the ball off the boards and get it out to you.

This is one reason why New York is so successful, why Milwaukee is so successful. When the Lakers had Wilt everything revolved around him. They got the ball in to Wilt. Wilt wasn't scoring but Wilt was doing his thing. He was dishing it off, letting others score. Same thing with Jabbar. If you get the ball to them they are happy, but if you have them standing around not moving they have a tendency to be unhappy.

You play against the other teams so many times that pretty soon you know what the other players are going to do. I've played against Jimmy Jones or Billy Keller for so long I know the moves they are going to make when they come down on the fast break. You can stop them sometimes by getting ready and being in a good defensive position, but sometimes you get caught up in a game where you completely forget these things. That's when you get beat.

The ballplayer I respect the most is Jerry West. I've watched Jerry for so many years when I was a kid in L.A., and in college. Jerry West was always involved in the game regardless of the situation. That's why they called him "Mr. Clutch." I don't think it was because he was making lucky shots. He just never lost himself in a ball game. He always had that poise about him regardless of the situation on the court. Eight seconds left and he's always got control.

I try to pattern myself after him. This is what a ballplayer has got to be able to do: remain poised and cool. Jerry West does this better than any other guard I've seen. John Havlicek too. These are your great ballplayers. This is what makes superstars, remaining poised. A lot of guys have talent, but they don't hold their cool.

I like to study ballplayers. I have a book on all the guards in the league. That's something I picked up from Bill Sharman while I was a rookie with the Los Angeles Stars. I kept a chart on all the players: what they do offensively, what they do defensively, who are the poor ball handlers, where they like to shoot the ball, what I can do offensively against them, where are their weak areas. Certain little things.

We were playing the New York Nets last year in the playoffs. We had played them three games in two weeks before, and I had noticed one little flaw about Bill Melchionni. He liked to come down the left side of the court and turn his back. When he made that turn he picked the ball up with his right hand, which enabled a guard playing fairly close to him to flip the ball and steal it. I noticed it in one of the games and put it in the back of my mind because I knew we had to play them in the playoffs in about two weeks.

I let him make these moves, never tried to steal the ball or anything, because I knew there would come a time when we might need it.

New York gave us hell in the playoffs. We beat them something like four games to two, but in one of the games we were down by one point. Sure enough, he came down the left side, made the move, and I reached in and flipped the ball. It was like with a minute and a half to go. I took the ball down, scored, got fouled. We won by five or six points.

Walt Frazier does this well. In the second quarter he might be playing good defense, but he never tries to steal unless it's an obvious steal. But he remembers certain little things that a ballplayer does and he will take advantage of them in a close situation. This is what you call awareness, being a student of the game, being a heady ballplayer, doing it when it counts.

Before each ball game I look at my book, find out what I did against certain players, and who I have to guard, and go over this in my mind. You are playing so many different ballplayers on different nights and they do different things that you have to be ready for. Just like pitchers. They just can't go out and pitch. They have a book on who they're pitching against and what batters have weak spots. Basketball guards should do this too. Once you're on the court, you might think you know everything, but if you get caught up in the game and haven't gone over things in your mind you get lost.

You have an excellent field goal shooting percentage. Is there any secret to shooting free throws?

I think concentration is the key word. They say that practice makes perfect, but I cannot concentrate as well in practice even though I take the shots. When I get fouled in a game is when I really start to concentrate. It's a routine. It's something that's conditioned, where you get in the proper stance and follow all the correct fundamentals. I gear my mind to shoot the ball and putting it up right.

So many ballplayers fail to concentrate and that's why they

92

are poor free-throw shooters. I'll give you an example. Joe Caldwell on our team. I think Joe must be the worst free throw shooter in basketball. He's shooting about 48–49 percent, yet he'll shoot 51 percent from the field.* Well, how does that coincide? How can a guy hit a jump shot from 15 feet out and can't even shoot a free throw with nobody around him. Joe practices and practices, but when he gets up to the line he doesn't concentrate. He forgets all about the fundamentals and the technique that goes into shooting free throws. When he's shooting a jumper he doesn't think about it. He just shoots.

You mentioned earlier that you also have to know the referees?

Right, I think that's important too. In my five years I've had like maybe four or five technical fouls called on me, and I probably complain a great deal more than a lot of other ballplayers, yet they get technicals. You have to remember one thing about officials: They don't want to be embarrassed. Just like a ballplayer who doesn't want to throw the ball away or miss a basket in a tight situation, because that makes him feel bad. Officials are human, too, although we ballplayers have a tendency to forget that.

I try not to embarrass them. If one makes a call against me, I might say, "Explain that to me," and I might go down to the other end of the court and literally cuss him out, but I won't embarrass him at the moment the play occurred. That's another trick I picked up from Jerry West. I'd never seen a guy really cuss out officials more than he does and get away with it. It's not because he's Jerry West. He just knows how to get away with it. You wait and go down to the other end of the court or wait until a call goes against another player, then let that official know how you feel. I talk to them. If they're

*During the 1973–74 season, Joe Caldwell shot .496 at the freethrow line, .494 from the field. Mark Calvin shot .875 and 471.

officiating a good ball game, I'll let them know it after the game. They respect you more and remember it the next time out.

I'll sometimes apologize to an official. About three weeks ago I was having a terrible ball game. John Vanek was officiating, and I got a technical. It was the first call I got all year, and it was because I got caught up in the game and forgot what was happening. We were winning, too, but I was playing terrible. There was a call that went against me, and I got upset, and he stuck me with a technical. Two minutes later I apologized. He told me later that he respected me for that. Instead of having a bad ball game and taking it out on the officials, you should be man enough to take it on yourself. But you can't go through an entire year and play every game perfectly, and they can't have a great game every night. They have bad games too. It just seems that everyone thinks they have a bad game every night.

15. Don Murphy

"Most people don't realize how hard we work"

Don Murphy wears a gray shirt, carries a whistle in his mouth, and sweats a lot. "They can't play without us," he says. "The only time they worry about us is when it's time to start a game and we're not there." Don Murphy is a referee, third in seniority in the National Basketball Association. He and his brother operate a garage door distributorship in Cincinnati, a business which reaches its peak during the summer. This is fortunate, because during the remainder of the year Murphy officiates as many as four or five NBA games a week. His travel schedule is even more hectic than that of the players, because he appears in as many games but has no

94

home court. Despite the fact that he clocks more floor time than even the most durable player, few fans would recognize him walking down the street. He is an invisible man, which is the way he wants it. The only time you notice Murph is when he calls what you consider an unwarranted foul against your team. Then the boos start.

This is a very quick and fast game played by very big and agile men, consequently we have to be in good shape ourselves. We run approximately seven to eight miles in a game, and we have to be on our toes every minute. The players have schedules where they play 41 games at home and 41 games on the road. We have 82 games on the road.

Our life is a lonely life, because we are on our own most of the time. We travel alone. The only friend we have is our working partner. We don't meet until we arrive in the city where we are assigned to referee a game.

The league office gives us our assignments by the month. The name of our working partner is on this list, so we may be in contact with him to see if we can rent a car together or share a cab to the hotel. We stay at different hotels from the teams. We have a master roster of the hotels where all the NBA teams stay, and we are designated two other hotels. Every once in a while you may run into a team at the airport the day of a game, but that's the only indication they have until we walk into the arena who will be working their game.

We have what we call lead referees and nonlead referees. We don't like the words "senior" and "junior." To qualify as a lead referee you need four or five year's service in the league and you must be stable enough so they can turn you loose with someone who has less experience.

There are 20 referees on the NBA roster and 12 are listed as lead. A couple of them work a schedule part with younger men and the rest with those higher in seniority. This is done for a purpose because you can't stick two younger guys together. From a rules standpoint this game is a lot different from high school and college. You need someone out there with experience.

The lead referee is not out there to overrule a nonlead referee when it comes to judgment calls. We let everybody referee their own game and hold up their end of the court. But if a rule interpretation is involved we step in and help the other guy out because our philosophy in this league is to get it right. We have enough mistakes as far as judgment goes without also getting mistakes on rules too.

To pick up fouls and violations you've got to have an angle. Angles are very important in our game and we work very hard to obtain the angle we want on any particular play. The flow of the action has a lot to do with what kind of angle you need. We don't like to guess on plays that we don't see. A lot of times when there is a whistle on a play, we will look at the other referee to see if he can help us. This is something we have a hard time teaching younger referees, particularly when you have a double whistle, to look at the other guy if there is any doubt in your mind. Let's get the play right. This is what we strive for: getting it right.

I've been to a lot of games where I sat up in the stands. Sometimes I say to myself, boy, you do get a good view from up here on certain plays. I look at the position of the referee and realize that I can see it better than he can see it. A lot of times, with the players so big, you can get too close to the play because there is not enough room, or time, to back off. I'll tell you a play that gives me a lot of trouble. A player will dribble along the base line as though he's going to throw in a reverse layup, then will jump up in the air and fire it back out to somebody. A lot of times he's very close to coming back down on the floor, which is a walk, before he releases that ball. You can't tell for sure a lot of times whether he got back on the floor or not. The spectator in the stands 40 feet away may have a better picture of the play because he can see the player's entire body.

At the same time it's amazing how fans will react to certain plays that happen on the opposite end of the floor and you know darned well that they can't see it. Or players on the bench. They can't see the end line and whether the guy stepped on it or not, but invariably they complain.

In an average game a referee may blow his whistle 60 or 65

Preceding page:

Elmore Smith, Los Angeles Lakers center, gets ready to block a shot by Chicago Bulls guard Norman Van Lier, as Gail Goodrich looks on. Van Lier, however, appears to pass to the man Smith has left.

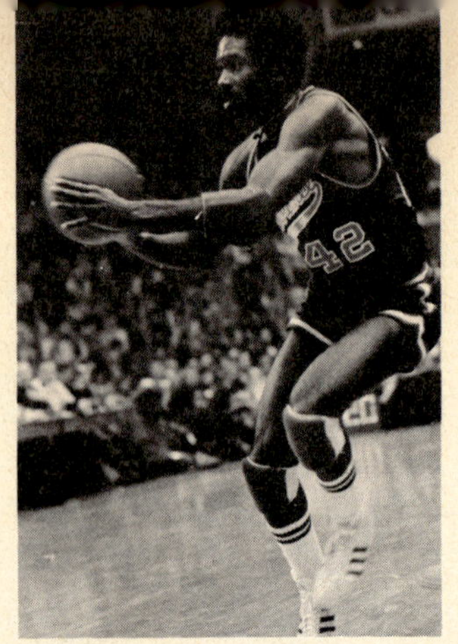

Lucius Allen of the Milwaukee Bucks.

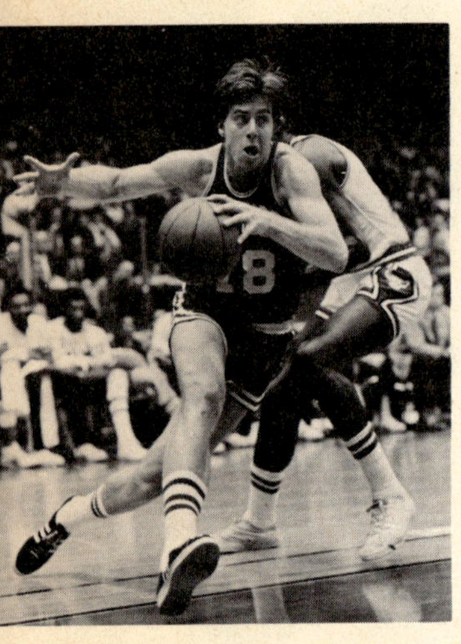

Dave Cowens drives toward the basket.

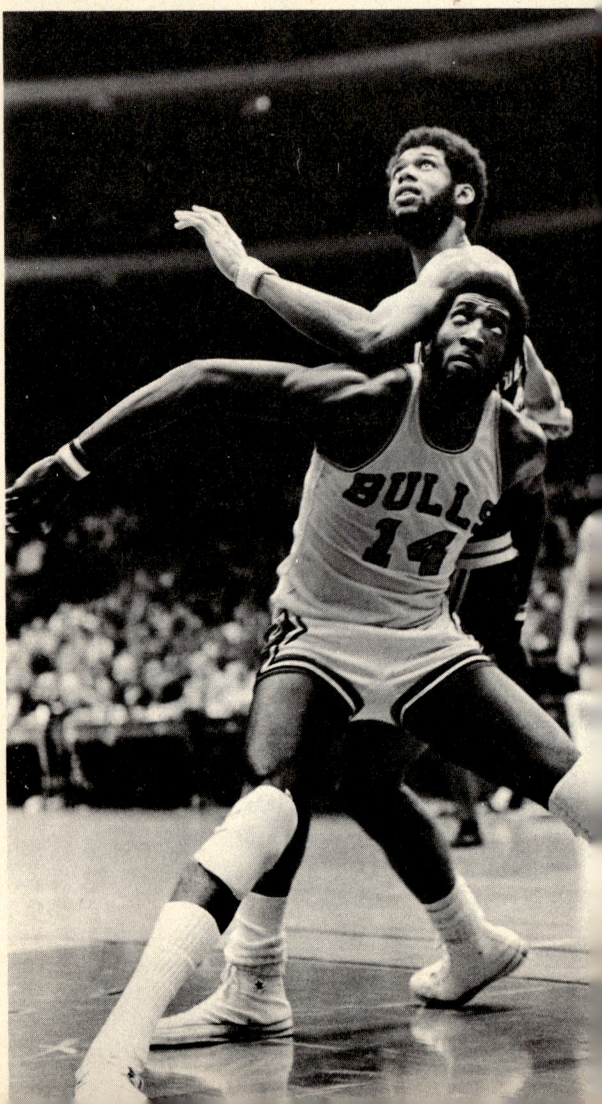

Clifford Ray, Chicago Bulls center, effectively boxes out Kareem Abdul-Jabbar of the Milwaukee Bucks. Despite Jabbar's height advantage, he will be unable to take the rebound away from Ray without fouling him.

Jerry Sloan of the Bulls in a characteristic pose: flat on his back with the Lakers' Keith Erickson.

Jim McMillian (before being traded to the Buffalo Braves) attempts to drive around Bob Love.

Charlie Scott, Phoenix Suns guard, drives for a layup.

Dave Cowens, Boston Celtics center, makes easy layup during NBA All-Star game as Sidney Wicks, Portland Trail Blazers forward, looks on helplessly.

Gail Goodrich runs Norm Van Lier into a pick set by Wilt Chamberlain and moves to get open.

Kareem Abdul-Jabbar,
Milwaukee Bucks center,
intimidates Chicago Bulls
forward Bob Love, as he
goes up for a shot.

Mismatch, left: Dave Cowen, Boston Celtics center, has switched to cover Nate Archibald, Kansas City/Omaha Kings guard, during NBA All-Star game. Archibald can drive around the larger man guarding him or pass to the man Cowens should be guarding, who now has a smaller man on him.

Ray Scott, coach of the Detroit Pistons and NBA coach of the year, signals a play from the bench.

← *Nate Thurmond, center for the Golden State Warriors, accepts a controversial call by referee Don Murphy with reasonably good grace.*

Lou Hudson, Atlanta Hawks forward, in action against Bob Love of the Chicago Bulls.

Walt Frazier, New York Knicks guard playing in the NBA All-Star game, brings the ball downcourt on the fast break, finds himself covered by Jerry West, so passes the ball to a teammate coming down in the outside lane.

Mismatch: Gail Goodrich, Los Angeles Lakers guard, has switched to cover Chet Walker, Chicago Bulls forward. Goodrich is in trouble, not only because Walker is taller and thus can shoot over him, but also because Walker is one of the NBA's top one-on-one players.

John Havlicek, Boston Celtics forward, cuts around a pick set by Dave Cowens.

times, and I would say if he keeps his errors down to five or less he's got a pretty good game. That's between 90 and 100 percent. We can pretty much tell when we've had a good game. You just can tell. You feel it. You know you're really sharp, catching everything. Other nights you find yourself working as hard as ever to get the right angle and you just can't get it.

This is why you sometimes may see us take a little guff from players without hitting them with a technical foul. There may be doubt in our mind. Maybe we did miss what he's complaining about. We take guff, but not abuse.

When players are shooting 50 percent, the games are easy to referee, because there are not many plays you have to call. But when they start shooting 30 and 35 percent and you get a lot of board action, that is when you learn who can referee. You also may get physically tired so your reflexes may not be as sharp. When a player gets tired his coach knows enough to jerk him out. When a referee gets tired you can't pull him out and put in a fresh man. We go for the full 48 minutes.

The key to the officiating trade is being able to set yourself a tempo. Every game has a different tempo. We can't go out tonight saying this is going to happen, because we never know. We always let the players develop the tempo, then we work at that tempo. If it's an overaggressive game, you just have to blow, blow, blow. There is no way out. You've got to do it or you'll have a fight. You'll have all kinds of griping, technical fouls, and all that.

I always make a point to say to my fellow referee when we start the game, let's try to make our first call a good one. There's nothing worse than getting off on the wrong foot with a questionable or debatable call. When I throw the opening toss I concentrate on getting that opening toss up just right, the right height, the right angle, so I don't start the game off bad and have them hollering all over the court: "You didn't throw it up straight." Maybe I'll get into the third quarter and have to make a questionable call, but if I have gotten the game off to a smooth start, I won't get as much flack on it.

Our cover varies with the flow of the game. It depends on

where the ball goes. One of us will be refereeing off the ball watching for three-second violations, watching for holding on the weak side. This is another thing we have trouble getting the younger guys to concentrate on: working off the ball. In high school and college you always find them looking at the ball. That's not important. You don't need four eyes on two players.

We don't move our heads a lot. We can get better peripheral vision just by moving our eyes. By the time you move your head, you've missed something.

We do have certain responsibilities, like the goaltending call. Most of the time this is called by the outside referee, because he has the best view of it. The underneath referee, a lot of times, is blocked out because when he looks up he is looking through the glass blackboard. Sometimes if there is a quick bust-out play you have to pull up a step short because the other guy will still be in the back court.

Three-second violations primarily are called by the underneath official. Once in a while the outside man will call it, particularly if the ball goes over to the corner. Then the outside man may look down the key and pick up any three-second violations.

Most people don't understand the three-second violation. First of all, the three-second count does not start until the ball is in the front court. Once it moves across the line any offensive player in the 16-foot lane with any part of his body is subject to a call if he stays there longer than three seconds.

But any time the ball is deflected or knocked away by a defensive team, a new three-second count starts. After a team has been taking three or four shots and one guy is standing in there, you'll hear people in the stands hollering: "Three seconds!" They don't realize that every time a shot goes up, you start a new count. Also there is leeway given to a man who receives the ball in the key and who in one continuous motion starts for the basket. It may take a four- or five-second count, but you let him go. Now if he passes it back out to someone else, then you whistle the violation. But you let him complete the play if he is going to the basket.

Another thing is where we let a guy finish a play even

though he has been fouled. He may be getting ready to shoot and someone may hack him on the arm. We hold the whistle a second longer and let him finish. If he has his man beaten and gets fouled, he shouldn't be penalized for making a good move. This is what you do if you call the foul too soon, because now it's a one-shot foul. You deprived him of the basket. This is what we call our continuation play. The only stipulation is that you can't put the ball on the floor again after the foul is committed. But if you continue with your motion you may get the basket and then the foul shot.

That's another thing that young referees have trouble adjusting to: sucking on that whistle and letting the play develop. The same way with a bust-out play. If the player catches a full court pass, heads toward the basket, and the defender pushes him to prevent him from scoring a basket, we call a two-shot foul. He either gets the basket or he gets two free throws because he was pushed.

Our philosophy is to let the foul mean something. Somebody has to gain an advantage before you call a foul. Like with rebounding action, you are going to have body contact. Two guys go up and one guy crashes into the other guy and prevents him from rebounding, then you have to call a foul. But if two guys go up and they bump bodies but the other guy gets the rebound cleanly, you just suck on your whistle and let the play go on. He still has the ball. Why call a cheap foul and march all the way to the other end and shoot a foul shot?

Every year we preach to each other, let's control the hands out front, guards who place a hand on the man they're guarding. This makes the game look bad; also the players get irritated when one guy is holding the other guy's hip and he takes his arm and swats it away. Our mechanics on that is we allow them to touch and feel, but no pressure. We will let them touch, because maybe he wants to fight his way through a pick and not lose his man, but when he starts trying to steer his man, then you have to call a foul. We do that early in the game. We let them know we're not going to allow it, then they'll play the way the rule books wants.

Each team is obligated to film at least two games a year

with a wide-angle lens as a check on the officiating. Periodically when we pass through New York we will go to the league office and watch these game films. You would be surprised how you can pick yourself up doing things you don't realize out on the floor. When the ball changes hands and I run downcourt I never turn my head, because before you know it: zingo, there goes a pass out of bounds. Now who touched it last? You may find yourself getting lax on three-second calls, or walking violations. The league also sends out observers to watch us at certain games and they sometimes will point up bad habits we have developed.

We are looking for perfection. Nobody wants perfection more than the referees. We don't like getting complaints from the players, from the coaches, or from the fans. Most people don't realize how hard we work. We are working a game that is almost impossible to be perfectly worked. I really believe that, because it is so fast and the line you draw is so fine. You never find any former players who officiate on the professional level. Most of them tell you that they don't want the job. They holler and gripe at you, but they know how tough a job it is and they don't want any part of it.

It takes a certain temperament to work this game. You need to be tough-skinned and have a tremendous amount of intestinal fortitude. The pressure is there and you have to know how to cope with it. You have to be able to make a big call no matter who it's against, or what the score is. It may decide the game, but you have to have the guts to call it. You may have to fight your way out of the arena, but if in your own mind the play happened the way you saw it, that's all you need to know.

Some guys don't get tough until they've refereed in this league for a year or two. They're used to refereeing in high school and college leagues where the players call you "Mr. Murphy this, Mr. Murphy that." They don't give you guff in high school and college. This is why you'll find a lot of our younger referees calling technical fouls, because the players are testing them, seeing how far they can go, trying to find out how tough they are. Once they start reacting, the players will back off.

We are not supposed to talk on the floor, but it is very difficult to work a professional game without some conversation. We try to keep it to a bare minimum. A lot of times a good sharp answer will settle some problems for you, whereas ignoring a guy will cause more problems to build up. Maybe give the guy who complains about being held by his opponent a quick answer, like: "Okay, if that's what he's doing, I'm going to take a good look at it the next time." You get him off your back.

Jerry Sloan commented to me that he had a hard time trying to figure out what officials called blocking and charging.

That's a tough call for us. You have to see the start of that play and the finish of that play. You can't catch the middle of it and call it. The rule states that you must have your position on the floor before he crashes into you. This is where Jerry gets caught all the time: When does he get there? He's a tough player. He's willing to get in there and take that rap hoping to get that call and it makes it tough on the referee.

They're all out there fighting for their rights. None of them want to look bad, and we don't want to make them look bad. They want us to be as fair as we can on our judgment of plays so they should be fair with us sometimes too. They don't like to admit they're wrong. But then most people who come to the games don't pay to see Don Murphy referee. They could care less. The only time they care about Don Murphy is when I make a call they don't like, then they let me know what they think of me. But when one of their players throws the ball out of bounds, or walks, or misses the basket, you don't see them booing. Yet that's just like making an error in refereeing.

I've often said to players that they may be right, that I may have made a mistake, that I'd like to bring that play back and have another look to see if I would call it the same way.

The league office wants us to control the coaches because they have such a bearing on crowd reaction and player reaction. We insist that they stay in the bench area. Once they step across the boundary line, they're dead. That's an automatic technical foul.

We want them down, but if they're up we don't want them waving their arms or gesturing. I'm usually involved in the game, running up and down the court, and I don't have rabbit ears. I'll be going past the bench and the coach may be saying something directed at me, but I don't pick it up because I have my mind on the game. Only if he gets loud enough or boisterous enough, will I pick it up out of the corner of my eye. Then I'll have to turn and get him.

A lot of times I think they try to bait you to call a technical foul. They get them called on purpose. They figure it will make their players mad enough to play harder. The key to being a good referee is being able to control coaches. Getting the respect of coaches and players both.

I once made a charging call that went against the Bulls. Dick Motta was irate. He jumped off the bench and said he was going to run a special seminar during the off-season for referees to teach us the difference between blocking and charging. Said he would pay my way first class to Chicago from Cincinnati. I went back out on the court and told my partner who responded, "Gee, can we bring our wives?"

As far as I'm concerned every call is difficult, because you have to react. You are asking a person to react first with his mind, then with his whistle. I had a play ten days ago where I could have jumped in a hole. We had a game between New York and Capital. For three and a half quarters, we had a super game. Tough physical game, but we're right in there blowing.

Phil Chenier comes down the base line and I'm underneath the basket. He goes up for a jump shot and I see Walt Frazier block the shot. I'm pointing out of bounds and that it's going to be Capital's ball. All of a sudden Frazier comes from nowhere and saves the ball, tips it off Chenier before it goes out of bounds.

Now I've already called the play "White." My partner hasn't called anything. So Frazier says to me: "Murph, I saved it off him." I asked my partner and he agreed. So I say, "Blue ball." Now Elvin Hayes gets mad and insists it's a jump ball because of two different calls. I told him I had made an error and our philosophy was to get the play right.

Now we get into a hassle. All hell breaks loose. The fans are throwing trash and paper on the floor. You never saw the tempo of a game switch more quickly. We couldn't do anything right and nobody is happy, particularly Capital after that call. We are refereeing like hell the last five minutes. My partner Lee Jones finally had to hit K.C. Jones with a technical. Coming off the floor he got all the flack, but it was me. I should have gotten it for anticipating that out-of-bounds. It was very embarrassing.

I always tell referees when they come into this league, if you are going to get in trouble, get in trouble blowing the whistle, because you are going to get fired if you don't. I remember the first game I ever worked, an exhibition game between New York and Cincinnati played in Anderson, Indiana. It was with Richie Powers, and we called 97 personal fouls in that game. I thought when we got in the locker room he was going to tell me to pack my bag and go home. He just patted me on the back and said: "That's all right, Irish. Keep blowing the whistle. I'll slow you down when the time comes."

He wanted me blowing. He didn't want me out there thinking! He wanted me reacting. He figured that after I got to seeing the flow of the game I would find out how it was refereed, and he was right.

16.　*Mike Riordan*

"All I wanted was to make the team"

Mike Riordan, sitting on the edge of his motel room bed in Cleveland following a practice session, offered an interesting contrast. He was wearing the red-white-and-blue, stars and stripes, warmup uniform of the Capital Bullets, yet he had this face that was so Irish he could have just stepped out of a Dublin pub.

Riordan exists as an anomaly in professional basketball, an indictment to its scouting system. In 1967 when he graduated from Providence College he was drafted only twelfth by the New York Knickerbockers. But while it is easy to measure height (Riordan stands 6 feet 4 inches tall, quite small for a forward), it is more difficult to measure desire. Riordan, who has had most of his front teeth knocked out, defied the scouts and stuck with the Knicks. Later he was traded to the Bullets where he established himself as a starter on a team leading its division.

When I came out of college I was the twelfth-round draft choice of the Knicks. They were pretty well stocked and I could see the handwriting on the wall. They already had six guards, and Bill Bradley came back from the service and they had to lop one off. I played a year in the Eastern League.

That year helped me quite a bit in adjusting to the higher level of competition. It was like a transitional period, from a college to a pro job. It gave me time to concentrate on some of the things I knew I had to do. It gained me more maturity and experience.

The following year the NBA expanded, and the Knicks lost three guards. That created three openings, and I had a better opportunity to make the team. That's all I wanted the first year—to make the team. After that I wanted to play a little bit more. After you play a little bit more, you want to start. You just look for higher and higher goals.

It's hard for a late-round draft choice to make it today, because there aren't as many opportunities, especially with some players with no-cut contracts. I was fortunate enough to come into the league before there were too many no-cut contracts or I might have been frozen out altogether. A lot of players may get drafted in late rounds because in college ball they might not have had the role of superstar. Yet often they may be able to fulfill that same role on a professional team if they only can make the transition and get the break.

104

There were three of us who came off the bench in 1970, the year the Knicks first won the championship: Cazzie Russell, Dave Stallworth, and myself. They called us the Minute Men. And each one of us performed a different role on the floor. We were specialists, but it was a difficult role to fulfill because you didn't know how many minutes you were going to play. You couldn't take time in the game to get warm. If you missed a few shots you weren't going to be in the game long, whereas the starter knows he's going to play 35 to 40 minutes. He'll have time to find his shooting eye, so he's going to be relaxed, and he can get into the groove. With a bench player, that's very difficult. The hardest job in basketball is to consistently come off the bench and play well.

So I would go work out the day of the game, shoot around, break a sweat, do some loosening-up exercises. In other words, I'd work hard enough so that by the time I got into the game that night it was almost like my second workout of the day and I felt much more relaxed. I had burned off some of the edge of energy. I knew I wasn't going to get tired because a bench player wouldn't play more than 15 or 20 minutes. I not only felt more relaxed, but if anything did happen to one of the starters I would be in better shape. I wouldn't be like a zombie if I had to go for 40 minutes.

Then even while I was sitting on the bench I would concentrate on who I would be playing when I got into the game, what plays were going well, which players were shooting well, how the officiating was going. If the officials were strict in calling fouls, I'd have to back off when I got in the game. If they weren't calling something, maybe I could take advantage of it. I tried to keep mentally alert while I was sitting on the bench so that when I did get in the game I was ready to play.

A lot of things that come easy for a lot of talented players didn't come easy for me. The only thing that comes easy for me is running hard and playing at an intense pace. The finesse moves, the shooting, the ball handling, passing, and the finer points of the game took me a long while to acquire. Defense is another thing that requires just a lot of hard work and practice.

I had to change from forward in college to guard in the pros and now I'm back at forward again, so I've had to work on a lot of different things as far as shooting, making the move off the dribble, using the pick and roll.

I hear the term "pick and roll" used quite frequently by ball players, but actually just what does that term mean?

Well, pick and roll is one of the most basic offensive moves in basketball. It involves two teammates, usually a small man and a tall man, like a guard and a center. The reason why you want a small man and a tall man is that the small man is going to run his defensive player into his big teammate and pick him off, or screen him. When this happens the defensive players are going to have to switch, and this creates a mismatch. The tall man who has just picked off the small defensive player now rolls to the hoop. Then they dump the ball into him and he can get either a layup or a jump shot over the head of the smaller player.

It's a nice play to watch. Oscar Robertson is probably one of the most adept at using the pick and roll, because he is clever at knowing what the defensive player is going to do. He'll drop the pass off, take the jump shot, or go all the way to the hoop. West is another good pick and roll man.

These are some of the things I've had to work at. A lot of guys coming up through high school and college do these plays, but you have to do them against a better level of competition at each successive step. You have to do it against bigger and quicker and more talented players. You try to improve by working on your game.

I say *working* on your game, but actually a lot of it is fun, especially because you can see you are going to derive some benefit. There also is the satisfaction of improving yourself as a player. Sometimes there is a degree of work in it, because you have to keep repeating and repeating and repeating certain drills to eliminate mistakes.

When I was talking to Tom Van Arsdale I asked him

106

which defensive forwards gave him the most trouble, and he mentioned your name.

Yeah, well he's a tough guy to stop because he has no weaknesses offensively. He shoots from the outside. He drives well. He comes off the picks good. He's a smart player. I just try to stay with him as much as possible until I get in foul trouble. We are both about the same size and same speed, so we are both banging at each other. He's physical and I try to play physically, so it's usually a good, rough matchup. Sometimes I'll know the keys on his plays and he'll know the keys on my plays because our teams run similar plays, so we often prevent each other from getting the ball. We both curse each other for knowing each other's pet spots. We find it hard to score off each other, because each of us defensively seems to be one step ahead of the other.

Do some players have pet spots where they like to shoot from?

Most of the players do have preferences, or favorite spots depending on where they catch the ball on the floor. They have favorite moves, favorite areas where they like to shoot their shots from. Most of the guys tend to go to the things they do best from the areas where they work best, so defensively you try to take some of this away from them. Force them into an area, or move, or shot which they are not accustomed to.

For example, Tom is very good at taking that jump shot to his right. Sometimes I try to force him to his left, but after a while of being forced to his left he gets shooting as good going left as going right. It's hard to stop a guy when he's going good, and the only way you can handle him is if the referees let you play with a little contact, let you get a hand on his elbow, or slap his wrist a bit.

I'm left-handed and they force me to my right all the time, and I'm aware of this. Other times a player might want to catch the ball at the top of the key and fire up jump shots. You have to take that away from him and force him to another area.

Before you play a team, you go over mentally who you are going to play, what he likes to do, and how he scored off you in the last game. You watch the other teams on TV and try to get a picture of their favorite moves. You only have 24 seconds to shoot so players don't have a lot of time to be fancy or cute. They have to do something simple and quick. A lot of times a defensive player will anticipate a bit and that's when he gets beat. The only trouble with knowing a player's moves is you don't know when he is going to use them. If you knew when he was going to use his favorite shots it would give you some kind of advantage, otherwise the advantage goes to the offensive player. Only he knows when he's going to do what.

When you shifted from the Knicks to the Bullets, you moved from a team that uses a pattern offense to one that likes to run. Did this cause any problems?

I found it a nice adjustment, because on school yards and in college I always liked to play the running game. I felt it was the best use of what ability I had. I like to run and I like to change from offense to defense. I don't get tired as long as I'm in good shape and I think this is one of the edges I have: running, covering the fast break, changing back over. If I had to go back now to a slow-down type of game, I wouldn't be happy because I don't think I would be used as effectively.

There is a trend that has come into the game the last four of five years where each forward has a different function to perform. Elvin Hayes, being a big and strong forward, does a lot of rebounding and often works inside as a second center. My job is more like being a third guard on the floor. So it is almost as though you have three guards, two centers, and no forwards. You know what I mean?

I move around a lot. I try to get down the floor on the fast break. I get involved in the ball handling, because I'm a former guard and I think I can make certain passes to get Elvin or the guards open. The small forward's job on our club isn't one of rebounding. He's more of a running, shooting forward as opposed to the bigger rebounding forward, and his job is to try to get loose, move away from the ball, try to set the other guys up. He should be versatile enough to work inside and out, and this helps create a faster team.

You can move with greater speed if you have two big guys rebounding on the ball. I usually just box out and then release, since with Unseld and Hayes in there they usually sweep the boards pretty clean. When I release on the fast break, that gives us a third man out. With the two guards going down we have three on two and that puts pressure on the defense right away. I think it makes for a faster more interesting game.

Usually on the fast break you have two wing men and a man controlling the ball in the middle. Normally when the ball comes off the boards I'll head for one of the wings. If one of the guards is already on my side of the court I'll circle over to the other side to balance the floor. If you don't have floor balance the two defensive players will be able to guard the three of us. If I can beat my man out on the break that means that one of us should be open. We try to get the ball down as quickly as possible so we can get a good jump shot or preferably a layup before the defense catches up.

17. Elvin Hayes

"You make them play your game"

Elvin Hayes was known as "Big E" at the University of Houston where he played center and engaged in several classic duels with UCLA's Lew Alcindor (now Kareem Abdul-Jabbar). Houston and

Hayes won one match in the Astrodome, but lost to UCLA later in the NCAA tournament. Drafted by the San Diego Rockets, Hayes led the NBA in scoring (28.4 average) his rookie year and in rebounds (16.9 average) his second year, but his team lost more than it won. The San Diego club moved to Houston and Elvin Hayes later was traded to the Baltimore Bullets (which eventually became the Capital Bullets). Wes Unseld already held the starting center job, so Coach Gene Shue moved Hayes to forward. Big E scored less, but blended well with his winning teammates, and during the 1973–74 season led the NBA in rebounding with a 18.1 average. We spoke in the coffee shop of his motel in Cleveland, the morning after my conversation with Mike Riordan.

We like to fast break. Wes Unseld is out right now, but when we have all our players healthy I feel we are one of the finest fast breaking teams in the league. Just before Wes went out we played four games in a row and in one of those games I had 21 rebounds and Wes had 21. And it was just *Goom! Goom!* That was the best fast breaking I had ever seen a team run since I've been in pro basketball. And, you know, Mike getting out. Phil getting out. Arch getting out. Any time you get those guys out on a three-on-one situation down the floor, you are going to get a basket.

Wes by himself, or myself alone, is not that effective, but when you have two players rebounding, getting 14, 15, 16 rebounds a game, then your fast break will work because you don't need that other forward helping out on the boards. You can let him release with the guards. Now when Wes is out, Mike has to stay in and rebound, so we can't run our fast break as well. We have to play more of a settle down, pattern offense.

The fast break is something that can get you a big lead, momentum, movement on the court, because once your fast break is working everything will work for you. It adds to your offense. You get a lot of easy rebounds, because the other team is worried about the break. They are rushing their shots on offense and missing them because they want to get back and stop that break. You put so much pressure on them that it throws their whole game off. It creates a lot of problems. It can be frustrating. You're trying, but you can't stop them. Every time you go down and shoot they come running by you. So then you decide to try and hold it up. You walk the ball down the court, but then you begin to make turnovers because most teams have favorite rhythms. Whenever you throw off another team's rhythm by running the fast break, this creates more situations for you on the basketball court.

Isn't this one of the reasons for the Bullets' success against the New York Knicks, your ability to fast break before their defense has a chance to get set?

That's right. The Knicks like to send their team to the offensive boards. Now if we get the rebound, we can run on by them. We played the Knicks five times this season and beat them four of those times, and once we beat them by 20 points because we just run them.*

You see, their offense is geared to protecting their defense, and if they don't crash the offensive boards and get the rebound, you can break them because they're all in there and they can't get back. Once you begin to break them it's just like any club: You make them play your game. Then they can't play that deliberate style of basketball they like to play: cut and move, cut and pick and roll. Now they have to get back *into* the game and this is not the Knicks' style. They have problems playing running, catch-up basketball. They are more pattern oriented and although they can break, it almost has to be given to them. They don't specialize in getting the fast break going.

I feel this way about basketball: The team that can control both backboards, offensively and defensively, and the team that can have the fewest fouls will win the basketball game. I

Later in the season, however, the Knicks eliminated the Bullets from the playoffs in a seven-game series.

don't care how many other field goals the other team scores, you will win.

Boston is a fine basketball team, and they cause us problems. When you have two teams matched up like Boston and Capital, you are going to have a lot of points scored, because everybody is out of position. The team that comes out most aggressive from the start of the first quarter will win. We played Boston three times this year and only won once, and I believe it was because they came out very aggressive.

They can put a lot of pressure on you. When Don Chaney gets the ball it's just like a hundred yard sprint down to the other end. We'll be running back in the middle trying to spread them out, but they get their front down line out so quick that Havlicek and Nelson will already be down there taking pot shots at us. When we're running well I think we can catch them off guard, but when things aren't going well and your shots are not going in, then you have to resort to something else. Then we try to pull it in, slow it down. If you get in a running match with Boston and you don't go well in the first quarter, you just have to call a halt and regroup. I think we can go to the slow down game better than Boston. I don't know if they can play that kind of basketball. They run and shoot. That's it. They don't care if they lose by 30 points, they're still going to run and shoot with you.*

We try to go into a game with a set game plan, but our game plan can alter during a game. It depends on what the other team is trying to do to us. If we find a team trying to run us, then we attempt to neutralize that with our offense. We'll put more pressure on their fast breakers to play more defense. We will run a man into certain situations. Make him go down low so he can't get out high. We just try to play smart basketball, because most of the clubs have improved and are playing fine defense now. The Knicks and Celtics

*Later in the season I saw Boston play at Capital. The ball crossed center court so often and so fast, it was like watching a tennis match.

have been pioneers in this respect, and a lot of other clubs are copying their defensive patterns.

Last year I thought we had a fine defensive club and this year, with K. C. Jones coaching us, I feel we have improved even more. But we've had injuries. We didn't have Arch Clark at the beginning of the year and Arch is hurting now. Wes Unseld has had problems with his knee and has missed a lot of games. When you have a link break in the chain it's hard to repair. You can do the best you can, but you can't replace those kind of players. When we had everybody playing nobody scored over 100 points on us.

We want to be number one and the only way to get there is by hustling, scrambling, and going out and playing hard every night. Defense is something that nobody wants to play. It's a phase of the game you don't want to do, because it takes guts. It takes getting scratched up. It takes connecting with the guy, shaking hands, greeting him, and saying: "I'm yours tonight." A lot of players don't want to do that. It takes work, and if you don't want to work you can't play defense. But if you can begin to play defense, it opens up so much more for your offense.

What about rebounding? Are there any secrets to doing it well?

There is only one key to rebounding. The thing that makes a good rebounder is never saying to yourself that I can't get a rebound. Never saying it's too far away from me. The whole thing is knowing in your mind that you're going to get every rebound, and if you don't get it you will get that finger on it. No matter where it's falling. That's what makes a rebounder: tough determination. Wanting that basketball.

You have to want it, first. If you want it, then you can say you're going to get it. If you don't get it, at least you're going to touch it. Those things have to be inside a person. You can't teach a person to rebound. Nobody made Wes Unseld a fine rebounder. That was something inside the player, instinctive. Like with Bill Russell: Nobody taught him to play defense. He knew how to react to a situation. With any good player, you can do certain things to help your ability, but those things have to be there.

Was it a big change coming from a losing team like the Rockets to a winning team like the Bullets?

I had an 80 degree reversal. It helps so much to be with the caliber of the players we have on Capital. We had some fine players at Houston and San Diego, but there never was any kind of organization. We had no cohesiveness. Everybody was individualistic. We had the talent to play fine defense, but we didn't work together. We tried to play defense individually instead of as a team. You can't play good defense individually. If you stop your man, then the other guy's man scores 30. Defense is looking after the other guy, trying to help your teammate and everybody on the court.

Here at Capital we stress teamwork. We stress togetherness. We stress helping out, and when you can build this relationship between players then you are going to win ball games. This is our biggest asset.

At San Diego and Houston there was so much division. At Capital it's more like a team. Everybody talks to one another. At San Diego it wasn't like that. Nobody socialized together. Maybe for two days people wouldn't even speak to you. But that's the way it is when you're on a losing ball club.

When I was in college I didn't *think* basketball as much as I think basketball now. In college you've got a lot of energy. You've got a lot of spring. You want to go out and just run and jump and rebound and shoot the ball and just play the game. Once I got into professional ball I discovered it was more of a mental game. It's not how high you can jump. You can jump high, but if they keep blocking you out, you won't get nothing. I was jumping, but I was getting nothing. So then it's more of trying to outthink your opponent, get him out of position.

If I'm guarding a player who likes to shoot five feet from the basket, I'll put him in an unfavorable scoring position. I'll put him two or three feet further out.

114

When I first came out of college Bill Russell taught me a lesson. He came out speaking to me, just laughing with me: "Hi there, Mr. Hayes." I went to the corner and took my first jump shot. He blocked it, and I had to sit on the bench for the whole game because it totally destroyed me. He was standing under the basket and I was in the corner and he still blocked my jump shot.

Right then I started watching players and how certain people would set me up. They would get good shots and I kept asking myself, how do they get those shots? How can I be giving that up? And they kept burning me on mistakes. It was just that I wasn't thinking basketball. I hadn't gotten into the game mentally.

It's the mental strain, not the physical strain, that gets to you. Before I go into each game I check each player out. I study him. I find out the things that he does best and I try to take that away from him. This year I learned something new about a couple of other players that I had never learned before. There's one all-pro forward, for instance, and all you have to do to him is one thing and he can't do anything on a basketball floor. And I never realized it until this year. It's totally surprising that something like that would go over-looked. He averages 24 to 25 points a game and he wouldn't average four points a game if players went out there and did that to him every night. It's really surprising that you can learn little things about a player, and if you weren't thinking he would go out and score like 40 points on you. So you go out there and you look at him, you figure him out, you see what he does, and he does the same thing over and over. He doesn't change. So you concentrate on him, you blend in with him, you play him. I'm a much smarter player than I was back in college because then I was just playing physical, not mental basketball.

18. *Austin Carr*

Austin Carr has an automatic answering device on the telephone in his Cleveland apartment. You dial his number. the phone rings once, and you hear wild jazz music followed by his voice: "Hello, this is Austin—" and a request that you leave your message. It blows the minds of long distance operators. With four and five games a week, it often is difficult to find basketball players at home, but I finally got through to Austin and we agreed to meet after a luncheon for the Cleveland Cavaliers sponsored by that team's booster club.

Neatly dressed in a blue sports jacket, Austin Carr, despite the presence of the rest of his team, seemed to be the center of attention. He had played for Notre Dame when the Irish defeated UCLA during the 1970–71 season, the last loss before the UCLA record 88-game winning streak. The last-place Cleveland Cavaliers selected Carr in the first round of the NBA draft, and although he has consistently averaged more than 20 points per game, he has been unable single-handedly to improve his team's finishing position, or even earn himself any All-Star game invitations. Austin Carr remains a good, solid ballplayer, patiently waiting for a winning team to be developed around him.

I try to do everything fingertip control, because I have better control in my fingertips. When I dribble the ball on my palm I tend to lose it. When I make a mistake dribbling the ball that means I probably lost my concentration, but usually when you dribble the ball with your fingers you have some control over it. You can spread your hand over a greater area, so that's better for ball handling.

Where did you learn to do this?

Well, you just learn it. I learned from my high school coach, and my junior high school coach, plus just playing on the playgrounds. Usually when you play on the playgrounds in your younger years you don't have adequate balls, or the pavement is not good, and it teaches you to be a good ball handler just playing in those type conditions. You have to adjust and that's sort of like a learning period.

There were a lot of guys on the playgrounds in Washington who did not make it to college, but who were very good ball handlers, very good basketball players. The competition was always superb. When I was younger I played against players like Dave Bing, Elgin Baylor, Artie Johnson, Willie Jones. Some of these guys never quite made it all the way through college or into the professional ranks, but they were very good ball players and you learned quite a bit playing against them. It was a good experience and I'll never forget it, because I still revert back to a lot of things I learned and used then.

Like what?

Like inside play, playing on the inside. I was always large for my age, so I grew up playing forward. Playing against players from the inside position, I learned quite a bit about inside play. Then after I started playing with older guys, I began playing at the guard position. I started putting both positions together, and my basic position now is more that of a swing man, because I like to play inside and out.

I did an earlier interview with Mike Riordan of the Capital Bullets. He plays the forward position more like a guard. You play the guard position more like a forward.

Right. You actually do more rebounding when you are a swing guard. You do more rebounding offensively and defensively. You play like a third forward. Your team has four rebounders defensively instead of only three. Offensively there are more possibilities as far as filling the lanes on the break. Naturally being a guard you're one of the main characters on the break, but when another forward is in on the break you match him so you can stabilize the unit more. It opens you up more to second shots.

I'm 6 feet 3 inches, and when I have a height advantage on the other guard I'll try to take advantage of that by posting him to the inside. But a defensive man, if he knows he's at a disadvantage, he won't let you post him. So you have to take him away from that position. If I want to take the low baseline position on the left side of the key, I'm going to start to my right to try to get him out of position. Then I'll come back and try to get him behind me. And just little things like that, like moving without the ball which I like to do. That's the basic part of the game.

I always try to go in the opposite direction from where I want to end up. Then if the defense collapses on a certain play, you want to be in a position where the offensive man can see you and get you the ball. It's no good to move to an open spot if you are behind him, or out of his vision, so you try to get in his vision so he can get you the ball when they converge on him.

How do you and the other starting guard, Lenny Wilkens, work together?

Well, Lenny has done a lot for me. I didn't realize it my first year playing with him. I've become more aware of patterns of the game. Being basically a swing guard, my thing is rebounding and scoring and playing defense on the other team's scoring guard and only once in a while playmaking. But being with Lenny for two years I've come to realize more what a play maker's game is. During the off season I'm going to try to develop that part of the game to my advantage, because usually I'm more on the scoring end of plays. Playing with Lenny I've become more aware of how he calls plays. It's a tribute to him that he's willing to give up his knowledge, where a lot of players won't.

What are some of the things he's taught you?

Little things, like calling certain kinds of plays in certain situations. Like when you really need a bucket, most teams

118

try to get it to certain players. When you need a point or two and a player is going well, you have to come up with a play where he will get the ball with time to shoot it. Certain plays: how to execute back doors from the forward positions, then from the guard positions, or center position.

Will he call all the plays for Cleveland?

No, I get to call plays too. It depends on the situation. Some games he will do more than he normally would, and some games I'll do more in the area of play selection. This year I've done more play calling, but see, he runs the team differently. If I run a team I run it more without the ball, because that's my game. Lenny controls the ball more than I do. It's two different versions of playmaking and the team has to get used to that. Now he may dribble into a situation where I may pass and get it back. It will be the same situation, but we do it differently.

There are definitely different patterns in basketball. Some teams run more patterns than others. The Celtics don't run much of a pattern offense, yet in a way they do. They run more fast break patterns, which depend on a secondary break. Like the initial break doesn't work, so the trailer comes into the situation. A team like Chicago, instead of fast breaking will come down and call a play, execute well, and score. The Celtics play better when they don't have to execute every time down. It's still a system. It's just a different system. When Boston runs a play there is more movement, with all five players moving and the other two not into it. Then as soon as it doesn't develop on one side the other two men immediately go into action.

Most of your successful teams running such systems have played together four, or five, or six years. They understand each other. They have the timing down. We had a major trade last year and it took a while to adjust to that. Only in the latter part of the season did we get adjusted to it, because different players have different roles. Now we are very optimistic about next year, especially moving into a new arena. That should provide an unbelievable amount of incentive, plus attendance should pick up. I'm hoping we have a good year.

19. *John Killilea*

"Basketball is not a game of thinking"

John Killilea is an assistant coach with the Boston Celtics. He also operates as chief scout, scouting both Celtics opponents and college stars. I talked with him during a scouting trip when he had come to observe the Milwaukee Bucks.

In October and November, we try and build a book on everybody in the league: exactly what they like to do, their plays, their personnel. We want to know everybody on their ball club because sometime we might want to know their offense, their defense, how they change up. Maybe we can pick up keys.

New York and Boston play seven times a year and we also scout each other. Their scout Dickie McGuire sees us. I see the Knicks. We know Milwaukee. We know Chicago. We still go see them so that we don't lose that edge, if you want to call it that.

After that, my own particular job is to make training films. We made a film last year of what the Celtics do, our execution. We make films on every ball club in the league, taken when they play us, showing all their plays. We think film is an easy method of showing the players what you want. Then, any advice I can give Tommy Heinsohn, and that's pretty much my job. Of course, there's only 24 hours and it's a 26-hour job.

120

How much scouting of actual games goes on in the NBA? As you say, it's not like pro football where the teams meet only once or twice a season.

At the beginning of the year you'll probably see a team a couple of times before you play them. You might see them one other time later in the year with the purpose of finding out whether or not they're doing something different. One of the reasons that scouting has become more prevalent in the NBA is that back when there were six or eight teams, you played each other so often you knew what everybody had for supper. Now we'll play Milwaukee four times, but two of those times were in October. I've seen Milwaukee play against other people this year without really concentrating on them, so when I look at Milwaukee today I'll be looking at them like I never saw them before. We have a book on them and we compare it. Ninety percent will be the same. But I have not seen Cornell Warner play for them. I have not seen what they do without Lucius Allen being in the back court. If one of their players is injured, how are they compensating for this? Things change from day to day with a ball club because of personnel.

Will you diagram plays?

Yeah, I will, a little bit. But you see, the thing with basketball is that any play, to be any good, has got to have three or four options off it. The options are predicated on how the defense reacts to different parts of the play.

Basketball is not a game of thinking. No one can convince me that the great plays made in basketball are all thought out, because the game changes so quickly while the play is being run. It's a game of reflexes. We recently beat New York. We had been coming over the top, over the top, over the top for the last three games in a row and all of a sudden John Havlicek, probably one of the greatest players that ever played the game without the ball started over the top with probably one of the best jab steps that Earl Monroe ever saw. Then he reversed and went back door. Cowens hit him with a pass for an easy layup and that was the ball game.

Now, why don't others on our team run that play? Well, they do. We use some people, but John fundamentally is probably the greatest. He'll work on the jab step, set the man up, then take it away from him, and that's it. Others will try that and never fool anybody because they're not convincing enough. They don't work hard enough at making it believable. Or they won't run hard enough to get open. I watched the replays on TV and Earl Monroe wasn't a quarter step behind John, yet that quarter step was enough for them to lose the ball game in Madison Square Garden. So you have to look back and determine the basic fundamentals in basketball that won the ball game for you.

Fundamentals win ball games for you. It starts long before the ball goes through the hoop. It starts when kids are just learning the game. When I look at a college kid I like to watch and see what kind of attitude he's got, and how hard he would work to maybe become another John Havlicek, or even get close to becoming a Havlicek There aren't going to be many to come down the pike like him.

When you scout college players, you are looking at many things. You are looking for attitude. How much? How smart is he? How intelligent is he? Who is his college coach? How much do you think he learned? Will he improve himself so that when he finally gets a shot at playing regularly, he can do the job? You look at our recent draft choices: Paul Westphal from USC with Bob Boyd as his coach. Steve Downing from Indiana whose coach was Bobby Knight. Phil Hankinson coming out of Penn where Chuck Daly coaches. All these kids are highly intelligent and they had excellent college coaching, so if they don't make it, it's sort of our fault. They are not gambles. None of them were superstars, but Westphal right now is a very big part of our ball club. The thing that all three have in common is attitude, super attitude. You know, being a star in college and coming here and sitting on the bench for two or three years can be a tough thing.

But you can't detect attitude from a stat sheet.

You are absolutely right. It isn't on the stat sheet. If I'm watching a college game, I look for —well, we call it "hiding." I know who I'm looking for, but if I don't notice him in the first five minutes without really looking hard at him, he must not be doing too much out there. That's going to tell a little bit about his attitude.

There are four things you look for. First, you look at a person's body. Second, his agility, quickness, and the speed that goes with this body. What's he doing with it? The third thing is brains, his intelligence. The biggest way his intelligence shows up is how he plays without the ball. Basketball is a great game of playing *with* the ball. That's why it's a great game of one-on-one. But what does he do without the ball? How does he get it? What kind of position is he in when he gets it? This shows his court sense. The fourth thing is the size of his heart. I think a person's heart is displayed on the defensive end of the court where it's nothing but hard work. I probably spend more time looking at the defensive end than at the offensive end.

And another thing: This may sound trite, but you sit there and watch when the boy comes out of a ball game. The manager tries to give him his warmup jacket and he flings it to one side or slams it on the floor. That's a minus. I think you've got to have attitude. You watch sometimes the arguing that goes on between a coach and a player. It happens, and you wonder what kind of player you're buying if his attitude is such that he can't take criticism, or whatever the coach took him out for. Another fellow may come out of the ball game and he'll tap his teammate on the fanny heading toward the bench. Encourages him. Yet he's the superstar coming out. I think that attitude will show up.

It takes 12 people to win. It takes 12 players playing together. You cannot have club house lawyers causing trouble. You can't have the guy walking around saying, "I scored 27 points a ball game for Oshkosh College and therefore I'm super and should be playing." You're going to get your picture on the cover of *Sports Illustrated* if you're tops in the NBA, so the Oshkosh *Journal* and all its publicity is down the drain. You're into another avenue of life and it's so much bigger and tougher.

If you were to just go out and watch college people, then your perspective would be: a great college player against what? Another great college player. By my being assistant coach and going with the ball club at least one third of their games, my perspective comes back to the pro level again.

In the NBA we draft 170 people the first ten rounds. Most teams know deep down that when they are drafting after the third round it's just going to be a matter of luck if someone comes up and makes the league. There's a simple reason. Only 25 people are going to be capable of coming into the league in a given year. Out of the group probably six of them will be gone the next year. Twelve of them will play an insignificant role in the league as long as their career allows. Probably there's only six players who really play a part in any given year. And one of them will be a superstar: a Chamberlain, a Jabbar, a Walton.

The turnover in pro basketball of the first seven or eight people on most teams is very insignificant. People sit their way out of the league; they don't play their way out of the league.

The good clubs are good because they go seven or eight people deep. If you check the boxes, very rarely you will see more than eight or nine people playing at all, and usually you see seven people getting probably 220 or 230 of the 240 minutes total playing time per game. We took Paul Westphal last year. He hardly played the whole season. He sat. He learned. Now he's our third guard. Downing and Hankinson came in this year. They were our first and second choices in the draft, but they were picked 17th and 35th overall. They haven't gotten many minutes. We know the role we want for them, and if they don't fit in, eventually we can let them go.

We are more fortunate than say, Portland or some of the expansion teams that get more help from their rookies. This is not a knock on Geoff Petrie, but Petrie came in with Portland and was co-rookie of the year with Dave Cowens. As good as he turned out to be, he probably wouldn't have had the opportunity to start with a number of teams. Could you imagine him coming to New York as a rookie and moving Walt Frazier or Earl Monroe to the bench? Or going to Los Angeles and doing the same to Jerry West and Gail Goodrich? Petrie went to Portland and started, but being a guard it was hard for him to affect things. David came into that center position with us and changed our whole ball club around, and now we have an opportunity to win the championship.

Anybody can subscribe to Basketball Weekly and learn enough about the game to draft in the first round. It doesn't take much basketball knowledge to pick a Bill Walton. But what about the less visible players, the Mike Riordans, people who perform a specific unpublicized role in college and who may be able to do the same as pros if given the chance. How do you find them?

Get lucky. Just like I said earlier, the big factor is luck. John Havlicek played at Ohio State with Larry Siegfried and Jerry Lucas. John was a defensive specialist. John now is the greatest scorer in the history of the Celtics. So how do you predict that? But John was blessed with a tremendous fundamental game, tremendous intelligence, and a super amount of team attitude, or whatever you want to call it. Jerry Sloan: if you asked what is the greatest attribute that Jerry Sloan has? It's his spirit. It's a mystic type of thing. What does Don Chaney do the best? Just makes you win. You can't measure that; I wish you could.

You look at a player's fundamental shot. You look at his release. You look at the spin he puts on the ball. You try and judge the quickness of his release. Now I say that like I know what I'm talking about: I really don't. Somebody will say to me: "Boy, he's got a quick release." And I always agree, but I'm never quite sure, because when he gets up in the pros he's got a Van Lier on him, or a Duck Chaney. There's no man in the world that's got a quicker release than Earl

Monroe, and he's got 97 different moves to go with it, but the last time we played New York, Duck Chaney made him eat his first three shots.

How quick is his control? Can he get his own shot? That's what I'm interested in. Does he need help to get his shot? If he needs help, will he use the help you give him? Does he know what it's all about?

Is it easier today for a small man to make it in professional basketball? Calvin Murphy. Norm Van Lier. Ernie DiGregorio. Nate Archibald. They're all listed at 6 feet 1 or under and they're all stars in the NBA.

It's not easier. What happens in the game of basketball is that people become geniuses because they do something that works. For example, ten years ago coaches wanted all the front lines in pro basketball to be as big as they possibly could. Then somebody came up, and I don't know who it was. Maybe it was a Havlicek. And he was so quick at 6 feet 5 that he left the Big Trees just standing there and growing. Now everybody said: "My God. What an innovative idea." So somebody else said: "Mike Riordan isn't that great a ball handler, but he's tough and moves well without the ball. Let's put him up front." So now every other team in the league was almost forced to go get a small fast forward to cover Havlicek and Riordan. Now Nate Archibald comes along and he just eats up all the big guards. Everybody else starts thinking: "We've got to get a small, quick guard to cope with Nate Archibald." So suddenly you have an influx of small guards, but nobody can convince me that shortness is a criteria. We are not looking for somebody that's 5 feet 11. We're still looking for somebody 6 feet 6 who can be fast as well as tall and cover Archibald.

The game is a lot more mobile now than with the Big Tree people. But somebody may come along with three giants who are very agile and mobile and he will win with them pretty easily. Take a look at Milwaukee's front line with Jabbar, Warner, and Dandridge. People keep saying they should ban

126

the 7 foot players, or raise the rims but that's ridiculous. That would be like saying that interior lineman in the National Football League can't weigh over 245 pounds. Some people have an advantage and it's up to the coaches and players to take advantage of those advantages. There are things that the 7-footers can't do. We've had good luck because we have a small, quick center in Dave Cowens, and he compensates a lot for what Jabbar can't do. Some of David's stronger points are Jabbar's weaker points and vice versa. Larry Costello is probably one of the finest coaches in the NBA, and he just anchors the defense around Jabbar. If you want to beat Milwaukee you have to take that anchor out of there. If you let Larry do what he wants to do, you get licked.

We talked earlier about diagramming another team's plays. Basketball moves so swiftly, how is it possible to watch the game and get all the X's and O's down on paper before three more plays have occurred?

I don't know whether you can. This is screwy, but when I was coaching I could watch all ten players on the floor at the same time, go home, lay down in bed, and almost see the entire ball game like an instant replay with ten people involved. Not only that, but I would see them as though they were moving in slow motion. You can get an idea of what they're trying to do, which is all you need to know. It's like a doctor training himself for diagnosing patients. It is simply a knack. I don't know what it is. I really don't.

You know, it's a funny thing. It's like when you get involved in the playoffs, and you go down to Madison Square Garden and the fans are going absolutely crazy. The only thing I hear is when they start the cheering during the playing of the national anthem. They start to clap, getting themselves psyched up, then I lose track of the crowd. I don't hear any noise after that. I concentrate on what I'm doing. The players do the same. It's just an involvement so that you are able to wipe out other things. You probably miss a great deal of the fun though.

20.   *Spencer Haywood*

"I like to put down a move and get open"

Coaches frequently speak of ballplayers as being quick as opposed to being fast. Often this term is used to describe a defensive lineman in football, who, though somewhat cumbersome going from point A to point B, has the ability to move with unusual speed while rooted at point A or point B.

But Spencer Haywood not only is quick, he is fast, exceptionally fast. You notice his speed when he runs downcourt with smooth-flowing stride to defend against the fast break, or when he strides from the corner to across the top of the key for a pass that leads to a twisting jump shot. The broad-chested, long-legged Spencer Haywood, you think, would have made an ideal Olympic 400-meter hurdler had his talents been channeled in that direction. He did run on the cross-country team in high school. Of course, he went to the Olympics (Mexico City, 1968) anyway in basketball and has his gold medal. He also has more money than any 400-meter hurdler will ever earn. Shortly after his Olympic trip he returned home and became the first collegian to join the ABA on a so-called "hardship" clause before graduation. He later moved further upward in salary by jumping to the Seattle Supersonics of the NBA with a six-year $1.9 million contract.

I visited Spencer Haywood in his hotel room only an hour before he was to leave by bus for a game at the Chicago Stadium. "Getting yourself up for the game?" I asked after we had shaken hands. I meant the remark as a conversational gambit, a space-filler while I connected my tape recorder for the interview. But the Sonics forward, ever intense, regarded the remark as a serious question. "I don't psych up," he responded. "A lot of people psych up for the game, but I try to stay as calm as possible. You're only at your best when you're natural. If you try and stay as natural as possible and combine this with the emotion behind the game, you can operate much better."

During the 72–73 season Spencer Haywood had averaged 29.2 points per game, third highest in the league. But the team had done poorly. Before the 73–74 season, Bill Russell came to Seattle as general manager and coach. Soon the team began to function more smoothly, even though Haywood was scoring less. "I'm taking about ten shots a game less than when I was playing before," he explained. "Before I had to carry the load in terms of scoring. Now we're trying to build a more balanced attack."

Scoring comes natural. When the shots are there, you take them. But a lot of shots can be there and you won't take them, because you're trying to get more adequate distribution of the ball. Take the top teams that are winning now. Boston doesn't have anybody averaging over 21 or 22 points. Chicago is the same type of team. Atlanta has two fine shooters on their club at the top of the scoring stats, but they're not winning games.

The game has changed in terms of offense. You need a five-, six-, seven-man squad rather than a two-man squad. They can always stop a two-man offense.

I like to shoot a good percentage, and I like to win. You can't win a game with outside shooting. In order for us to win, I think we have to take the high percentage shots. This is what we're doing now.

My best shot is the turn-around jumper. I like to shoot it around 15 or 20 feet from the hoop. I don't like to shoot from way out, because that's not my shot. I feel I'm invading the guards' territory.

Playing on a basketball court is like painting a floor. You work your way inside, and you work your way outside. That's the rule in basketball. This is the way I play. In terms of working my way out, I don't work myself beyond my perimeter. If I work myself from underneath the basket all the way out to the free throw line, then the guards take it from that point. The centers have their area to work with too, which is right in the free throw lane.

How did you make yourself into a great basketball player?

I always just played basketball. And I always shot, and I always was a rebounder. I like to drive. I like to put down a move and get open, you know. I like the way we're playing now, which is basically, if you don't have a shot—one, two, three—then you make your move or give it up because we don't have time to waste in jockeying for position. In terms of how you develop your talent—it's just by shooting. But as far as shooting baskets a certain amount of times, I did not do it.

I was coached in high school by Will Robinson, who is now coach at Illinois State. I refer to him as a genius because he taught me all the things I know. This was one of his philosophies. If you can't run, you can't play. There are a lot of shooters who can shoot but can't run. They are out of the league.

Another thing he had us do was ballet dancing for balance. I danced, and I ran a lot of 40-yard sprints to develop quickness. I also would run cross-country during the off season. I didn't do any playing.

The basketball court is a triangle in terms of getting open. Once you come down to the offensive end, you can run up to the top of the key. You can run down to the corner. You can run over to the other corner. So I concentrate on running in the triangle. In that triangle I won't interfere with the plays, and I also can work to get open.

If the ball is on one side I don't like to force myself to be over on that side. I like to work the opposite side, making movement. And in terms of making movement, if you are moving constantly your opponent will find it hard to box you out from rebounds and getting to the offensive board.

Before a game I like to know the man that I'm going to play. I make a study inside my head how he normally plays. Then I captivate his style and get his rhythm down and combine it with my team defense, because nobody can guard another man by himself. I would never do that, because you need teamwork.

You make your contribution by playing your man as honestly as possible, doing as much as you can with the other men, because we play a switching defense and a pressing defense, man-on-man. If the man gets away from me, the center will pick him up, so I have to get in front of their center to keep him off the boards. That's the kind of defense that basically all the teams have gone to now. It's impossible to play a particular man, because in the NBA no one man can stop another player, but a team can stop a player or team from scoring. That's what's important.

You go over your scouting reports and try to pick up the style. Chicago plays a slow, deliberate style. If you play their pattern they are going to beat you, because this is just Chicago. They run their players well so you have to counteract by moving the ball and running more.

Our team is doing much better with Bill Russell,* and that's because of his philosophy on the game. His philosophy is that you take one game at a time, and give it 100 percent. If you win, lose, or draw, you do things that he wants you to do.

In terms of myself, I looked on it at the beginning of the year as making a sacrifice in terms of averaging say 29 points to going to down to say 23. But after evaluating it and looking at it—wow, how silly can you be in terms of your own personal goals, to want to score 30 points and your team is losing. What you want to do is score down near 20 and maybe get the average of the man next to you up to 18 or 19 and have a good balanced attack. That's most important. And this is what he has been doing with us. Everything we do is as a team.

Statistics are for the fans. There's only one score that's important and that's the final score.

I play as hard as I can on any occasion. If I'm playing my brother, same thing. It's my philosophy. You can't take it easy at any time. When you're on the floor, you should give your all. If you don't, and the next player doesn't, then you end up with a flop team. You take the teams that are winning big: They give it all they have. They give the maximum and they are specific in what they are doing. They do the things they do well. Not do the things they don't do well. Leave those to somebody else.

*Russell became general manager and coach of Seattle before the 1973–74 season.

Spencer Haywood, at times during his professional career, has played center, even though at 6 feet 8½ inches he is relatively short for that position. At Denver, Haywood sometimes would play center on defense and forward on offense. Russell also tested Haywood at center early in the season, then moved him back to forward using him at center only occasionally in relief.

I found playing center difficult. I didn't master it as well as I have forward. I don't think you can ever master a position, but I didn't play it as well. I didn't feel as comfortable at center as at forward, but that could be because I didn't spend enough time as a center.

Center is, just like you said, center. You are the center of attraction, because everything has to come to you in terms of offense and defense, so you have to be thinking constantly.

I got good playing center defensively. In fact, I really dig that end of it, because I like to block shots and I like to try to intimidate teams, so I had a lot of fun doing that. Offensively it was just a matter of getting my timing down, scoring and that sort of thing.

What about the art of rebounding?

Yeah, well, rebounding is timing, of course. One way to get your timing is by tipping and by jumping. In high school Coach Robinson had me do a drill which consisted of touching the basket thirty times. I would touch it ten times to the left, ten times to the right, then ten times with both hands. That way you get your timing down.

Then you have to learn how to box your man out: get position on him so he can't go for the ball. You box, then go for the ball. If you don't box it's no good. With two players side by side, once he gets his hands on the ball the ball is loose, so if you box before you go to the boards then you'll have a clear shot at it.

I used to think of rebounding in terms of that. Also while practicing rebounds we used to put a cup on the basket that kicked the ball out each time it was shot.

132

You also have to read the ball. If the ball is being shot from the left side, then 75 percent of the time it is going to come off the right. It won't usually hit the back of the rim and come back. So you read the ball and try to get in position where you think it's coming off.

The easiest shot to rebound is your own shot, because you know where it's going to go off. You would be surprised at the number of players, however, who don't follow their own shots. In fact, I don't follow mine consistently.

As for blocking shots, you don't jump forward to block a shot. You jump straight. That's important. That's where a lot of ballplayers make mistakes, pros, college students, and high school. They make the mistake because everybody likes to be spectacular in terms of blocking shots and slamming them to the floor. You know: pinning a man down. But the idea is to try to control the ball as you block it. If you jump straight, you can control the ball as you block it. If you jump straight, you can control it more than if you only lean and slap. If you slap, you might slap it against the floor, or against the man, but if you jump straight, you can tap it. Nobody ever did that as well as Bill Russell. He used to block a number of shots and keep them in bounds because he would jump straight and just tap.

Bill Russell and I talk a lot of basketball. We spend many hours off the court discussing the philosophy of the game, because basketball is a mental game. Spontaneously going out there and playing won't let you win anymore. All of us have the same amount of talent, but you have to go out there thinking.

21. *Sidney Wicks*

"When you get that sour taste of defeat in your mouth, you don't want to taste it anymore"

Sidney Wicks is catlike when he makes his move to the basket or pops in the air to take a jump shot. He is catlike, also, on defense as he stalks his opponent, threatening him with his deep eyes, daring him to shoot. "I try to turn that glare on as much as possible," he admits.

But when I watched him one afternoon in practice, he was loose, relaxed, gaming under the basket with his teammates, practicing flat-footed dunks and fingertip basketball spinning. The Portland Trail Blazers, except for the second-stringers who at the other end of the court were playing a three-on-three game with their coach, seemed calm, relaxed in this, the last month of the season. It is the kind of relaxation—resignation perhaps might be a better word—that comes upon a team when they realize that even by winning every one of their remaining games they cannot make the playoffs.

For Sidney Wicks it was not always thus. He was the middle man in the UCLA dynasty of superstars: after Jabbar and before Walton. In the two years Sidney started at UCLA, his team lost only three games and continued its annual pillage of the NCAA championships. From the top team in collegiate ranks, it was a long fall to the bottom club in professional ranks, the Portland Trail Blazers, who were able to draft Sidney as the most coveted 1971 graduate only because of their low place in the standings. Perhaps it is understandable, then, that when you ask Sidney Wicks to talk about basketball, he relates backward through time to a point when he was part of a winning team, in fact, the winning team in basketball history.

My style of play is different from that of a lot of forwards in the league. I bring a completely different outlook to forward. My particular strengths are being able to play the all-around game. Some guys just shoot well, rebound well, or play defense. I like to think I can do everything, and do it exceptionally well.

Playing one part of the game is easy, because you can concentrate on it. When I went to UCLA we couldn't specialize in anything. We had to be all-around players, because our team was geared so that any given night a person might have to take up the slack for someone else.

The guards did the same drills the centers did. The centers did the same drills the guards did. That way the centers would know how to handle the ball. A full-court press might come up, and Kareem Abdul-Jabbar would bring the ball up the court. Bill Walton might bring the ball up the court. Or Sidney Wicks might bring the ball up the court. You have to be able to do that.

I keep relating back to UCLA because that's where I got my basic fundamentals. That's where they worked to perfection. Everybody was doing the basic fundamentals right, and we just clicked. That was the last time I played with a team that clicked as a unit. We were winning all the time, and we were able to isolate things down and say: "We are winning because when this man drove around him you helped out, and he knew where to go to help you out."

The UCLA coach Johnny Wooden presents the game to you in a fascinating way. It's really a trip the way he presents basketball, as a theory, to the players. He has a play where the high post is here, the forward and the guard are there, and when you draw it out, it's a triangle. So he said the whole game was nothing but angles. How well you can use the angles in your favor decides on whether you win or lose.

The game is made of triangles. When you come down on the fast break you make a 45-degree angle cut to the basket. When you box out, you box out on angles. When you rebound, you rebound in a triangle. The center boxes out his man. The forwards box out theirs. Everything is angles, like how you cut off a man on the base line. There's an angle on him. The base line is helping you out. When you are pressing a man you can run him to the corner, here, or run him into another man, there. What you really made is a triangle.

He's a very astute man. When he says things, they are

really profound. I read in the paper the other day that Johnny Wooden said he was having trouble with his team this year, because they listen, but they don't hear. You understand? People just read right over that, but I understood what he meant, because he would tell them to do something and they would go out and not do it. When I played, his whole attitude was hung up on a ball player being able to do exactly what he said. He'd say: "If you do this, we'll win." The guys would do that and we'd win. And the times we didn't win were the times we didn't do what he said. He *let* us lose. I lost two games in college where he let us lose.

Many observers felt that when Notre Dame broke the 88-game UCLA winning streak, Coach Wooden let his team lose. Notre Dame scored 11 unanswered points at the end of the game, yet Coach Wooden failed to call a time-out to halt his team's slide.

Right. He lets them lose when they don't play the way he thinks they should play. And he'll say: "That's what happens to you. You may not lose all the time, because you're talented enough to make up for it. But when you play against a nationally ranked team, on national TV, at their home, and you don't do what I say, chances are you're going to lose.

He let us lose when I played against Notre Dame—I felt. That's really strange, because you don't want to lose and what he does is let you taste the bitter taste of defeat. Like everything is going hunky-dory for you. You win 17 or 18 games in a row and have tasted the sweet taste of victory. Then when you get that sour taste of defeat in your mouth, you don't want to taste it anymore. You say: "Hey, I'll do anything rather than lose again. And he uses that to get you over trying times in the season. He feels that the team needs something to get them through the NCAA playoffs.

Swen Nater has become an instant success in pro ball even though he barely played in college. He feels it was because he was able to learn so much even while sitting on the bench at UCLA.

136

I feel another thing that helped Swen out a lot is that he went to the ABA. If he had come to the NBA many things that he's doing now he wouldn't be doing. The NBA is a lot different from the ABA, and it's because we have more veterans, older players with more experience. They know how to play a rookie. A rookie coming in, they would take all his strengths away from him and deal with his weaknesses. That's what the league is all about: People taking your strengths away from you.

Whether you survive depends on how much you can diversify and still play within your own capabilities. For example, if you can go to your left real well they'll overplay you to that side. So now you have to do something to make them respect your right, so you can fake and still go left, if that's the only way you can go. Or be able to go both ways.

Elvin Hayes commented that there was one all-star forward from whom he had discovered the secret of playing, and that if everybody played him that way, that forward would be through as a player.

Different people play different people different ways, you know. Elvin Hayes probably uses his God-given talent in some way to stop this guy. Now, everyone doesn't have Elvin Hayes' talent. He may be able to take something away from this forward and still use his talents to make up for what he's giving away, because if you take away something over here, you are giving up something over there. He can do this and still be able to come back and make up for the slack.

Some people may be able to stop a certain individual. Yet you play against him and he's going to burn. It may be that he has your number. It's really a trip. You try a lot of things on him, but nothing seems to work for you.

It's the matchup.

Definitely so. That's what the NBA is all about. There are a lot of things that the NBA is about. Taking away strengths. Knowing weaknesses. How teams match up with other teams. The Capital Bullets, for example, present problems to other teams trying to match up because of the way they are able to play a Riordan as a swing man between guard and forward. They spread him out to keep the court open. They use Elvin Hayes almost like a zone to block all the shots and get the rebounds so the guards can flare out and run. They play good defense and send everyone up the middle into Elvin, and he's able to block the shots while the rest of the guys pick up behind him.

A couple of other teams in the league are hard to match up against too. New York, for example. It's hard to defense them, because of that perimeter offense that New York uses. The forwards are 30 feet away from the basket, whereas most forwards play in closer. Now the defensive forwards must move out into a new environment 30 feet away from the basket. Not many forwards are accustomed to playing defense that far away from the basket. You understand? Okay, now you have DeBusschere shooting 30-foot bombs and making them. Bradley comes flying off picks shooting 20-foot jump shots. All of a sudden they present another problem for you. And their guards, Earl and Clyde, go inside and that presents a problem for the guards, who are not used to playing the whole game being backed inside and shot over. But that's Earl and Clyde's game. The Knicks take people away from their environment and present a problem for them.

What happened to Sidney Wicks when he came into the NBA as the first choice in the draft and had the old vets clamp down on him?

I didn't change my style, because I was able to do a lot of things. If someone played me to my left, I went to the right. A lot of people can't dribble well enough to use both hands. The main adjustment I had to make was not to come out there and try to show the other guys they're bad. They try to do too much, get themselves tired out, and here we have a whole other three quarters to go and they're dead tired. I found myself doing that the first two or three exhibition games. I had a tendency to run like I was on fire. I took about 89 shots the first quarter, only made like two. The guy playing you is intelligent enough to work on your weaknesses.

They thought my weakness was having to shoot the ball out on the floor. Don't let me penetrate. Get off me. Stop me from driving around them. Whenever I take my shot just jump up and try to make me shoot over. It worked real well during preseason and it took me a while to make an adjustment, and what I did was I just passed the ball. Once I passed the ball, they had to be aware of me passing the ball and cutting away and using other guys to help me get open rather than having the ball all the time. You know, maneuver.

But maneuvering for a guy my size, having to make a quick move to get by my man and shoot, takes a lot of energy. You're draining yourself. The Knicks and Bulls with their slow-down pattern offense just pass and pass and all of a sudden somebody has the ball and he's wide open. Their whole game is made easy. Different teams do different things. The Capital Bullets have people who are able to create their own shots and make them. The Celtics are able to create shots because they are running.

A pro basketball player has to pace himself, but I don't think he should pace himself necessarily for the fourth quarter, because there may be a time in the game where if you don't start putting out right *now,* the game is going to be out of hand before the fourth quarter. It has to be an intelligent pace. Most guys who have to play the whole game are able to pace themselves calmly, taking what they give you, and no more. You can't take any more than what's there. If you try and take more, that's when the fatigue factor starts coming. When you come down and say, "Okay, I have to shoot all the time."

If you feel you have to score 30 points—

If you have to score 30 points, you'll never win, because that gets away from the whole element of team play. The next guy on your team could be feeling the same way, and the next guy, and the next guy. All of a sudden there are not enough basketballs out there for a team to do anything. When we were at UCLA, for example, we used to love for schools to come in there with two high scorers—one guy averages 24, the other guy 25. We'd say: "Fine, we are going to hold the rest of the guys to their average or less. We also are going to hold these guys to their average, or less. And we're going to win."

They would have three or four plays for their hot shots. All you would have to worry about was box them out, keep them off the boards, just deal with their strength, and once you take away that from them, those other guys have to shoot. Now this other guy has a wide-open shot, and he doesn't even want to take it because he's not accustomed to taking it. He shoots, misses, fast break, layup, all of a sudden he's thinking: "I'm not going to shoot the next time I get the ball." So he passes off the next time he gets a good shot. Once he does, that means that our strategy is working. And it worked, and worked. When I went to UCLA our margin of victory was something like 20 or 25 points. We just blew teams out of there.

What about the adjustment you had to make, coming from a team like UCLA where you won practically every game, to a team like the Portland Trail Blazers, where almost the reverse was true?

I had to mature and learn I wasn't in college anymore, and here I am playing professional basketball and I am playing with a team. My first couple of years a lot of the guys I played with in Portland weren't as good as the ones I played with at UCLA. Yet I'm playing against better ballplayers. Once I started thinking about that, I didn't expect to win. What I expected to do was get out there and play well. That's all you can do. Get out there and play like a team ball player and let everyone else know that I know how to play team basketball, if nobody else does. I go out trying to do as much as I can for

140

the team, and there is no more that they can ask of me. They
can't ask any more.

22. *Geoff Petrie:*

"It's like the ball is floating off my fingers"

*Geoff Petrie attended Princeton University, only an hour's drive
from where he grew up in Philadelphia. "If I honestly thought I was
going to be a professional basketball player, I probably wouldn't
have gone there," he admits. "It didn't do great things for me as far
as publicity goes, or didn't help me get into the NBA that much, but
I got a good education, and I'm here anyway. Princeton can't
compete recruiting-wise with some of those other places. We had
some good players come out of there—Bill Bradley, John Hummer,
Brian Taylor—but they just never got five good players in any one
year."*

*When the Portland Trail Blazers were founded in 1970, they
chose Geoff Petrie as their first-round choice in the college draft,
although few of the so-called experts expected him to go that high.
Nevertheless, he became an instant success in the NBA, averaging
24.8 points, playing in the All-Star game, and being named Rookie
of the Year along with Dave Cowens. In 1973 he won the
one-on-one contest featured at half-times of the ABC telecasts of
NBA games. Geoff is not so much what you would call a quick
guard as you would call a shifty guard, and on nights when he is
shifting in the right direction the basketball soars off his fingers and
through the nets with machinelike regularity. In his first three years
in the NBA he ten times scored more than 40 points, twice reaching
51 points.*

The good players in the league and the good teams in the

league are the ones who can play within their limitations. They know how to play to their strengths rather than to their weaknesses. A lot of players don't understand what they do well and what they don't do well. Shakespeare talks about when a man gets out of his element, it brings disaster. The same thing happens in athletics. A player who tries to do what he can't do is not a good player. Not only is he not going to help himself, but he is not going to help his team.

So I try to look at myself and ask: What are my strong points? What are my weak points? If I'm honest I have to say, well, I think I'm a pretty good shooter. I'm as good a shooter as anyone else in the league. So that's one thing I can do. All right, I'm a good passer. Now I cannot penetrate like Nate Archibald and snap off quick passes, but I can see open men and throw them the ball. Defensively, I can play good position defense. I can keep my man under control and make sure that he doesn't get any easy baskets, but I'm not going to go out and steal ten balls a game, so I try and limit myself on that.

You have some guys who are playing third forward, and they will come in and play maybe eight minutes a game. The first thing they do when they get in is see how many points they can score rather than see if they can play good defense and help the guys that are out there. It comes to playing within yourself, just trying what you do well. If you know you can't pass the ball, don't try to make passes. Let somebody else do it, and just do what you do well. That's my basic impression of the game.

Since I play in the backcourt, I've got to make sure that things run well, or that we are running the plays. But basketball is unlike football or baseball where one guy isn't that important. In basketball, from junior high, to high school, and even in college, the good players dominate. But when you get to the professional level, one player can't dominate the game. Not Bill Russell. Not anybody else. Even Kareem can't dominate the game, because he has only won one championship in five years. Sure, he's always going to have a good team, but he hasn't dominated. But when you

142

get to the professional level you have a number of players who, from past experience, think they still can dominate, and they all want to do so much.

Sidney Wicks told me that when he first came into the league he wanted to do everything.

You can talk about Sidney in this way. I think Sidney has improved tremendously as far as the way he plays now compared to the way he did then. He's a very intelligent guy, and he really understands the game and how it can be played. When he doesn't play well, it's more out of frustration rather than being selfish. A lot of people think that Sidney and I don't get along, but that's not really true. There are a lot of others on our team that Sidney hasn't gotten along with besides me.

When he was a rookie he felt a lot of pressure because he was the number one draft choice and everybody thought he was going to turn our team around. I was hurt and didn't play well. We both probably said things we didn't mean, but the last two years we've gotten along well.

With two players the caliber of Sidney Wicks and Geoff Petrie, why hasn't Portland been able to win more games? At times, the Trail Blazers have seemed only one step away from being a winning team.

With the team we have this year, that's true. Move back and see who we played with a couple of years ago and it just wasn't possible. First of all, we were in a situation where we had such a turnover in personnel every year that nobody knew who was going to be on our team and who wasn't. Most of the guys were rookies each year, and rookies just don't win games for you. Experience wins games for you. The winning teams in the league are experienced teams.

Then this year came along and we had more experienced players than we ever had. We were 19 and 23 at the All-Star break and with a little bit of luck we could have been about a

.500 ball club, but we had injuries, and things just deteriorated to a point where we'll probably finish with a worse record than we had last year. We'll have around 25 wins this year, but with luck we could have had 45. Things just didn't work out.

The last time I saw Portland play, you got beat when Jerry Sloan hit a jumper with two seconds to play.

We've lost about six games just like that, and in seven of our last ten games we have been ahead with three or four minutes to play and still lost. There really is no excuse to lose that many games that way, consistently. We haven't had guys in the lineup, and we just don't have the depth to be able to win those games. Before the All-Star game I was probably averaging 40 minutes a game, then I got injured. After I came back I went a whole string of games probably playing only 15 minutes. It's a difficult experience when you come back after an injury and you play only 15 minutes when you're used to playing a lot longer. I'm just glad I'm feeling good again.

When you play 90 or 100 games a year, it causes a lot of wear and tear on people. I've been injured off and on for the last four or five weeks. The last three games are really the only ones I played close to full since the All-Star game, because I sprained my ankle, then I hurt my knee, then sprained my other ankle. J. J.* broke his elbow and our team really hit the skids, so to speak.

My biggest problem mentally has to be injuries. My senior year in college I had a herniated disc in my back and I missed all my early practices and the first few games into the season. My first year in the pros I played every game, then the second year I tore a cartilage in my knee.

It was around August and I just went down to the gym to shoot around. I wasn't doing much and all of a sudden I had a pain in my knee. The doctor took a while to diagnose the problem, but eventually he ended up operating.

*Forward John Johnson.

144

I missed the first 20 games. I never got back into playing shape until about the last 20, because they played me way before they should have. Then last year I had a good year again and this year I was off to having the best year I ever had, but I got hurt again. I'll probably miss 15 or so games this year.

When I hurt my knee it was the second operation I had on it. I had torn ligaments playing football in high school, so I've had two operations there. And this year I've got tendonitis, so it's really a delicate thing. There's nothing so wrong with the knee that they have to operate, but once in a while it gets sore and I can't play as well as I should.

What about the problem of playing four or five games in a row on the road, and not getting home for two weeks?

No question about it, when you play at home, you are more rested. You're more comfortable if you're not traveling every day. I don't mind playing on the road. I don't get that tired either, but you have to be careful and watch yourself so you eat right and get as much sleep as you can, otherwise later in the season you can get yourself run down. Playing on the road is a mental challenge more than a physical challenge. You can get yourself to thinking: "This is our third game in a row," and if you're mentally tired you might as well forget about playing.

It's an 82-game schedule, and you're going to have your ups and downs and I don't think you can overplay the importance of any one game. You have to look at the long-term result. In college one game can be a total disaster, because you have five days to prepare for two games over the weekend, then you have five days to recover after the last one. In this league if you tried to make every game an emotional experience, you just couldn't do it because you're playing too many games consecutively. You have to play hard all the time, and play well, but not because you jre psyched up. You can get a lot more out of yourself when you are emotionally up, but you can't do that for 82 games.

The pro game has really helped me though, because in

college we were a defense-oriented team with a slow-down offense, and we used to beat teams like 54 to 38. We never ran with the ball, so when I got into the NBA with the game being so much more wide open that really helped me.

What about the techniques of scoring? What allows you to average 24 points per game and have hot streaks where you hit 51?

I have about four or five moves that I have some confidence in. I know that if I make one of those, I can get a shot that I can make. If you just want to talk about shooting in general, I think shooters have to be confident. Every time they shoot the ball, they have to think it's going in. If you don't have that kind of positive attitude, I don't think you ever can be a great shooter, or even a good scorer, because you're going to have nights where you are going to miss three or four in a row, and maybe even more than that. A lot of people have a tendency to say, "Well, I'm off," and stop shooting. My idea is that if I miss five in a row and I stop, I'll never know if I might have made my next five in a row.

I have certain places that I like to shoot from, and I try to work to get to those spots. When I get there it's like positive feedback. Every time you do it and it works, you get just that much more confident. That's one reason why I've been scoring. Another thing is that our team plays to Sidney and me, so we are going to get more shots than the other guys are, but that's true with any team where several players are scoring a lot. They have a bit more freedom, a bit more leeway, as far as what they can do and what they can't do on the court.

You say you have favorite places that you like to shoot from. Don't the other teams realize this and try to take those spots away from you?

That's true. I'm sure before every game, the other coach will say, "This is what Petrie likes to do." And we know what

146

every other team is going to do before we go out there. But just because you know that someone is going to do that, that doesn't mean you can stop him. Like we know that Lenny Wilkens is going to dribble with his left hand the whole game. He's been doing it for fourteen years. But it's not possible to stop someone from getting his shots for a whole game. Or it may be possible for one game, but over a long period you can't because you have four other guys that are helping him and getting him shots.

The thing about basketball is that no play is ever exactly the same, because the game is kind of a collage. Every play is always a little different. You're never really in the same situation twice. It calls for a lot of split-second decisions. If you play smart, you can get shots.

When I'm hot or in a streak I have no conscious control of what I'm doing. It's like it's no effort at all for me to shoot the ball. It's like the ball is floating off my fingers and just going in the basket. That's the way it feels to me. It's almost like I'm separate from everything else that's going on. It's an unbelievable feeling, because no matter what you do the ball is going in. It's like a dream.

It doesn't happen that often. It goes in streaks, but any time you shoot 15 for 21, or something like that, that's the way it seems. Some people find that hard to understand because they go out in their backyard and they can't make one out of ten from the foul line.

I've had a couple of 50-point games. I've had quite a few 40-point games, but I think shooting is a mechanical thing. If you do things mechanically right, you can do them over and over again competitively. Finally you'll get to a point where you can do it consistently, and you'll become a good shooter.

There are guys who are good shooters who aren't great scorers. Take Dick Snyder of Seattle. He's a great shooter, but he's only averaging 13 or 14 points per game. Guys that are great scorers are the ones who know how to get fouled, who have the ability to get their men out of position and get shots. A lot of times a person wmo has always been a greater shooter has never had to work to get himself open. He's never had to move without the ball because he's always been able to make shots just standing around. On the professional level it's much harder to do that.

You can be a great scorer without being a great shooter. When you have a player who is both, like Oscar Robertson or Jerry West, then that's a player that probably comes along once every ten years. Those two not only are great shooters, but also great scorers. They know how to get shots, how to get fouls.

Getting fouled is all a matter of having some fakes and getting your man off balance. You don't necessarily have to drive to the basket to get a lot of fouls, because if the defensive man is aware that you can shoot, he is going to try and block those shots. So you just have to fake him sometimes and get him up in the air.

Pete Maravich is a great scorer. I don't think he's a great shooter. Goodrich is a great shooter. Kareem is a great shooter. McAdoo, same thing. Havlicek is a great scorer. He can have a terrible shooting night, but he's still going to end up with 20 points just by the way he plays. Charlie Scott is another guy who is a great scorer even though he's not a great shooter. He just has fantastic physical abilities, to the point that he can get off shots where a lot of players couldn't get them, but I don't think he'll ever be a great percentage shooter.

Jerry Sloan is a good example of a player who knows how to get fouled. And he can get fouled even when he doesn't have the ball. I don't think he has great quickness. He'll give you certain areas of the court, but don't try to come in on any of his. He doesn't try to overplay you to prevent you from getting the ball too much. But you can't penetrate on him because he plays good position defense. You can shoot good jump shots over him on the perimeter, but it's difficult to go around him. He's a good example of a player who knows that he doesn't have the quickness to go out and overplay a guy. He couldn't play full court defense, but he'll pick you up at the top of the key and that's it.

That's the way the Bulls play. They don't give you any-

148

thing inside, which is a good concept in defense, especially in this league. In college they can full-court press because they only play 25 games. You can't do that for 90 games. There's just too much running with the 24-second clock. You'll burn your guys out if you try to do something like that.

Because of the 24-second clock, the professional game is much faster than the college game and high school game. People say there's more scoring in the NBA, but there really isn't more scoring. If high schools and colleges had a 24-second clock and they played 12-minute quarters like we do, there would be more points in their games than there are in ours. The defense is unbelievable in our league. There are so many games now where under 100 points are scored. And when you think about how many opportunities there are in a 24-second period, then you realize how good the defense is.

What about the art of dribbling the ball?

Dribbling is just something you have to work on from the time you first pick up a basketball. I never try to turn my back on the man. Oscar is a great example of that. He never would turn his back on his man unless he maybe was on the base line about to shoot. He always faces the man. He always has the whole court in front of him, so he can see exactly what's going on when he makes his move. If a man is open he can see him.

A lot of young players get into a position, especially when they're being pressured, where they start turning their backs. It's a bad position to be in. Some players contradict that. Earl Monroe turns his back all the time, yet he's still a great passer. But to be a great passer and ball handler you have to be able to play facing the basket.

Take Ernie D. There are a lot of things I don't like about his game, but one thing he can do is pass. For some reason when he was a little kid, he thought passing was great, where some other kid may have thought that rebounding was great. So he just built his whole game around that. He's as great a passer as I've ever seen.

I can get any guy off the street here and show him the proper way to throw a two-hand chest pass probably in five minutes. In that time he could throw the ball back and forth to me. But in a game you have to do these things when you're running and moving and there are other people involved who try and stop you from doing that. That's a whole different situation. If I just stand there and throw a two-handed chest pass to somebody it's going to be intercepted. You have to know when to throw the ball. You have to know how the defender is playing the man. It's a whole series of things and the only way you learn them is by playing the game. I could take somebody out on the court and spend two years with him, teach him how to shoot, how to pass, how to dribble, and stick him in a game with nine other guys and he probably would be the worst basketball player you've ever seen. You can't have the jctual skills of the game without the game itself. You've got to learn how to play the game. You only learn that by playing.

You need a mental conception of what the game is like, what is going on, because the game is basically made up of two- or three-man plays. Well, it's a five-man team, but most of the plays only involve two or three men at one time. No more than that. But you have to have some idea of where all the other people are the whole time. That's why it's a mentally demanding game, because it's split-second. Things are changing every second and unless you can conceptualize the whole game you have problems.

I'm not saying that all five men are not totally involved, but you try to isolate people on certain plays. It's much easier to play two-on-two basketball, or three-on-three, than it is to play five-on-five—from an offensive point of view. Defensively you always want to play five-on-five. It's a constant battle between the two.

That's why so many teams put emphasis on the fast break, running the ball upcourt as fast as they can, because they want to get the ball up there and play three-on-three before the other team gets set. Once the defense gets set, it's much more difficult to be effective.

If I'm just standing in the backcourt on defense waiting for the team to get down, I have everything in front of me. I know where the ball is. But if I'm running back on defense, and the guy is running over here, it's much harder to stop somebody.

23. Nate Thurmond

"I wanted to drive the Rolls-Royce"

I spoke with Nate Thurmond the day after his team, the Golden State Warriors, had defeated the Chicago Bulls by three points. "Nate had a good game," Rick Smith, the team publicist, told me. "He scored 31 points, got 19 rebounds, blocked three shots, and broke up one fight." The balding Thurmond did all this despite having missed the previous night's game because of an ankle injury.

Nate was sitting in one corner of the hotel coffee shop at noon eating poached eggs on toast. Nate Thurmond owns a restaurant in San Francisco on which he has declined to place his name, not wanting it to be a typical athlete's restaurant. "I've got good food," he says. "I used to eat out seven nights a week and I'd go to an Italian restaurant and I'd see Orientals, blacks, Spanish people. I said to myself, if you got a nice soul food restaurant you'd see the same people. That's what I have." Nate named the restaurant The Beginning, after his grandmother. "She was the beginning of our family as far as we know. That's as far back as our history goes."

During a decade of play, Nate Thurmond has been one of the dominant centers in the NBA. Twice his team has made it to the final round of the playoffs, only to lose both times. He carries a career scoring average of 17.8 points with an even more impressive rebounding average of 17.1 a game.

If I was out recruiting someone, I would pick the person who could do a little bit of everything. I'm a good defensive ball player, but I can score. Too many people think of themselves as specialists in one area, rather than complete basketball players. I've had five seasons where I've scored 20 or more—when Rick Barry wasn't with us. Now I don't have to score 20, because we have guys who shoot better. But during those five years my man didn't score on me.

On offense I'm a rover. I don't just play in the hole. Centers are becoming more and more agile, like Bob Lanier and Dave Cowens. You just don't turn your back when you are in the hole and have your teammates throw it in and you hook. Those Mikan* days are gone. You've got to be able to shoot from anywhere on the court. If Wilt had learned to shoot from outside, they would have had to outlaw him. But you knew he was going to turn his back and stand in one position.

The really big guys in the past—the Mikans, the Pollards—couldn't run, couldn't move. The guys today are a little taller, but they are ten times more agile. That's what has changed the game around. People say basketball is getting rougher and rougher every year. It's not because the players are getting rougher. The players back in those days were rougher, but they didn't move as fast. We have players who are four inches taller, 20 pounds heavier, and who can run faster. You have the same amount of space, so you have more collisions. That's the reason it's getting rougher. Back in those days you had a fight every game. Guys would elbow you on purpose. It's not like that anymore.

Playing basketball is hard work, but first you've got to know what your opponent is going to do. I keep a book on everybody I play against. It's not written down; it's in my head. You've got to anticipate, because the offensive players always know what they're going to do.

The day of the game I always think about my opponent: what he likes to do, what he can't do, what you want to make

*The dominant NBA center between 1948 and 1954, when the Minneapolis Lakers won five championships in a row, was George Mikan.

him do. Some guys you can't really stop, but you can contain. Kareem, for example. You can't stop him, but what I do is I don't let him get the easy ones. He's got to work for everything he gets, and that way if he gets 30 points, by the end of the game he's tired.

I've had fairly good success against him. I can't block his hook shot, but people put too much emphasis on blocked shots. You can intimidate people and not get credit for a blocked shot, but it's just as good because the ball doesn't go in the basket.

I'll be thinking about my opponent all day, but right before the game I'll give him about 15 minutes. I like to think about all the things he's tricked me on before, what areas he's going to look for a shot in. Maybe the left side. Some guys don't like to shoot on the left side of the basket. I sometimes think of him as part of an entire team. Things he does to help their team. Like maybe I should set a lot of picks because he doesn't like to switch. Or maybe I should set a lot of picks because he *does* like to switch and I'll have a smaller man on me.

You can't go into a game and play well without giving some thought to the player you're going up against. A perfect example was my last game against New York. Gianelli, their center. I made a mistake because I thought someone else was going to play. The first time I played Gianelli I didn't know anything about him. He had his best game against me, so I really owe him. He made a couple of funny moves and threw me off my game. Generally speaking, if you know your opponent, it helps.

Everybody has a pattern. If I had to analyze myself, I've got a pattern. And I don't care who you are, you're going to go to your strong points when it gets tight. If the score is tied and you need a bucket, you're not going to go for a shot that you haven't tried for a week, unless you're forced into it, which is what I try to do. I take you away from what you want to do. You don't have to block the shot. Just intimidate your man. Make him shoot four inches off. Just as good. It didn't go in. A blocked shot excites the fans, but it doesn't mean much. Just like dunks. A dunk shot is still only two points.

Before the game in the locker room, everybody talks about the individual he's going to play. The other guys on the team fill in the rest of the roster. Cazzie Russell doesn't start so the coach may ask him to talk about their third forward. You go right down the line. You talk about everybody, so the entire team gets the general idea. Then you go through their playf. It's like when you go in for a test and you want to refresh your mind by looking through the text book.

We start our pregame talk about 7:15 for an 8 o'clock game. We go on the floor for an 8 o'clock game at about 7:40, so that means we have 25 minutes. Fifteen minutes you spend talking about players, then ten minutes discussing their favorite plays. The last two or three minutes we'll talk about what we can do against this particular team.

For example, should we run them? Now you don't want to get in a running game with Boston. That's their game. With a slower team that likes to set up, like Chicago, you're going to run them, because they want to slow it down. We want to get Chet Walker tired so he can't shoot as well. As hot as Howard Porter is, I'd rather see him in there instead of Chet. He was hot yesterday, but he's not as consistent.

I guess after ten years teams try to run me, especially if they have a young center. So you discuss all these things. Maybe the guy has a bad knee; got to take advantage of it. Ankle bad; make him run. It's not dirty. It's just trying to win the game.

What do you do when you come up against a team like Los Angeles which has almost completely turned over their personnel in the last year? Wilt is gone and they have Elmore Smith at center. McMillian was traded and Connie Hawkins plays forward. With Jerry West injured, Jim Price is now the other guard with Gail Goodrich.

We still have a book on them. They're still a Sharman-coached team. Individually they do some things different, but they still try to run everybody into Elmore. Of course, Wilt was more intimidating. Elmore is blocking a lot of shots, but I think he leaves his man too much. I could block maybe

154

five shots a game when I was young, but I also was still playing my man. See, I look at the box scores and he blocked seven shots, but Lanier got 34 points and they lost. You know what I mean? Lanier got 13 and 19 against me in the last two games. Now I got 29 rebounds against Elmore. He can outjump you, but he's going everywhere to block shots and I'm left under the boards by myself. I shouldn't get 29 rebounds against L.A. He'll get straightened out—in about three years. By then, I'll be gone.

How long did it take you to become a polished player?

It definitely took the whole first year. I didn't play center at first. I was on the team with Wilt for a year and a half before they traded him. I played forward some of the time. When Wilt left I was ready, because I had played against him in practice a lot. As a matter of fact, that first year I was better than I thought I was going to be. I kept improving, but I worked hard. I don't work as hard now, but at that time I was impressed by the fact that the players who are your so-called stars are the ones who drive the Rolls-Royces. I knew that if I didn't work I'd always maybe be on the same team with the star as a backup. I wanted to drive the Rolls-Royce and there are never two guys on one team driving one.

So I worked hard in the summer, lifted weights, played a lot of ball, and I'm glad I did. We have a young guy on our team named George Johnson who is going to be a fantastic ballplayer. He can jump, run fast, block more shots than I can, but he has to decide that this is what he wants to do. He was working in a bank. What do you make at a bank: $9,000? If you go back in the summer you'll make maybe $4,500 more. I told him to play summer ball. Take advantage of his talent. He's got enough of it. The NBA requires hard work.

In order for your team to be a winner, your center has to be able to play both ends of the court. Then you need a tough defensive forward, who possibly doesn't score much, but he's a tough rebounder. Then you've got to have another tough defensive player at guard. Your other two guys are your scorers. In other words, you've got a center who's a scorer, a forward who's a scorer, and a guard who's a scorer. You might have another scorer on the bench, but you need at least two guys who can hold the defense together and two guys to put the ball in the hoop.

That's why it hurt us when Clyde Lee was out, because he provided our defensive balance. We lost nine games in a row when he was out with an injury. We had to take Rick Barry and put him on a tough player, or Cazzie, who's not a good defensive player. Plus it takes a lot away from these guys who are shooters. They can shoot better when they're not tired. Our guys got tired out and we went into a tailspin.

What's it like when you go through a long losing streak?

It's unbelievable. Everything seems to go wrong. We were playing bad, but it's still hard to lose nine in a row. We would get beat at the buzzer, or we'd throw the ball away with nine seconds to go and they would score. I mean little freaky things happen to add to your lack of playing well.

The reverse happens when you're winning. We won nine games in a row after that, right? And we are down in Houston. With two seconds to go Calvin Murphy makes a shot that puts them one up. We figure we are dead. We call a play in the huddle. Rick gets a shot off from the deep corner and we win. We keep our streak going. It happens both ways. Now we should have lost that game. With two seconds to go and down one, most likely you're going to lose. But it works both ways.

What about the art of rebounding?

You can learn all the techniques, but personally I feel that if you just go there some of them will just drop into your hands. I'm talking about offensive rebounds. Defensive rebounds, you're already on the inside and should get them. Offensive rebounds, you have to go to the boards and it takes effort. People are trying to block you out and you are going to get hurt.

Defense and rebounding are things you just have to work

156

at. You've got to want to do it. A lot of guys come down, wave at the man, and he goes up and scores, so they just run down to the other end where they hope they can score to even things up.

You've got to want to rebound. Just like Clyde Lee. He doesn't get any publicity. He gets beat around on the boards, but he does the job. He gets well paid. Same with me. I'm not getting the publicity that I should, but I get paid well. As long as the owner of the team thinks I'm worth it, I don't care about publicity. I do, but I don't, because it doesn't add anything to my bank account. It does in intangible ways which I've missed out on, but I'm just talking about salary.

Most of the things that are hard to do on a basketball court, people just stop. They don't go to the boards. They don't try to defense their man. Other than Bill Russell, how many people have gotten a lot of publicity playing defense? Nobody that I know of. I mean, Sloan gets a little. K. C. Jones got some and Satch Sanders, but they were with winners every year. Nobody else. So that's why a lot of people forget about defense.

Of course, the trend is on the guy who scores. Kids coming from college, they don't think about defense. But defense is the name of the game in the NBA. You've got a perfect example right here in Chicago. These guys shouldn't be winning 60 games a year, but they do it. I've never played for Dick Motta, but he has to be a fantastic coach. He's got those guys out there killing themselves on defense. They ain't going to let nobody get 100 points. If you don't let the other team get 100 points, you ought to be able to get 102 or 103 and win.

You play 82 games a season. In how many of those games do you come off the court feeling that you have played up to your potential? All 82? Maybe half? Or none?

I'd say it would be more like half. If you come out of the season and you think none, then you're not trying. One thing about me, I think I give it my all. Now everybody takes a blow. I'd be the first one to admit that, but I play hard at both ends of the court. Last year I played more minutes than anybody except Nate Archibald. That was my tenth year and I always have played a lot of minutes unless I was hurt. I enjoy playing hard.

Sometimes you try your best, but things go wrong. But even though you shoot bad, you still can do other things. This is what I mean by being a complete ball player. I've seen Jerry West have an off night shooting, which is not too often, but he stole seven passes. Same with Oscar. Maybe he didn't score, but he got ten assists, or got eight rebounds, which is a lot for a guard.

I twisted my ankle in San Francisco Friday night. I went up for the second half tipoff. Somebody was trying to get in and get the ball and I came right down on his foot. I didn't play Saturday, and the ankle was really sore after Sunday night's game, but it feels better today.

Everybody in the NBA has to play hurt. I'm not crying, because we all get banged up. You get bruises and you forget about them. Sometimes in a game you are really warm and hiked up because of the crowd and you don't realize that you got bumped pretty hard. After you take a shower and cool off you think—wow, I've got a lump on my leg. Well, the next day you have to go right back out on the court. You can't stop for a lump on your leg. The fans probably don't understand that.

I've been in some games where I was skre the flu was coming. My head was hurting. People will stay home from the office because they have a terrible cold, but you don't stay away from the basketball court. I've been sitting on the bench when they had to have a separate towel for me, and a separate cup, because my cold was so bad. And you might play bad. The fans will boo, but they don't understand the problems you have. Saturday's game was only the second one I missed all season. One game I missed because I had a 24-hour virus and I just couldn't get away from the toilet. Other than that, you've got to play.

I don't know if I want my son to be a professional athlete. Sometimes it's cruel. The money is good. Some of the glamor is good. But you never have anything to yourself. You don't have any privacy. People are fickle, but after a while you realize that's the way sports people are. Now I love baseball. And you get to the last of the ninth inning and a guy is three-and-two and he lets a pitch go by and strikes out. That burns me up, because he's got his bat on his shoulder. I'll get mad at the guy and I won't say anything out loud, but I'll think to myself: "Oh, goddam!" But the same thing happens to me when I miss a free throw. You know what I'm saying?

But you see these movie stars and they say they get tired of signing autographs. And people sometimes can get a little obnoxious. But when they stop asking, then it's time for you to hang it up. It's the good with the bad. You've got to live with it.

24. *Elmore Smith*

"I have a lot to learn"

Standing in the middle of the key, Elmore Smith resembles a lighthouse, whose long arms switch like beacons to locate and deflect any balls aimed at the basket behind him. Smith is a master of the blocked shot. In his second year in the NBA the native of Macon, Georgia, blocked 300 shots, an average of four a game.

He then was playing for the Buffalo Braves, a team that had picked him third in the college draft in 1971. The choice proved sound since he was the leading vote-gainer in the balloting for the NBA all-rookie team. But before the 1973–74 season Wilt Chamberlain left the Los Angeles Lakers to coach the San Diego Conquistadores. To replace Wilt the Lakers traded forward Jim McMillian one-on-one to Buffalo for Smith. Smith's arrival in Los Angeles caused problems. First, his $300,000 salary in his third *year already was higher than that earned by perennial all-star Jerry West in his fourteenth year. A brief holdout by Jerry remedied that. But the 7-foot-1 Smith had problems fitting into the Lakers concept of team defense. "He doesn't seem to know what Bill Sharman expects of him," commented CBS colorman Elgin Baylor, "whether he is supposed to stay inside like Wilt and let the defense funnel people into him, or move out to help out. He picks up most of his fouls when he switches onto someone else's man." (The previous season, Smith fouled out of 16 games.)*

Elmore Smith is like an unpolished diamond. Seven feet one inch tall and still learning, he may still become one of the premiere centers of the league.

I didn't think much about sports when I was growing up. I played sports, but I didn't care. It was just a pastime: football, baseball, basketball. I never cared that much about any of it.

I went out for basketball my freshman year in high school, but I was about 5 feet 11. I had a friend and we both went out for guard. He made it and I didn't, so he quit. My senior year in high school, we both went out again. I was 6 feet 10. I made it and he didn't, so he joined the band.

I really didn't want to play. I just went out because it was something different. I usually worked summers and after school. But after I went out for basketball I started liking it. I could always jump, but I didn't know how to play, so I made a lot of mistakes, and the coach didn't have time to try to help me develop into any kind of ballplayer. But I did get scholarship offers and I went to college.

That's where I developed my abilities. I went to Wiley College out in Texas for about three months and didn't like it, so I left and went to Kentucky State. Things looked better. I didn't play when I first got there. I sat out a semester, but I learned a lot of fundamentals. Coach Mitchell worked with me before practice, and after practice. Four or five hours. Just a lot of running, jumping, and stuff. I used to jump rope two or three hours before practice. After I started playing, it didn't take long to learn.

160

They would have me dribbling, catching the ball, kicking it out, rebounding, shooting foul shots, pushups and stuff, everything. Doing all that stupid stuff paid off.

When I came into the NBA I figured I'd be here awhile because I was still learning and after seeing a few guys play, I thought that with what ability I had, if I could continue to develop I could make the pros. I was hoping that I would just not get hurt.

I have a lot to learn, but I think I'll get there sooner than most people think. It'll just take a lot more hard work. I don't mind the work. It's just that I like progress. A lot of times with the hard work you can't see progress, but I think with this team it will come faster than it would have with the Braves, because I really didn't know my role there. They would ask me to score, so I would score. They weren't satisfied. They asked me to play defense. Okay, I played defense. They were still losing.

It's a lot better playing for the Lakers, because they have more experienced ballplayers. They know what to do, whereas younger guys are always guessing. I'm able to pick up things quicker here. It would have come sooner or later, but I'm learning faster with the Lakers.

You've got to get out there and do it. Depending on what you can do, you do it. My problem is being consistent. I have a lot of things to work on, but being more consistent would be about the biggest thing.

You're filling some fairly large shoes.

Well, I think the last couple of years Wilt sort of settled down and just tried to play defense. The two years I played against him, he would just pass the ball, rebound, and play defense. That's all I wanted to do all along. That's what I did in college. I feel comfortable here playing defense, but I figure if I have to score I can, which is the same with Wilt. But I don't look at it as coming in and filling shoes. I look at it as coming in and playing my game.

Centers have big roles. We contribute to the defense. With

the Lakers I try to fit in on offense as well as I can, setting picks, making the pass, but I'm not considered an offensive ball player. I'm more or less a defensive player. Price, Hawkins, and those other guys are scorers, so I don't even worry about it.

You can tell whether or not we played good defense according to how many shots I block. I can only block the shots if my teammates make the offensive players come to me. If they're forced certain ways I can block the shot. If I get only two or three blocked shots a night, you can tell we didn't play good defense.

If someone is taking a short jump shot, I'll take a chance to block it. I may take myself out of position for the rebound, but I'm hoping that the forward will help out. Usually Happy Hairston comes through and gets the rebound.

A lot of times I don't get as many rebounds as I should, but I figure blocking a shot, keeping a guy from putting the ball in the basket, is better than a rebound. If I can block a shot and one of my teammates can get it, that's just as good as getting a rebound because they didn't score plus we got the ball back.

I used to try and block every shot. Coach Sharman showed me that it wasn't necessary to go after every one. Lots of times on a fast break I would get caught under the basket by myself, three-on-one, and if I went after one guy he would pass it to the other guy, and when I went after him he would pass to the third guy, and he would lay it up. It's not necessary all the time to jump. Presence alone will make teams throw the ball away a lot of times.

I like to play my man honest, but I have to protect the basket too. If my man goes out, I have to be able to go with him yet still get back. That's what I concentrate on. I go out as far as I can. If I don't think I can get back I'll let somebody know. They'll cover. If not, the guy scores.

Some centers go out more than others.

As far as going out, I would say there's Lanier, Lacy, and sometimes Cowens. He's not that consistent. Sometimes

Cowens can't miss from out there, other times he can't hit. I play him to drive most of the time. Big guys like Lanier and Lacy, where the guards kick the ball out to them at the top of the key for a jump shot, give you a lot of trouble.

How do you defense someone like Jabbar or Thurmond?

A guy like Jabbar is deadly going from his right, because he's right-handed and he's more accurate with his right hand even though he does shoot a left-handed hook sometimes. So you try to force him to go left, trying to put as much pressure as you can on him to keep him from turning. A guy like Thurmond you would try to force him out from the basket to take the shot, because he's more dangerous under the basket. Someone like Lanier who can go inside and outside can create problems, because if you push him one way he'll go the other way. Nine times out of ten, if you don't block his shot he'll score, or you'll foul.

McAdoo, you have to keep ahead of, because he's really a forward and a good shooter, so he won't come in low that much. You know he's going to take the shot outside. The only thing you can do, is keep a hand in his face and hope he misses.

When we're on offense and I feel I've got my man beat I'll take the shot. When we need some points I'll start going to the basket. If I'm caught with the ball and nobody is moving I'll take the shot. Other than that, I'll probably pass off and try to get in position for the rebound.

If I'm close enough to the basket and I figure I can get a rebound, then I'll go get it. But if it's only about a 40-60 chance I'll just take a couple of steps forward, then if I see we're not going to get it I'll start back to protect the basket, because I figure I'm the last resort as far as a layup. If a guy makes a layup, even though he's not my man, I feel responsible.

A lot of times our guards don't get back. I would take a shot at the foul line, but I wouldn't be concentrating on it because I would be worrying on getting back and protecting the basket. I would miss a few shots and Coach Sharman would tell me it's better to concentrate on the shot and let somebody else worry about getting back.

I have a hook shot that goes on vacation every now and then, but I'm working on it. My jump shot is not bad. Not bragging, but I think I can make 70 percent of my shots if I really concentrate on shooting.

I'm working on setting a better pick, because if I could ever get the pick and roll together I probably could score quite a few points. Right now I'm concentrating on being in the right place. A bad pick is just like no pick at all. A good pick you get results, because maybe the guy can get open. A lot of guys get hurt off picks. They run into picks they don't see and it knocks the wind out of them. The guy is open and can take the shot.

Some nights you can push a guy out of position any time you want to. It depends on the official, because some officials will allow quite a bit of pushing. Some start out early by breaking it up, and there's hardly any contact under there. When there is, it gets pretty rough.

I'm used to pressure. When they apply pressure that makes me know they're concentrating on what I'm going to do, and nine times out of ten I can make a good pass. When they're concentrating on you, you can do other things.

25. *Bob Love*

"You must move smooth and easy"

Bob Love of the Chicago Bulls owns perhaps the most distinctive shot of any forward in the NBA. If you could see only his fingertips and the ball rocketing. toward the basket you could recognize it as a Love shot. It is almost without an arch, like an arrow shot. The

164

lanky Love will hold the ball over his head, pump once or twice to get the defensive player off-balance, and then: Thwak! Two points! To get in position to take this shot, Butterbean (his boyhood nickname) will race like a madman, here, there, everywhere, running his defender into the bodies of other Bulls before finally breaking free.

Butter was no immediate sensation when he arrived in the NBA from Southern University, a small, predominantly black college in Louisiana. He spent three years of relative inactivity as a pro. Two were at Cincinnati where he occasionally played guard in the backcourt with Oscar Robertson. "They had a lot of forwards," Butter recalls, "and I was lucky to make the team. My main job was to play defense." Milwaukee selected him in the expansion draft, but didn't play him and traded him midseason to the Bulls: "I got the chance, the chance to play, the chance to show what I could do." He then averaged more than 20 points for five successive years.

My game is moving, moving until I can get an open shot. Whether it's from the right side or left side, it really doesn't matter. I can shoot right-handed hook shots, left-handed hook shots, jump shots, or go straight up, whatever it calls for. I don't have a spot on the floor where I like to shoot from, but I do have a range. My range is about 18 feet. From 18 feet in I think I'm as good a shooter as any forward in the league.

I shoot flat. A lot of guys have flat shots, but shoot it hard. I have a shot that is straight but soft. A lot of times I get bounce-in shots off the backboard. Each guy has his own style, and this is my style of shot. This is the kind of shot I've always shot, all through my life.

I don't jump very high on my shots, but the game of basketball is a game of timing, a game of getting your man off balance. A lot of guys have to jump on shots because they don't have the timing. If a guy is guarding you and jumps to block your shot, you can get it off if you fake him. Once he commits himself he has to get back into a crouch before he can jump again. That's my thing, see, I just hold the ball over my head and use it to fake him out of balance. I fake the ball and if he jumps I hold it, and if he doesn't jump I go through and shoot. It's a simple process, but you have to practice that shot all your life.

Moving without the ball is one of the hardest things to do in basketball. The easiest thing is to get the ball and go one-on-one. To be a truly effective forward, you have to wear the defensive man down. You have to bring him in and bring him out. When he gets tired and you keep doing it, you're going to get the open shot. It takes a lot of energy to guard someone who moves well without the ball. I don't think there is anyone in the league who can keep up with me the whole game if I'm moving well, but if I stand still anybody could guard me.

Chet Walker and I work well together. We both have different styles of play, so we complement each other. Chet likes to have the ball and I don't, so I know that every time he gets the ball he's going to try and make his move and shoot it. What I try to do is break free from my man and go to the basket for the rebound. He knows that every time he gets the ball I'm going to be moving loose. He'll give me passes. When I get the ball and I'm not over 10 or 15 feet from the basket I'm going to try to shoot it. Our third forward Howard Porter has his own distinctive style, but he's also like Chet. He'll shoot when he gets the ball. The Bulls' style of play is to get the ball in to the forwards so we can score. We have a team offense. You've got to pass the ball to each other, help each other on screens, stuff like this.

When I was in high school I used to watch Bob Pettit play. He didn't jump very high on the jump shots, and he didn't dribble the ball very much. I think this saves guys legs and saves energy all through the game. You're not fighting the pressure that the defensive players give you all night and game after game. You just move smooth and easy. I don't fight pressure. Usually if someone is trying to keep me from moving right, I'll go left. If he bumps me, I'll go another way. It's like automatic. I don't fight the guy. I want him to move, because sooner or later he's going to get tired.

But to lead the league on offense isn't going to win very many games for you. You've got to have a team defense. This is what the Bulls do very well. Very seldom will a guy go all the way down our lane free. If he does he's going to get scratched, slapped, knocked. They just don't drive against us. Other teams will let people drive to the base line and nobody picks them up. Nobody switches. Usually these are the losing teams. The winning teams are defensive teams: New York, Boston, Chicago. The Bucks play real good defense.

I know what every forward in the league does. I know their weak points and I know their strong points. I know what they're going to do when they drive in and I know what they do on the outside. A lot of players if they go left will drive all the way to the basket. Others, if they drive left, will shoot a jump shot. It depends on the players. This is my strong point as a defensive forward: knowing what people are going to do. If I want a guy to shoot a jump shot, I'll make him go the way he shoots his jump shot. If I want him to drive I'll make him go the other way. Then I'll stop him before he gets all the way and make him pass the ball back out.

Whenever I meet a new player I play him head on. I want to see his best moves. Then I'll overplay him on his right to see if he'll drive. I'll overplay him on his left to find out what he does then, maybe shoot a jump shot. Once I get him down, well, that's it. I've got him. I know his weak points and his strong points. This is what I call being a smart defensive player. A lot of the guys in the league who have the reputation of being good defensive players really just beat guys up. I like to play the smart game. I think I do a better job, or as good a job, of this as any forward in the league. I can guard anybody, really.

Nine times out of ten, each guy in the league has a pattern. Every player, whether he's good or bad, has a pattern, and the smart defensive guy forces him away from that pattern. This is what happens when players have off nights. The defensive player has forced him off his offensive pattern. That's what the game is all about.

I need to play only one game against a player to be able to

learn all I need to know. You can tell whether a player is fast or slow just by his moves. I make him show his best moves the first time I play him by playing him head up. This is what most guys like you to do. They like to be played head up. By that I mean not playing them right or left but straight front. And nine times out of ten a guy is going to show you his best moves right then, so you can tell whether he's real quick, a good ball handler, or what.

If you watch me play you'll notice that very seldom do they drive on me. They very rarely are able to post me down low, because I refuse to let them get the ball down there to that base line. This is what I mean by knowing your man. I think I play a very smart game. I'm not going to do anything fancy or try to muscle you off the floor, but I'll make you do what I want you to do all through the game.

Is it because defense is something that Dick Motta emphasizes over and over again each day in practice?

No, I really think that Motta found a bunch of guys that have played defense all their life. Defense is not something that you learn to play in one year. Defense starts in high school, or even grade school. You just can't wait until you get into college or into the pros to play defense. I've been playing defense ever since I started playing basketball. With my coach in high school, if you couldn't play defense you didn't get on the team to play ball. The same thing in college.

Did you think back then that you might be playing professional basketball?

This is really what I wanted to do. I wanted to play sports. All through high school and all through college, I geared my life to this. While most guys were trying to get girls and stuff like that, I was either running or shooting baskets in the gym. I played ball every chance I got. I geared my life to this and conditioned my body too, and this is my life. It paid off. It's hard work. It's hard as hell. A lot of times you get

168

discouraged, but I stuck in there and didn't let anything on the outside distract me.

We keep the defensive pressure up on the Bulls. If a team does that to you game in and game out, hey, it'll either make you or break you. We're going to break you because you will have to consistently play your best ball. You've got to come and play to beat us.

26. *Phil Johnson*

"Basketball is a game of reaction"

Phil Johnson grew up in Idaho under the shadow of Dick Motta. He played for Motta in high school, later became Motta's assistant coach at Weber State, then took over as head coach of that college when Motta became head coach of the Chicago Bulls. Johnson won three consecutive Big Sky Conference championships for Weber State, then in 1971 rejoined Motta as Bulls assistant coach. On November 28, 1973 (following Bob Cousy's resignation), Phil Johnson, at age thirty-two, became head coach of the Kansas City–Omaha Kings. The Kings were in last place when Johnson took over and they remained in last place for the remainder of the season (behind Milwaukee, Chicago, and Detroit in the NBA's tough Midwest division) but he succeeded in improving the Kings win/loss percentage from .250 to .402. A sorry-looking collection of individuals in October, the Kings, by March, had become a well-disciplined team capable of battling (if not beating) any team in the league despite the absence of All-Star Nate Archibald, out with injuries. Toward the end of the season I spoke with Phil Johnson in the Kings' office in Kansas City.

My basic philosophy is that basketball has to be a team

game. Everyone has to be involved. Everybody has to feel like he's participating in the offense and defense. Now, you are going to take advantage of the strong points of each player on the team. That's basic basketball. But you cannot tell one man, "I never want you to handle the basketball." In other words, you can't emphasize the negative aspects of basketball. Things take their course. The guy that can't handle the ball particularly well will end up not handling it as much.

If you introduce your plays, and introduce your philosophy, and sell your players on the idea that if they execute they can win, then it will work. And they seem to like that. They like the fact that they all are participating, and all have a role, and know what their role is. So far our team has enjoyed playing that type of basketball.

That's the approach to basketball that Dick Motta preaches in Chicago. Is Phil Johnson bringing the Motta system to Kansas City?

People ask me that a lot: Am I bringing the Motta offense here? Well, that offense is as much mine as it is his. It was half mine. My philosophy is the same as his, but I have a different personality and I exemplify that to my team. I communicate to my team differently than he would. I don't try to be like him: I try to be like myself. It's not a Motta offense, or a Chicago Bulls system, that I want to use here, it's a Kansas City Kings offense, and I emphasize the strong points of my team. For instance, my guards score more. My guards are emphasized here and his forwards are emphasized there. It's as simple as that.

Basically our offenses are similar except the Chicago Bulls end up giving their forwards the shots. They have plays for their guards, but we emphasize those plays more here. My forwards still score. They score more now than they used to, because I like a more balanced attack.

We have about seven offensive plays and we must have about four options off each of those, so you are talking about possibly 28 to 30 plays, but basketball is a game of reaction.

170

Action to a reaction. It depends on what the defensive man does. The offensive players react to that. The plays are simply a crutch in place of fast breaks. For instance, penetration to the basket is so important in basketball. Nate Archibald going to the basket, or Jimmy Walker going to the basket, or Mike D'Antoni going and penetrating and kicking the basketball off to a man who can shoot. That's not a set play, but it works.

It's action in response to a reaction, and each team will defense that move a bit different. That's why basketball is such a tough sport, because you can't say this play is going to be run exactly the same way every time. You can do it within the realm of movement of the play, but something will change each time: the defense, or the situation, or the spot, or the time on the clock, or fatigue of the players. There are so many variables that each time the play ends up being different. That's why this is such a great sport, because the players react to these subtle changes and it looks like, man, they must have worked on that forever. They've played so much basketball that they can react to these certain situations.

How much is there in professional basketball that is new and original? You'll play a team in your division six times a year, and play them year after year. How often does an original thought come along?

Very few things are new in basketball. There are a few innovations each year, and I guess maybe four or five years ago professional basketball was a one-on-one game where there was very little team offense involved. All of a sudden, they started getting college coaches who had used offensive patterns to give players shots, and it worked. Now so many of the teams run more offensive patterns, but it isn't new. It is simply that they hadn't used it.

There's very little of what I call clearing out, going one-on-one, anymore. You still play one-on-one basketball, but it's done very quickly. So there aren't new things, but there are new approaches. Coaching in the NBA is teaching;

it's a selling job. You've got to sell your players on the idea that your system will work if they know what they're doing and believe in it.

The big change in the NBA in the last few years has been defense. At one time defense wasn't too strong and the top players could get a shot almost any time they wanted without much movement or using screens. Then suddenly coaches started emphasizing defense, stressing it, and now a man can't score easily on his own, so he needed a crutch, which was a pattern offense.

I've heard the term "position defense" used frequently, but I'm not certain I understand the meaning.

Well, there are several theories on defense, but position defense is basically a zone principle. In other words, you are communicating with the other team and telling them you've got to beat us from 15 to 18 feet out. You've got to beat us from the outside. You've got to hit jump shots. You're not going to get anything from the inside, because we're going to help each other and position ourselves on the court so that you are not going to penetrate to the basket and get a good shot inside. That's position basketball.

Now there's the other theory. We are going to press. We are going to try and make you turn the ball over. We are going to press you all over the court and try to make you make mistakes, take you out of your offensive patterns, and make it tough for you to execute your plays. Some coaches believe in that, but you have to have the personnel to execute that way. Philosophies are built, very often, on the personnel you have on hand. Kansas City used to play a pressing defense, but I felt it was a mistake to play that way with the personnel we had, so I changed that. We ended up dropping our defensive average since I took over the club, but if I had different personnel, I may have wanted to press.

Will you adjust the style of your team depending on who you play on a given night?

172

I would like to get my team to the point where other coaches have to adjust to me. In other words, I'd like to not make a whole bunch of changes. I want to run what I'm going to run and let the other team adjust to what I'm doing. Now you need good personnel to do that. Your players can make individual adjustments as far as personalities are concerned. We make little adjustments depending on what team we play, but any time you try to change too much from game to game you'll have trouble. Now you're expecting your players to do something they can't do.

What are your plans for Nate Archibald? You haven't had much of an opportunity to use him this year.

Nate's got to help us. I don't think there's any question about it. It's been hard for him because he had a really great, fantastic season last year, and he's never been healthy this year after the first game. So I haven't had the opportunity to coach him full speed, but even when he was at what had to be 60 percent of his ability he was great for us, because he did what I wanted him to do. He adjusted his game a great deal to complement the rest of the players.

I doubt if you will see him average 34 points, or lead the league in scoring again. I'm sure he could if he wants to. He's going to have games where he scores a great deal because of the situation, but his basic need to this team will not be to be the leading scorer in the league—unless we're winning, unless it's worth it. That's going to be our goal, to win basketball games.

27. Nate Archibald

I called Nate Archibald one afternoon at his apartment in Kansas City and he said: "We're going to be practicing tomorrow afternoon at the arena." Then he corrected himself: "They're going to be practicing tomorrow afternoon at the arena." Incredibly, sadly, the NBA's most exciting guard during the 1972–73 season—when his averages led the league in three categories: points (34.0), assists (11.4), and minutes played (46.0)—no longer thought of himself as a member of his team.

It had been a hard year for Tiny, as he is called. In the Kings' opening game of the season in Chicago on October 10, Bulls center Tom Boerwinkle accidentally crashed into him. The result was a sprained Achilles tendon. In and out of the lineup, Tiny reinjured himself on February 1. His leg had to be placed in a cast, and he had not played or practiced since.

Nevertheless, when he appeared at the arena for a team practice in late March, the day after our phone conversation, you could almost feel the crackle of excitement the instant he walked in the door, even though he looked overweight and out of shape. During a television interview he admitted to having gained 10 pounds, yet he looked heavier than that. While his teammates practiced under the supervision of coach Phil Johnson at one end of the basketball court, Tiny practiced shooting, alone, at the other end. After every few shots he would pause and gaze, longingly, almost fearfully, downcourt. Only six months earlier he had signed a seven-year contract, which according to the Kings was "the largest amount ever committed to a professional athlete." Now he had to wonder whether he could recover sufficiently to deserve that money. After practice ended he ran several laps (about a mile) in the arena corridors, then paused to talk before going downstairs to the training room to lift weights to strengthen his leg.

At a listed 6 feet 1 inch, Nate Archibald is small for an NBA player, but his nickname "Tiny" actually dates back to when he was

174

still in grade school, growing up in New York. "That was my father's nickname," he explains, "and he just passed it on to me. He was Big Tiny, and I was Little Tiny."

I don't think my role with this team is going to be primarily scoring points anymore. It's going to be running the ball club.

When I was in school at Texas El Paso, my role was primarily just that. I think my average was around 16 points a game. I ran the ball club and when I had the open shot I took it. Most of the teams that we played against in college played zone, so there wasn't that much penetration on my part. You can't just run through a zone. You have to pass the ball. Most of the time when I got a layup it was on the fast break.

I take more shots in the pros than I did in college primarily because teams are not playing zones. With my ability I can go to the basket on anybody. My asset is to drive on most of the guys, because I'm a lot quicker than them and I can get to the basket and maneuver my body in such a way that I can score, and maybe even get the foul.

Phil Johnson has changed the offense. A lot of guys on the team now are getting into the offense, more than did last year. Last year primarily it was just a couple of guys that were scoring points: myself, Sam Lacey, maybe Nate Williams. We didn't have the offense distributed among the players. You have to get more than three or four guys into the offense. This is what Phil Johnson has instilled now. We have to get everybody playing together in order for us to win ball games.

The backcourt man's responsibility is to primarily run the plays and get the guys into the offense. Not mainly yourself, but the other guys. A lot of backcourt men are just shooters, and they take their shots. They don't involve anybody else into the offense, or anybody else into their plays. Last year I was scoring points, but I also led the league in assists too, because I was driving to the basket. When a man would come over to defend me, he would commit himself and I would try to drop it down to the open man. You have to involve more guys so everybody can be satisfied.

We're playing better defense this year than last year, because we're not running as much. Next year we'll probably continue to play good defense, and, with me in there, will probably run a lot more, get fast break baskets. This is what we're lacking now. We lost a lot of games by one or two points. A few fast breaks, or easy shots, guys going to the basket, penetrating, throwing off to the open man, would have resulted in a win instead of a loss.

Take a team like New York with a guy like Dean Meminger, who is not considered a shooter. What he does so well is drive down the middle, penetrate to the basket looking for an open man, and when the defense comes over to help, he just gives it off to somebody else.

You have to know when you have an open shot and know when to shoot it. A lot of guys seem to take bad shots. Then again, a lot of guys don't take enough shots. Now Jerry West is classified as a shooter, but I think he can score points. He knows when to take the shot and he also knows when you are going to foul him so he can shoot the ball at the same time and maybe get a pair of free throws or maybe even a three-point play.

How much thinking do you do when you have the ball, or is it all instinct?

It's instinct. You have to think, but you only have a split second. You might think, dribbling down the court, that you are going to make a base line drive, but then the other team may protect the base line. You may have to drive to the middle. It's a split-second decision which way to go.

You may call a play, and the other team may put more pressure on where the ball has to go, and it makes it harder on you to throw it there. Sometimes a defensive man, after he hears the play called and sees the ball go to a certain position, may overplay where the next pass is going. So you have to go to a different man. So if you call a "one" play where the ball is supposed to go to the forward, the forward might be overplayed. You may have to throw the ball to the center and run a different play out of that one. If the forward is overplayed I may have to pick for him, so the play turns into a "three."

When you were ten or twelve years old, what did you do to make yourself a better player?

Well, it was sort of like a dream. Everybody has this dream while they are real young. The person I idolized way back then was Lenny Wilkens. I saw him play and I styled my basketball playing after him, because he was known as a driver and an assist man, and this is what I strive for. I was never known as an outside shooter, so I would always drive for the basket and try to create something. I liked his style of play and I practiced driving and shooting, not a one-hand set like he has, but a little jumper, driving around the basket, playing guys and passing off and creating different situations.

He's still quick. He might not be as quick as when he first came in the league, but with his experience he knows what he's going to do. His instincts are quicker than someone first coming into the league, because he has more experience. He knows that if a guy plays him a certain way he's going to drive the other way, and when a guy commits himself on a certain leg, or extends a hand, he will take him to the basket.

The book when I first came into the league was that Lenny Wilkens was left-handed and if you play him on his left side you can stop him. But he has a right hand. He might not shoot right-handed shots, but all he does is shift the ball to his right side and after he gets by you he puts it back in his left hand and lays the ball uv. I don't think you can overplay anybody unless they cut their right or left hand off. You have to play everybody honest.

How did you learn to dribble?

When I was young we used to play in the community centers. We had Floyd Lane, Ray Felix at one time, and

Hilton White. They would set chairs in the middle of the floor and we would have to dribble between them, changing hands back and forth and keep that up. We worked a lot going between chairs, played games, and just practiced, practiced, practiced. It's practice and a whole lot of desire if you want to become a good basketball player.

How is your injury?

My leg is coming along. Right now I haven't done a lot of running. I like to run outside because the track is longer and the air helps get my endurance back. I don't think running around inside a gym will do it. I run like six or seven miles every other day in the summer. Just now I only ran a mile, and I'll probably run a mile tomorrow. It's a slow process, but they think it's better to do it this way than reinjure the leg by doing too much.

I've been shooting around outside. I don't know what it is about the outdoors. I just like to play outdoors. A lot of guys don't because they say it bothers their knees.

A lot of guys get hurt. It was just an unfortunate season for myself. I just have to throw this one out the window and recuperate and come back strong next year.

28. *Ron Behagen*

"Got to keep everybody happy"

"You want to put me in your book?" said Ron Behagen, grinning broadly when I approached him one afternoon after practice in the Kansas City–Omaha Kings office. "Wonderful! Well, it feels so good." Behagen wasn't putting me on; he sincerely meant it. While

at the University of Minnesota the previous year, Behagen had become involved in an on-court brawl in a game with Ohio State that made national headlines. He had emerged somewhat of a villain, yet while speaking with this apparently gentle and mild-mannered individual, I wondered how it could have been the same person! The Kings had been attempting to promote Behagen for "rookie of the year" honors, but it was a difficult sell in a season when Ernie D. of the Buffalo Braves led the league in assists, playing with a team that made the playoffs. Still, Behagen had played very impressively as a defense-oriented forward on a guard-oriented team. After a slow start, he began to show signs of future greatness and finished the season averaging 7.1 rebounds and 11.0 points per game.

I came into this league thinking defense. That's what my game is all about. You can throw ball players off quite a bit if you're playing well on defense, especially top scorers. You take a scorer and play him well from the start, you get him thinking about you, and his whole game might get thrown off.

The main thing in defense is in wanting to play it, because that's all defense is: hard work. If you want to play it, you can do it. A lot of it has to do with anticipating where your man is going. If you do that you can beat your man to the spot and either draw an offensive foul, or cause him to put up a premature move.

The game is changing to where the better defensive teams are the ones that are doing things. Winning teams are not always the ones who have the high scorers.

I've had a strange year as far as adjusting, because we've had three coaches and three different systems. First Bob Cousy, then Draff Young, and now Phil Johnson. Under Coach Cousy, his big thing was our offense. He spoke of defense, but we never really worked on it in detail like we do under Coach Johnson, and I really enjoy this part of the game. You enjoy winning more when you do it by holding your man and the other team below their averages. It makes the job easier because you don't have to score as many points.

If you go hard on offense and not on defense, you have to put out more energy. To me it seems that way. But if you play hard on defense, your offense seems to come much easier. If you have a strong defense, you get the other team thinking about scoring and they forget to play defense.

I like to play team defense. A lot of guys you can't play one-on-one. No matter how good a defensive ball player you are, you are not going to be able to guard everybody one-on-one. There's just too much talent around. But if you get everybody playing defense, five men against five men, you do much better. If I get beaten somebody helps me. They get beat, I help them. If I get beat and nobody helps, then I'm in trouble. No one player can stay with another man the whole game. It's really impossible. But if you get everybody thinking together and have a team concept, you start winning. That's what I think Coach Johnson is looking for next year, a fresh start. I believe we'll come out and you'll see a different team than you saw this year.

A chain is only as strong as its weakest link. This is the same with defense. If you have one man loafing, you are not going to get the job done. No matter how hard four guys are working, if one guy isn't guarding his man and taking care of his assignments, it's not going to work.

I also believe you have to play together as a team on offense. Last year Cous (Bob Cousy) wanted Tiny to score. But in the years to come we'll have other scorers. I like it better that way. If you get five guys in double figures, you have a better chance than having only one or two. Somebody scoring 21–22 points. Somebody scoring 20. Somebody scoring 16. Somebody 15. Somebody 12. You're more likely to have a winning team than if you have a guy scoring 30–40 points a game and everybody else way less.

You need a balanced scoring attack. New York proves it every year. Boston does it. Chicago. L. A. You need to have scoring from all five of your scorers, then you have two or three people coming off the bench. Matter of fact, this is my first year playing basketball where I've had a losing season, and it took a while to get used to that. I'm not used to it yet,

180

but it took a while to realize that my team was losing. And I look at last year's team, and they also had a losing season with Archibald scoring. I don't believe that one high scorer or two high scorers is the way to win. Got to keep everybody happy, you know. A lot of guys say they don't mind not scoring, and I say that myself. I don't mind not scoring if we can win, but I do like to score. Everybody likes to score.

Does everybody like to rebound?

There's a definite science to rebounding. I think, number one, just like defense, you've got to want to do it. Another thing I find, the highest jumpers are not always the best rebounders. I like to position myself between the man and the basket and try to keep the man on my back as much as possible. That way you can feel where he's at better than when you simply try to outjump him. I've never been known as a great leaper, but I get my share of rebounds and that's probably because I go after the ball as much as possible and try to keep between the man and the ball.

There are certain angles where the ball comes off from. A certain percentage of the time the ball is going to come off in one direction. If I shoot it from the left hand side of the basket a lot of times it probably comes off the right side of the basket, you know. I'm not sure of the percentages, and I'm not sure if it comes off the right side all the time, but I seem to instinctively know where the ball is coming off a lot of times and get in the right place at the right time. As soon as the ball goes up, you have to turn and try to read the backboard to figure out where the ball is coming off. No matter how high you jump, if you are not around the ball you are not going to get your hands on it. Most rebounds are grabbed below the rim. Just try to follow the ball as it goes up, follow the path of the ball as it comes down. Another thing is quickness: Once you get your hands on the ball, get it out of there real quick. Don't play with it. Soon as you get your hands on the ball, snatch it out of there.

181

The Russians? At times I used to think it wasn't basketball we were playing. I played quite a bit against the Russians. I was fortunate that Coach Cousy played me a lot. I didn't like their brand of ball. They allowed more contact. What I couldn't understand was that a lot of times the referees called a lot of perimeter fouls, but underneath anything went. You could grab a guy and throw him down. A lot of times it looked like a free-for-all out there. We were fortunate to win four out of six games. Later in the year I was invited to go back and play against the Russians in Russia, and against the Chinese in China, and I kind of refused.

Theirs is a different game. Their moves are very awkward, but they are bigger and stronger. We are much more agile and have more quickness, so we just had to play our type of ball. As soon as we got into their type of ball where we tried to slug it out with them, it was no contest. Plus international rules are different. If we played under American rules, I'm sure we would have demolished them in all six games.

The game is rougher in the pros than in college, but the Russians were rougher still. But compared to college ball, pro ball is a little easier to play. You're not worrying about contact. They have to protect the ball players in college much more because somebody's parents might not want their sons to get beat up. But I played in the Big Ten and there was a lot of contact in that league. It helped prepare me for pro ball.

I was overweight at the start of this season. I weighed around 230 or something. I was having trouble in the beginning of the year because of my weight, but I got it down in the middle of the season to 204. Right now I'm 210 and as long as I keep my weight around there I'm all right.

It happened during the summer when I wasn't watching my weight like I should have been. Then during training camp I gained quite a bit of weight because we would eat a big breakfast in the morning, work out, then go home and eat a big lunch, then go to sleep, work out at night, and come home and eat a big dinner. I just started gaining weight because no matter how hard the workouts were, I was putting more pounds on than taking off.

I stayed with Tiny for a while and that's all we did, eat and sleep. He's gained a lot of weight since he's been injured. He weighs 190 pounds and he's 30 pounds over. He'll do well next year though. He's disappointed about not playing. I played this summer with Tiny in the Rucker's tournament. That whole summer I just worked on playing with him, running without the ball, trying to get open as much as possible, then he got hurt and I had to change my whole game. As well as Jimmy Walker plays, he's still a different kind of player than Tiny. He's more of a shooter, even though Tiny shot a lot last year. I thought we had a chance to do a lot of good things this year and Tiny got hurt and it all fell through. The times when Tiny and Walk played together, they played very well. Archibald handles the ball most of the time and all Walk has to do is get open.

I want to win. Everybody on New York's team is considered a star. They were the champions and they've got Frazier, and Reed, and DeBusschere, and they all are considered stars because they are winning. Take a team that's losing, and only the high scorer is considered a star, and he may not get superstar status. Frazier is not scoring that much, but he's considered a superstar because he does everything else so well. That's the kind of ball player I like: chipping in, doing something of everything, steal a few baskets, get a few rebounds, play good defense, draw some charges. That's it. I believe we're going to win next year. I hope so. I don't like this losing.

29. *Jim McMillian*

"You teach somebody by showing"

Earlier in the season when I had interviewed Elmore Smith, the Los Angeles Lakers center, one of my questions had been: "How does it feel to be traded from a perennial tail ender like Buffalo to a championship team like Los Angeles?" Several months later the question seemed rather ridiculous since the Buffalo Braves qualified easily for the fourth playoff berth in the east while, for a time, it looked as though the Lakers would be ousted in the west by Golden State.

Buffalo doubled its number of victories from one year to the next partly because of the play of two successive rookies of the year: Bob McAdoo (1972–73) and Ernie DiGregorio (1973–74). But the key to the team's success was the arrival of the veteran (at age twenty-six) forward, Jim McMillian, who came east while Elmore Smith went west. In McMillian's three years with the Lakers, his team had made the playoffs each year and won the NBA championship one of those years. Over that span the Columbia University graduate had averaged 15.3 points in the regular season, but 18.4 points in the playoffs. Moving from Los Angeles to Buffalo, however, forced Jim McMillian into a different role.

Certain situations were a lot easier for me at L.A. For instance, the task of rebounding. I didn't have to worry about rebounding, because Wilt was in there averaging usually around 20 per game. We also had Happy Hairston averaging in double figures. Even on offense, I played more of a passive role. I would take advantage of situations that Jerry West and Gail Goodrich would create. The offense would revolve around them. They would penetrate and the defense would collapse and I could move to the corner for the open shot. Now I'm playing more of an aggressive role with Buffalo, not only on the court, but off the court with the other guys of our team.

Right! And that's really amazing. It took me a while to mentally get over the fact that I had come from a team where I was one of the younger fellows to one where I was one of the oldest. In fact, I was second oldest behind Bob Kauffman before he got traded. So I had to make a mental adjustment to that. In L.A., honestly, I didn't have to contribute much to the conversations and discussions we had about strategy, because obviously my teammates had years and years more experience than me. But in Buffalo, none of my teammates here, except for newcomers Jack Marin and Matt Guokas, who we got midseason, ever have been in a playoff situation, so now I'm in a position where I can give the advice.

I've watched you play since you came into the league, and I've always thought of you as a strong defensive player with a picture-book one-hand shot from the corner, but until I checked your statistics in the NBA Guide, I didn't realize that you also have been averaging close to 20 points a game the last few seasons.

My type of game isn't very eye-catching. Very seldom during a game does anyone notice how many points I have, because I get free throws, a couple of jump shots, a couple of buckets off offensive rebounds, and for some reason those things don't register with spectators watching the game. As I said, I played a passive role in L.A. Now it's different. I'm initiating certain things which my teammates take advantage of. I'm looked to to carry more of the rebounding load with Buffalo, because in Bob McAdoo we have a smaller center than we had in L.A. with Wilt.

But McAdoo will put more points on the board than Wilt did. That means that on most nights it's not necessary for me to go out and score. A lot of people thought that because I was traded to Buffalo it would be an opportunity for me to average like 30 points a game and make the All-Star team. McAdoo is such a great offensive center, and is so good one-on-one, that you get the ball into him and he's going to create something. There's less scoring pressure on me, so I can concentrate on other parts of the game.

Management today is more aware of this, which is good, because in the past when you went to negotiate, statistics were the only thing you could use for leverage. Today management has gotten to the point where they are willing to pay a player based upon what he contributed to the entire unit. New York proved that you don't have to have everybody a superstar. If you played the game right, and moved the ball, and moved bodies, you were going to win. Those guys have been compensated very well for that type of play. Because of this more players have been able to relax and play their style of game without being pressured into going out only scoring and rebounding because that's where the money was.

It's usually tough to instill an attitude such as this into a rookie. To tell him, just do your job. If you are not open, go set the pick for the weak side man, then roll to the basket. It's tough, because players are indoctrinated with the idea that if you don't do something flashy, you don't get the publicity. If you don't get the publicity, you don't get the money. But there's still a job for unpublicized players, and they can make a nice living at it.

Another thing that's tough for young players to realize: This is a game where you specialize in something. That's important in putting a unit that fits together. If you realize your limitations and try to stay within those limitations, you become a much better ball player. You know that your range on a jump shot is 20 feet. You are not going to go outside of that. You should work to your strength and not try for impossible plays. This allows you to relax more. Like me. I don't have to score 30 points a game, therefore I won't force shots when I don't have the shots.

Will you take fewer shots from the perimeter now?

Not really, but I'm looking more for ball movement, body movement, because I've seen how well teams like New York and Chicago play with that type of ball. It's tough to play that way, but it's very enjoyable because you win more games than you lose, so you enjoy the game while you're playing it. As a result I sometimes pass up open shots, because you try to instill a certain philosophy in your teammates. With our young team we are at a stage where these little things mean a lot. I think we've got the type of club that's going to be together for a while, because we are young and have been successful, so it can be helpful in developing our experience. New York, for instance, does things that take years and years of playing together to do.

You have a rookie guard in Ernie DiGregorio who has led the league in assists.

But it's been tough for him this year. I don't envy him. People say he got all that money, but he's paying the price. The pressure has been tremendous on him, not so much now, but at the beginning of the year when everyone was getting down on him for lack of defense and shooting too much. He came into the league with a built-in reputation and was given a tremendous amount of responsibility, and I didn't envy that position. I think he stood up well though. Did you see us when we came through here the first time?

I was out of town.

You would be amazed to see the improvement. He's a much more relaxed person now. He's much more confident both on offense and on defense. We're number one as far as scoring, but we're also next to last in giving up points. Phoenix is last and we've given up almost as many points as they have. There was an article in the paper yesterday commenting on how unusual it is for a team to be over .500 with those kind of defensive statistics. I don't think we'll ever be a team that holds an opponent under 100 points consistently, because that's not our style of play. We give the ball back to the other team so many times simply because we score quickly.

A team that plays a slow patterned brand of ball is going to show good defensive statistics as much because of their offensive style as their defensive style. Last night New York came down five times in a row and took shots with only about three seconds to go on the 24-second clock. So naturally you're going to score fewer points against them, because you'll have the ball less. But each team has to take advantage of its players' skills and their talents. It would take away from our overall game if we had to play a pattern-type offense like Chicago. It wouldn't take advantage of Ernie's talent as a guard to direct a running attack. It wouldn't take advantage of McAdoo's talent going one-on-one. So a coach would be defeating the purpose, which is winning games. He has to figure out which method is best suited for his type of players, and for us that's a running game. Boston is also basically a running team because of Dave Cowen's talent. We do have a few patterns, but basically we're a running team.

How often will you come down the court running the ball rather than calling a set play?

On a good night running would be 80 percent of our offense. That's a lot of running, but you have to realize that most coaches incorporate patterns in their offense mainly to do things that you should be doing naturally. When you are running, if you are a guard, you usually throw the ball to the forward and go pick for the other guard. If you play ball long enough, that's what you do. You don't throw the ball and go after it unless it's a specific play. You throw, you go away. You throw the ball to the forward, he throws it to the guard, and it eventually goes to the other guard for a jump shot. We have plays like that, plays that try to make you think on the court, and make you do things that you're supposed to do naturally.

It's a matter of instinct, a conditioned reaction to situations instilled through repetition. You don't have to run plays. You see a guy maybe throw the ball to the center and start toward the ball then suddenly go backdoor and he gets the ball back and scores, and everybody says: "Damn! That's a

188

hell of a play." But in fact it wasn't. It was just two guys working well together, because they knew basically what each other was going to do.

And yet you have had success with a second-year center, McAdoo, who played forward last year, a rookie guard, Ernie D., and two forwards—yourself and Garfield Heard—who weren't even playing for Buffalo last year. Not to mention reserves Guokas and Marin who arrived midseason.

Well, when you saw our team on paper, you had to believe that we were going to be a halfway decent club. Then when you saw us play, you knew that because of the personnel and talent that was there, we had to get better. So however well we were playing in the first half, we had to play better the second half, because we were playing nowhere near our capabilities. I think a lot of why we are winning this year has to do with our coach, Jack Ramsay. He's been a tremendously hard worker, because he likes to win. And he takes it even harder than we do when we lose. It's unbelievable how hard he takes it in the locker room, not necessarily getting on us, but after we get dressed and are leaving he's still sitting there just shaking his head.

We've been working hard. We had our problems this year trying to get used to playing with one another. For instance, Ernie D. out there trying to anticipate on the fast break what the player on the wings should be doing. He lets the ball go because he knows the guy is supposed to be going one way, but he learned he can't think for the other man. The only time he can think with him is when he has been with that man long enough to guess what he's going to do. So he had to calm down a little as far as that play went. You have problems when anybody is new at their job. But it's beginning to work with us. When he comes down in the break I'm always looking now, because I know that at any time he may throw that ball.

The ideal situation is to have talented players and make sure they are young so they will have years to work together and be able to know what each other is going to be thinking.

Like when the ball goes in to Mac. I know that he's beaten his man before, so he's going to be looking for the shot. So I don't throw the ball to him and expect to get it back again. I throw it to him, relax a bit so my defensive man will relax, and when I think the shot is about ready to go up, then I go for the offensive boards. And I've been doing a lot better rebounding offensively this year than in the past, because of this.

You also talk to each other. Like Garfield and I. He's with me on the bus, or on the plane, or at each other's house listening to music, and basketball conversations come up. You talk to a guy and find out what side of the court he likes to play on. Some guys shoot better, especially right handers, when they are on the right side of the court. You put the player on the side where he enjoys playing and can operate from the best.

I also will try and watch his type of moves. For instance, I know what his shooting range is because I've been playing with him enough now. If I see that he has the ball out of his range, I'm going to try to work to get in an open area. I may fake to the foul line and then go backdoor, or I'll go around the center for an outside jump shot. But if I see him down in the low post, I know he is tall and can jump well, so I won't go over, which may cause my man to double team him. I will stay away until I see the shot go up, then go to the boards.

Sometimes you have to signal. For instance, the forwards may be overplaying us to keep us from receiving the ball, so we just crisscross and the guy on the strong side sets a pick for the forward coming from the weak side to get him open. It's a simple play, but it's amazing how many times that forward coming from the weak side gets picked off and you're open going to the other side. You may be open just for a split second, but that's enough to get that ball in for a jump shot. Our plays involve guard to forward a lot of times. The ball goes from the guard to the forward and then we start running our plays. If we can't get the ball in to our forwards then it throws our offense off because we're used to going that way.

190

I had a thing with Jerry West when I was with L.A. We would be playing and I would be in position near the left corner, and he would be up toward mid-court with the ball, and I would look at him, and he would do one of these [*Click! McMillian suddenly shifted his eyes right*]. I would know he wanted me to go backdoor. You don't have to talk at all. You find a lot of smart ballplayers like that. If you know the basics of the game you play that way. And Jerry and I had that type of thing. I could see him driving down the lane from the strong side and know where he wanted me to go. He just wanted me to back up in the corner where he could bounce a pass to me. You go to an open area, because if you don't, you're going to be in his way. And Ernie and I are getting that way now, you know. So it makes things a lot easier. Of course, we have signals. If I see someone overplaying me and I want to let him know I'm going back door, yet I don't have time to give subtle hints, I may just stick out my arm and go. He'll know I'm going and the ball will be there.

How much talking will you do before a game?

At this point of the year not as much conversation goes on about a game as during training camp and during the early parts of the year. Right now we know each other. Sometimes we might accidentally get in the wrong area at the wrong time, so occasionally you do have to have discussions. If you feel you have a small man on you, or you're playing a team that you've been very successful against offensively, or defensively, you may say, "Try and clear a side out for me." You may have a play where the ball comes down to you and you're supposed to give it back and you have an easy guy on you, you may say, "When you're running the three play, go the other way." It depends on game situations. Or if you think you can do a defensive job on somebody, you may tell your teammates when the ball comes into your man, they don't have to worry about giving you any help.

Most players are sensitive individuals, but we all realize

191

that we're out there to do a job. Sometimes my job might be to criticize you. No one likes criticism, but if you realize it's constructive criticism you should be able to handle it. You should be able to handle criticism as well as dish it out. Because I'm a member of a team, and I want to win, it may be necessary for me to say something to one of my teammates. You don't try to say, "Hey, you're shooting too much!" Most guys can't accept that kind of criticism, even though it may be true. [*McMillian laughs.*] You don't want to alienate your teammates, especially when you're going to be together so much during the year. You might say something like, "Hey, relax a little more on your shots. You're forcing things." Which is a nicer way of saying the same thing.

We're all out there to win. If my man scores 100 points and we lose, obviously he scored the points on me, but all twelve of us lost. Thirteen with the coach. So the object of the game is to make sure you work together as a unit. If somebody else's man gets by him, I've got to pick him up even at the expense of letting my man get an open jump shot, because if my teammate's man gets a layup the two points scored is against the team, Buffalo, and I'm on the team, so I can't say, that's not my man.

Those types of things are contagious on a club. One or two guys start helping out, then everybody starts playing team defense. Same thing with passing and moving your body. The guys who were great at doing this were Cazzie Russell and John Havlicek. The team gets a little bogged down. Those guys come off the bench and they are running and driving, diving for the ball, hustling their heads off, so the other four men say, "Damn! This guy is making us look bad. I mean, as fast as he's running it must be obvious that we're not moving." So they automatically start moving the ball. You teach somebody by showing. It's easy to say, "Ernie, you should pass up that shot because I'm in the corner, and even though we both are open, my shot is closer, a better percentage shot." It's easy to say that, but you have to go out and show a guy. A player will respect you more if you show him by passing up your shot for someone else who has the better shot. It's contagious, especially with a young team.

192

What about the art of defense?

It's a matter of concentration. If you have the talent, the ability of a Jerry West to anticipate the passing lane and quick hands, or quick feet like Frazier and Meminger, then it makes defense a lot easier. But if you're just average you have to work at it. You have to work physically to get your body ready, and even more important, you have to be ready mentally. You have to want to play defense.

Defense is psychological. Constantly throughout a game you are waging psychological warfare. You try to jump on the other team early in the game and take them right out of it. If you jump on them the first five minutes, the rest of the 43 minutes they're out of it. Some players you have to be on them all the time. You can't give them a break. Other players you jump on them early, it just makes them play harder. Some guys you don't want to antagonize. Wilt was like that. You never wanted to say a thing before the game about Wilt being over the hill, or that he can't jump. Certain things to certain guys, you don't say. And never say it to certain teams.

New York, for instance. The Knicks had beaten the Lakers twice early this season. Frazier said, "Well, we beat the Lakers tonight, but it was a very boring game. It was so boring I almost fell asleep. It was like playing the Buffalo Braves." Of course, Rudy Martzke, our publicity man, made sure we saw the article, gave everybody a copy of it. And, you know, we beat the Knicks like four out of the next five games. Certain things you don't say about certain players, coaches, or teams, because you never know how they will react.

If you know a certain guy gets upset if you bump him, then you bump him because it's going to throw his game off. When we went out against the Knicks the next night, we didn't let them dictate the pace of the game. They don't like to run and we are a running club. We went out and dictated the pace both offensively and defensively and it worked for us, even though it still was a close game.

At the professional level, there are very subtle things that make the difference between the star and the superstar, or between the good and great teams. And sometimes on certain days, it's just a matter that you have your rhythm better than theirs and your timing is a bit better.

Are you up for tonight's game? [Buffalo was playing at Chicago, although without the services of Bob McAdoo, who had the flu.]

We're up. We're up. Even though we already have clinched our playoff spot. You don't like to go into the playoffs having lost your last few games, because we are a young club and we need all the confidence we can get. We're missing McAdoo, but it's amazing: A team often plays harder when somebody is missing. If you have one of your starters out, you might lack overall talent, but for some reason you try and make up for it by hustling and playing hard. I hate to play a team at their home when one of their starters, or the coach, gets kicked out of the game. When I was with L.A., Motta would almost get kicked out of every game, and as soon as it happened they would beat us. Or Sloan would get kicked out. It does something for the fans, and it does something for the players, so you make up for it.

Chicago is the type of team that even when I was at L.A., we never beat them by many points. Very seldom did you ever blow a Chicago team out of the arena. They might be down by 20 and they would still come clawing and scrapping back. They might still lose by 4 or 5 points, but you could never relax against them.

People don't realize how good our team is. I think they got the idea the other night when we beat Phoenix even with McAdoo out. Phoenix is not having that good a year, but with our top scorer out we shouldn't be able to run away from a team like that. Yet we beat them by 30 points.

It's a funny thing, playing the Lakers now that I've been away. It's just a weird feeling. All of a sudden you've got a different colored uniform. Sometimes you almost want to pass the ball to one of your old teammates. For instance, in practice I'm always on the blue team. The second team is the gray team. Then suddenly they switch me to the gray and I

194

make a mistake passing because I look at the guy's face instead of his shirt. It was a weird feeling the first time we played the Lakers.

Your coach might get mad if you passed the ball now to Gail Goodrich.

[McMillan smiled.] Well, maybe I'd at least get an assist.

30. *Calvin Murphy*

"I'm still around"

I called Calvin Murphy on the house telephone and he told me to come right up. We were staying at a hotel across the street from Detroit's Cobo Hall where Calvin's team, the Houston Rockets, would play the Pistons that night. Calvin Murphy, while at Niagara University, had made the all-American team three times, averaging 33.1 points, fourth best mark in college basketball, despite being only 5 feet 9 inches tall. Professional scouts doubted he could survive among the tall men of the NBA, however, and nobody even drafted him in the first round. Yet he has great jumping ability to go with his scoring ability. He can dunk the basketball and occasionally gets called for goaltending. "Calvin's biggest handicap was, it took him so long to come back down to the ground," claimed Alex Hannum, former coach of the Rockets. The only active NBA player listed as being under 6 feet, Calvin Murphy averaged 15.7 points his first three pro seasons, being used mostly as a reserve guard. In his fourth year, as a starter, he averaged 20.5 points.*

When I knocked on his door and was ushered inside I was embarrassed to find a large shape hidden behind the sheets of one of

*Ahead of him were Pete Maravich, Austin Carr, and Oscar Robertson.

My situation is unique. Most athletes are influenced by
their environment. Their father starts them off, or their
brothers, or their cousins, or their friends. In my family my
mother was the basketball player, so she started me off
playing. She was very knowledgeable about the game.

I enjoyed basketball when I was playing in the playgrounds and I figured that sooner or later I would grow to a
good size, because my whole family is tall. My mother is 6
feet tall. I expected to be a big basketball star at around 6 feet
7 inches. It never happened.

As I got older and I saw I wasn't going to grow anymore, I
just had to alter my plans a bit. I had to do something now to
allow me to stay in the game playing against the 6–3 and 6–4
guards. I started developing my shooting and my touch. Ball
handling was something I always worked hard on, because I
felt that for me to score on the bigger guards I had to be able
to maneuver past them.

When I went to college I had a reputation as only an
offensive ball player, but I always had the defensive skills as
well. It was a funny thing. They said I could never play in the
pros, not just because of my size, but because defensively I
couldn't hack it. But whenever you have one part of your
game that overshadows the other, people never know what
you can do when you are forced into a different situation.
And this is my fourth year, so I must be doing something
right defensively. I'm still around and I've just signed a new
five-year contract.

196

There are no secrets as far as ball handling goes. I did the same things all good ball handlers did. I spent a lot of time just dribbling. I watched great ball players before me, things they've done. You watch a Bob Cousy. You watch an Oscar Robertson. You watch a Guy Rodgers. You watch a Jerry West. Those are the great guards, the ball handlers, the playmakers. What do they all have in common that makes them great ball handlers?

One thing they all have in common is that they were able to dribble the basketball without watching the ball. They're able to make that ball become a part of them. This is the main thing I try to do. Everybody knows that you've got to dribble the ball with your fingertips. You've got to have fingertip control to be a good offensive ball player. This, along with keeping eye contact with what's going on down floor. These are the two main things I worked on, and I spent hours, and hours, and hours just dribbling the basketball. I always kept my head up and I did this a lot on my own, not when we had five or six guys to play. I spent a lot of time alone just dedicating myself to the idea that I was going to be a basketball player.

The last few years I've done a lot of clinics, and I demonstrate. We start off with the basic rules of dribbling the basketball: fingertip control, eye contact. A good dribbler must learn different types of dribbles: a control dribble, dribbling waist-high for control. Body positions as far as protecting the basketball. There are about ten basic rules for learning to dribble the basketball, then from there we talk about some of the offensive moves in the game, and from there we go to team play, and you talk about the dos and don'ts. Overdribbling is one of the biggest problems of the young dribbler.

I worked hard dribbling so that it became automatic to me, and for a while I thought there was nothing else to the game but dribbling. This can become hazardous to a team. My lecture usually runs an hour and a half, and it would run longer if they would let me go. They have to stop me. There is so much involved in dribbling, so many different styles of dribbles, so many different types of offensive moves.

Every young player patterns himself after a star. All right, Earl Monroe. He's an unorthodox dribbler, A great dribbler, but if I were to teach young kids how to dribble, I would never teach them to dribble like Earl Monroe. But is Earl wrong in the way he dribbles? Not at all. He's very effective in what he does. He violates some of the rules of dribbling. He has a spin move that is fantastic. He got his reputation off that one move. But we don't teach high school and college players that move, because it's done above the waist. We teach that all offensive moves are done waist-high. Then they say: "Well, what about Earl Monroe's move?" All right. I don't tell people it's wrong, because it's not. All I can explain to them is we are talking basic basketball. The pro game is entirely different.

Geoff Petrie commented to me that you should never turn your back to the basket while dribbling the ball

Exactly. If I had to depend on backing my way to the basket I would never score, because of the way the defensive players can use their hands in the pros. The strong guards would just hold me out. I like to face my opponent. I'm more effective that way, because if I don't have the shot I have the pass, or I can make my offensive move to create situations. If my back is to you I have only one thing to do, and that's pass the ball.

Also important is to know your capabilities with the ball. A lot of young ball players don't know their capabilities. They still don't when they're in the pros. They still are trying to do things with the ball that you can tell they weren't able to do back in junior high school. They always saw these moves and wanted to do them, so they are going to spend the rest of their life trying.

Here in the pros, the defensive guards hand check so much that it is hard to protect the ball, whereas at other

198

levels of the game it is easier. Once the opponent uses his hands in college it's a foul. In the pros they push you off stride, so I had to change my protection of the basketball to fend off my opponent. If you're not ready to protect the ball no matter what happens, they're going to take it away from you. Believe me, this is an entirely different game. You try to tell young ball players that and they don't believe it. They believe basketball is basketball. I was like that too until I got here.

But I think hand checking is very necessary, because the players are so big, so strong, and so skilled, that if you just went by the basic rules of defense—keeping your body between the man and the basket—teams would be scoring 300 points a game because of the way guys can shoot. Hand checking neutralizes a lot of ball players. It makes the game more civilized.

In college you may have one or two great ballplayers on a team, so the other three will balance it out. In the pros you've got the cream of the crop from all over the country, all over the world, whatever. Everybody is a specialist and if you are not allowed to do something to stop this great offensive ball player, he's going to trim you to death. If they didn't hand check me, hey, I'd have big fun. I could score 40 points a night. Just being smaller and quicker than most of the guards, and if they weren't allowed to touch me, I'd just pick out the places I wanted to go for my shots and go there. But with hand checking, you have to alter your moves.

But doesn't this cause unnecessary friction on the court? Don't a lot of the fights result from what might be described as unnecessary roughness?

That's basketball. If we didn't have a flicker now and then, basketball would die. Unfortunately fighting is hazardous to the health of ball players, but we are in the entertainment business. We need something to make people pay to see us play. Just to run up and down the court, shooting the ball with nothing else, people wouldn't pay for this all the time.

One of the greatest sports in the world is hockey. Why? All right, it's a fast game, but people like to see physical action. They like to see somebody get his nose broken every now and then. It sounds harsh, but this is one of the facts of all sports. So if hand checking is going to cause these kinds of problems, this is something that we as pro athletes have to live with. But I also think that as mature athletes we've got to know our limitations as to what causes friction. If hand checking causes a fight a night, the officials will have to alter the rule. On the whole, I don't think it has been that much of a problem. I say this now, but tonight if somebody is holding me I'll be good and pissed off.

I've heard you comment before that the referees don't let you play your game, that you feel they often protect the superstar.

First of all, the referees in this league have their minds fixed on exactly what an individual's capabilities are. I keep using this word "capabilities," and I think that's very important. If I block a shot they automatically are going to call goaltending, because they say to themselves, "If this guy is 5–9, he has no business blocking a shot. He must have goaltended." This is wrong, but this is the way it is, which is a double standard.

All right. Right now, I am leading the league in fouls. Why? Is it because I'm a dirty player? No, I'm doing things that they are letting Oscar Robertson, Dave Bing, Jerry West and others get away with. But do I stop playing defense because of it? Of course not. If my fouls were going to hinder the team, I wouldn't be playing. So far this year, playing 40 minutes a game and averaging like close to five fouls a game, I must be doing my job. Like right now, I must have 250 fouls, and I've been—

You have 293 fouls and have been disqualified from eight games.

All right: 293. I'm leading the league in fouls, but I'm

200

leading the league in hustle also. I have around 150* steals also. I could easily just become an offensive player and not have any fouls at all. Just let the man score on me, and I'll go down and score on him. We'd trade baskets, but this would hurt the team. So if I commit a foul it's a hustling foul, or it's often where I have left my man to help a teammate after his opponent has beaten him.

To get back to that double standard thing, the referees having their minds fixed, I had to get used to that. See, I penetrate very easily. A lot of times I'm pushed, or when I go up for a shot I'm hassled. My elbow is hit, the ball goes straight down, but nothing is called. This used to upset me. Then I'd go down to the other end, use a little too much hand pressure, and they would call a foul on me. So on that score I think something has got to be done so that it's more equal.

Now referees say, "Hey, we don't have favorites." That's baloney. Just baloney. I'm not saying that referees cheat or anything; it's just that they'll call something on me that they don't call on Oscar Robertson. I'll get a technical whereas it would take nine statements by an established star to get the same technical.

Referees are paid to do their job. They have a very important job, because a referee can turn a game right around in an instant. A couple of fouls, a couple of traveling calls, or whatever. When I first came into the league, I used to have a lot of faith in my moves, not just to show off, but this was part of my game. I had a lot of moves that I worked hard on, and the referees weren't ready for. They figured I had gotten by my opponent so easily I had traveled or taken an extra step. When I was a rookie I would look at films where I would have five or six turnovers on traveling and I would go watch the film the next day with coach Alex Hannum. We would keep saying: "How could he have called that a walk?" They just weren't ready for my moves.

*Calvin Murphy finished the season with 157 steals. The league leader (with 217) was, appropriately enough, Larry Steele of Portland.

Like I shot off the wrong foot a lot of times. It gives me a half step on my opponent. This is something I worked on. Well, the referees think that because I went up on the wrong foot I must have been traveling. They had to adapt to my game, and eventually most of them did. Then you have a rookie referee join the league and he's calling the same stuff they called four years ago.

As a spectator, I have a hard time determining what is and what is not traveling. I watch the Bulls a lot, and Bob Love always seems to get called for traveling violations that I miss.

Ohhhh, not enough.

Not enough?

Not eeee-nough! And I say this because Butterbean is probably one of the finest people I know. I really like him. I tease him a lot about that. As soon as he gets the ball he starts into a little waltz. I tell him, "Bob, you've got to stop mamboing out there." He says, "Murph, you're just not hip to the move."

What about when you play defense. I would think that because of your size—most NBA guards being 6 or so inches taller than you—they would attempt to post you close to the basket. I also would think that Calvin Murphy would be a person teams would attempt to pick and roll on. How do you combat this?

Well, first of all, when players try to post me, I love that. First of all, I'm getting a rest because what they do is just go down to the basket and stand there and wait for their teammates to give them the ball. I'm getting a breather. I just front them. If they try to throw a lob pass the weakside forward or the center is backing me up, so what happens is they spend all night trying to post me for one basket and everyone on the opposing team is just standing around. Every now and then a team will take me low and score a few

202

baskets, but that's throwing their whole offense out the window, which is good for us.

But it's not only because I'm 5–9. If somebody 6–4 is guarding somebody 6–5, they'll still try to post him. So as far as saying, "Calvin Murphy is out there. Let's post him," they don't do that much anymore because it bogs down their offensive play.

What I do defensively to make sure this doesn't happen is that I try to pick up my opponent full court. I make him work as hard as possible. Like I'll be playing against Dave Bing tonight. Well, Dave Bing is in for a game, because I know if I let Dave Bing walk down the court and do what he wants to do he's going to kill me because he's one of the finest players in the game today. So I'm going to pick him up full court and make him aware that I'm out there. Right? I'm going to make him very cautious about protecting the ball. I'm going to make him second guess himself as far as making his move on me. Right? I'm going to make him realize the fact that maybe he's getting a little tired. Now that's going to benefit my team because now Dave Bing's edge has been taken off him. You've got to realize what a Dave Bing, or any great guard, can do when you let him. So I make him work, and I rely on team defense, because no matter how hard you work, the players in this game are so good that you are not going to stop anybody. What you try to do is cut their effectiveness.

For me to say, I'm going to shut off Dave Bing—hey, I'm kidding myself. Or Dave Bing saying he is going to shut me off—same thing. You try to say: "Calvin Murphy is averaging 20 points. If I hold him to 19 or under, I've done my job." Right? Dave Bing is averaging 18 points. If I hold Dave Bing to 18 points I've done a job, because the man is capable of scoring 40.

Some nights, no matter what you do, the other fellow just feels good. I've had fellows guarding me that were playing great defense, and they might as well have stayed home, because everything I did was right there. My moves were there. The timing was there. The ball was leaving the fingertips nicely. I was getting that good backspin. I was getting up quick and leaping real well. There was nothing more my opponent could have done to stop me. He had good body position. He had hand pressure. He kept me from getting in the key. But that's the way basketball goes.

You have to realize these things on defense. The only time I'm disappointed in myself defensively is if I watch films after a game and think I did a job on my guy, but I may have loafed somewhere where I hurt a teammate. Sometimes I may have stopped my man from scoring. My man may have gotten 9 points, but I caused my partner's man to score 25, because I didn't help him out in team defense. This will bother me.

A lot of youngsters have the delusion that all you have to do is score 40 points and you have a great night. If you don't score, you've had a bad night. Not necessarily true. When I was a rookie we played Baltimore, and Wes Unseld was guarding Elvin Hayes. Wes Unseld hardly took one shot that whole night and he was the most valuable player, because he did a job on Elvin that was unbelievable. Defensively, his rebounding was incredible. He was getting that ball off the boards and out into the fast break. It was one of the greatest performances I've ever seen anybody have. First thing after the game was over I said, "Wes must have had 35 points tonight." This was the kind of game he had. And I grabbed the stat sheet, and looked, and it was unbelievable: *He had not scored one field goal!* He had scored a couple of foul shots, that's all. Yet he was phenomenal that night. A lot of ballplayers think: "Hey, I did my job. I got me 25 points." Maybe so, but the man you were checking got 30. Or maybe he only got 5 points, but got 25 assists.

Speaking of assists, you're ranked second in the NBA right now in assists.

I'm glad you noticed that, because I've always been known *just* as a scorer. In college I was a scoring machine. My job was to put points on the board, so I just did what my job was. But I've always been able to set up teammates and this year I got to prove it. I got the playing time and I got the ball around. I've never been a selfish ballplayer. People at times thought I was, because I scored so big in college, but I always did what I was told. You know, I changed my game five times in five years to suit five different coaches. This year I played more of the kind of game that I would like to play the rest of my career. I got the minutes. I took the good shots. I wasn't handcuffed. I wasn't told I couldn't do certain things. I got that ball around to the open man, despite who he was.

See, my biggest problem, and I think my coach would agree, is that I've got to learn my personnel better. For instance, if we are coming down on the fast break and I have Rudy Tomjanovich, who is an excellent shooter, in one lane, and another fellow who is shooting maybe 38 percent in the other lane. But Rudy is covered. *Phooom!* I automatically give the ball to the open man, but I've got to learn maybe I should take the shot myself because I'm an excellent shooter too. This is just learning your personnel.

For instance, the ball is being set up. A fellow who is not a good shooter is open at the top of the key. Wide open, right? And Rudy has a small man underneath. Now who should I give the ball to? I should give it to Rudy normally because with the mismatch, and with Rudy as strong as he is, he may have a better chance of scoring. But seeing the open man my first instinct is to give it to him. So after I learn my personnel a little better and get a little more selfish with the ball, I'm going to become a better all around guard.

Of course, the argument to that is that if you always force the ball inside to Rudy, instead of giving it to the open man, no matter who he is, pretty soon that player will figure he's never going to get the ball and stop trying to get open and your offense will bog down. Or the defense will sag on Rudy to the point where he's double-teamed. Mack Calvin of Carolina suggested that particularly in the beginning of the game he tries to involve everybody in the offense, particularly the tall men. He wants them happy so they'll play harder.

See, I don't look at it that way. I don't go out and say, "Well, I'm going to give the ball to so-and-so the next time to keep him happy." Nine times out of ten, if you do that, you're going to mess up the play. I try to make my game flow naturally. I'm watching the whole situation. I may plan to pass to you, then see somebody breaking to the basket. Instead of giving the ball to you because I'm looking right at you, I've got to give the ball to that man breaking to the basket. This is the way I play basketball. I don't come down and try to get everybody involved quickly, because you tend to do this without purpose. Everything I do offensively I want a purpose behind it. Like on a fast break, I want to have that two-man option, and I want *me* to be an option. I don't want to penetrate to the basket and have only one man to give the ball to. I want to come down at that fast break, stop at that foul line, and have a choice.

When the NBA teams bypassed you in the first round of the collegiate draft, despite your all-American credentials, some people suggested that your best opportunity to play professional basketball might be with the Harlem Globetrotters.

The Globetrotters never impressed me. I've gone to see them play and I love to watch the showmanship, but as far as ball handling, watching them dribble, that never appealed to me as far as saying that's what I want to do. I knew that it wasn't legitimate basketball, and everything they did as far as ball handling was for show. I never had an ambition to be a showman-type ballplayer. I always wanted to play legitimate basketball. Everything I did to work on my game was geared to that, rather than to please a crowd.

What about last season? Were you very frustrated when you barely got a chance to play?

Frustration. That just isn't the word. Last year was perhaps the worst year of my basketball career. The previous year I had just come into my own. I ended up starting for the team. Not only did I average 18 points a game—and like I say, points don't tell the whole tale—but I was shooting like

206

48 percent. My year's average was around 45 percent, but toward the end of the year I was shooting even better. And I'm getting the ball around. I'm getting the feel of the pro game. I feel like I'm progressing and I'm optimistic. Over the summer I'm working hard and figuring I've got that starting job now and I'm going to really begin to show people.

Then for no reason at all, all of a sudden I'm not playing. Not only am I not playing, I'm not even a *part* of the team. Going from a starting guard to not even a part of the team, which happens in pro ball. This is fine, but they wouldn't trade me either. All right. Maybe nobody wants me. But I could be put on waivers and make my own deal. I'm just stagnant. I'm very frustrated, because I feel I have all this basketball in me that's not being let out. You can talk to anybody else who's on the bench and they'll tell you the same story, but I'm not talking about anybody else. I'm talking just about *me!*

Because it had never happened to me before, you know. This was another big thing. I had never been on a team where I didn't play, and it was a brand new thing for me. And here was a former college coach that came in who was telling me: "Calvin, you can't do this," and "Calvin, you can't do that." It was hard to accept, because I had been doing it for the two previous years in the pros and doing it effectively.

I actually felt my career was coming to an end. That was the last year on my contract. This was my option year. I said, "Hey, Murph. You've got to do something, because this could be it. You could sit here on the bench, being 5-9, and people having doubts about you anyway, and you sitting on the bench for a team that wasn't winning, this could kill you." So a lot of things jumped up and happened because of it. Some things I had to do that weren't nice. I don't mean hurting anybody. But I had to make some statements that I was hoping to be traded. But I wasn't traded.

I came back this year and said, "Well, the only thing I can do is give it that old college try again." Fortunately for me, things worked out beautifully—you know, individually. Naturally, the team could be doing much better. We're playing better ball now. But individually, the year worked out very well because I was given the chance to prove myself. I raised so much hell last year that they finally said, well, let's give the little guy a chance. And I think I rose to the occasion.

I also rose, to go. In the corner bed, the shape that was a basketball player hidden beneath the sheets had stopped stirring. It lay like a log, dead to the world. "Hey, I told you," said Calvin. "Nothing, I mean nothing, ever bothers Rudy. I've roomed with Rudy four years now and he has not answered the wake-up call one time. He sleeps through everything. We have gone to New York and I have had relatives up in the room having fun, but when he decides to go to sleep he just blacks out. It's no problem."

31. Ray Scott

"One hand watches the other"

Ray Scott played nine years in the NBA with the Detroit Pistons and Baltimore Bullets, and two in the ABA with the Virginia Squires. In 1972 he returned to the Pistons as assistant coach to Earl Lloyd, then midway through the season was appointed to Lloyd's job. The following year under Scott, the Pistons, who had failed to make the playoffs for six consecutive seasons, set team records for victories, had the fourth best win-lose record in the league, and Ray Scott was named coach of the year. I spoke with him in the Detroit airport just before he was to take off with his team to Kansas City.

Any time I went to play for a winning coach, he knew from the first day what he wanted the team to do, and that was the only level he communicated on: "This is what I want. This is

208

how I want you to do it. If it doesn't work, then I'm the guy that's going to pay. But since I'm the guy that's going to pay, why don't you give it a chance and see what happens. Then if you still have some ideas as to what we should do, or should not do, I'm open to suggestions." This is the way it was when I played for Al Bianchi at Virginia and Gene Shue in Baltimore.

The biggest thing you need to have going for you are some intelligent people who are willing to try the things that you know work. It breaks down to a situation of communication: How can you communicate the things you've learned about basketball to the people who are already there?

What we try to do is get the players to participate in the decision-making as far as floor play is concerned. They're the ones who have to go out and do it. Players are very honest about the things they can or cannot do, especially when they want to win. The thing that worked for us is that last year we began to win. We won 20 of our last 31 games, so we got a taste of winning. We felt the season just ran out too soon. We didn't have enough time to prove how good we were. We were just beginning to come together as a team because we had acquired some new people, and everything just fell into place.

And we had a plan. We knew what we wanted to do each night. During the summer break when the players got together we knew that when we got back together, one of the things we had to work on to get down pat was a strong defensive plan. As far as offense was concerned, all we wanted to do was to make sure we could execute, because we know we can run and we know that we can set up. This is one reason teams have difficulties with us, because if they shut us off from running, we are just as capable of setting up and playing a disciplined pattern offense.

But exactly how do you communicate? Do you just stand up in practice one day and say: "Okay, today we're going to start playing defense"?

It takes much more than that on a professional level. I

don't know what it takes on a lesser level; I don't even remember. This is why people aspire to get a pro job. Coaching at the professional level is very difficult, but what you do is you outline, you use X's and O's, you use different strategies at practice. You try different things. It's not a question of just saying, "Let's go out and do it." That's probably one of the big fallacies about professional basketball. It's not as simplistic as it seems to a lot of fans.

To many it might seem simplistic. You're theoretically prevented by the rules from playing a zone defense. You have to play man-on-man. So what do you tell your team other than, "Dave Bing, you guard this man; Bob Lanier, you guard that man"?

The idea is knowing the personnel of the other team. You have to do your homework. You have to be totally aware of your job. Naturally you wouldn't guard a Calvin Murphy the same way you would guard a Walt Frazier. When we play against different teams there are certain things we want to do on certain areas of the floor. We know, for instance, that some guys do not drive, so we try to pick them up high. There are other players who love to penetrate, so we try to cut the floor in half and let them penetrate only on one side of the floor. That means, if they do pass off, they can only pass off to one area. Then it becomes possible for our players to get into those areas to protect against the pass. It boils down to knowing your own personnel—and execution. You need to have intelligent people. A lot of intelligence is required. I think you'll find that most of the teams that win consistently are usually peopled with very intelligent and mature men.

I'm inclined to agree with you, but what information do you give your team? You're taking off this afternoon for Kansas City and you've already played that team five times this season. What new can you say in the locker room before a game?

Usually by this time of the year, the sixth time around,

210

you're pretty well programmed as to what they do. It's just a question of reminding people. We'll go over the team personnel, any new players, anything new they might be trying to do, who's playing well, who's not playing well. Then each player will give a dissertation on the individual he is going to guard and say what he will attempt to do, so that the other players on the team, who may be asked to compensate, know what to expect.

If we are playing Jabbar, we know we will not have to give Bob Lanier help in most situations, because we believe Bob can handle him one-on-one. By the same token, Bob will be so busy with Jabbar that he will not be able to help our other people. We have to come up with a plan where our other people can be effective. It's the old adage: One hand watches the other.

The player who directs the defense is your center. He has to do the bulk of the talking and explaining, to the other players what's going on on the floor, because in essence he's the middle linebacker. He's the one who sees the whole floor all the time. So he's the one who has the prime responsibility for directing the defense. That's why everyone looks for a very large, intelligent individual to play the middle.

Offensively, my guard runs my offense. Dave Bing runs my offense, or Stu Lantz, or Chris Ford. He has to be the extension of the coach. We have to think almost identically. There have been times this year when I began to call a play from the bench, and Bing already was calling that same play. We think exactly alike in certain situations. But Don Adams calls plays at times. Curtis Rowe calls plays. That's due to the fact that we have a lot of people with leadership ability. There's no conflict. We all get along. We realize winning is the greatest thing. In the past it was individual achievement. We've achieved more as a group, other than the Tigers going to the World Series, than any other sports team in Detroit during the last ten years.

Every fan who watches a football game knows that the quarterback in the huddle is calling a prearranged play—

211·

Yeah, and they have a whole week to rehearse it.

—but plays in basketball have to be called on the run. What situation might arise to cause you and Dave Bing simultaneously to think of the identical play?

Whatever is happening on the floor. We recognize a situation that we want to take advantage of. Maybe one guy is tired and the other is not. Maybe one guy is shooting better at this time than another. Maybe one guy has someone defending him whom he can beat very easily. Maybe Bob is shooting the ball real well, and usually in a key situation we want to go to Bob Lanier, because he's going to get the shot closest to the basket and he's one of our best shooters anyway.

What happens when you call a time-out? This is probably a mystery to most fans.

I don't think so. I think fans call time-outs for you. The play gets a little raggedy. The players get tired. Things aren't going right, so you just call a time-out to get things together. Sometimes you call a time-out to give a team a rest, or make adjustments on the floor. You have to use time-outs wisely, not indiscriminately.

But what do you say?

Whatever is necessary. It's hard to really describe it, because I'm not in a time-out. You call seven times-outs in a game, so seven times you're going to talk about seven different things. It would be unusual to continuously go over the same things with a good team. With a bad team I'm sure you do, but that's not the situation I'm in.

212

32. *Meadowlark Lemon*

"My bag is comedy"

Friday in South Bend. Saturday and Sunday in Chicago. Yesterday in Terre Haute. Tonight Lafayette. Tomorrow Kalamazoo. Several weeks after our talk I would pass a poster in Milwaukee and realize that he had preceded me there too. "This is what the Harlem Globetrotters are all about," says Meadowlark Lemon when you ask him about the back-breaking schedule that keeps him and the other members of the world's most famous professional basketball team (nobody has heard of the Bucks or Bulls in Berlin and Bangkok) traveling by bus to city after city to play (or perform) night after night.

I had first watched the Harlem Globetrotters a quarter century earlier when one of their traveling units appeared at Mount Carmel High School in Chicago, where I attended school. I had seen them occasionally since that time, and they visit Michigan City, Indiana, where I now live, every second or third year. Many of the routines (or "reems" as the Trotters call them) are the same old ones: the funny balls, the water bucket filled with confetti, the baseball and football takeoffs, Meadowlark sitting on a teammate's shoulders for the last second dunk, the whistling, finger-snapping rendition of "Sweet Georgia Brown." Watching the Globetrotters is like watching the umpteenth rerunning of The Wizard of Oz *on TV. It never fails to delight. Meadowlark Lemon has been called the "clown prince of basketball," no argument there if you can recall him functioning like an epileptic octopus in the pivot, hassling the stooge referee, shooting (and making) ceiling-high hook shots from half court, shucking and jiving with the crowd. Yet I was having a hard time connecting the strutting, grinning, arm-waving, loose-limbed, loudmouthed, on-court comedian with the serious, soft-spoken, almost gentle individual whom I spoke to one night in Lafayette. Pagliacci, take off the mask.*

A quarter century ago the Harlem Globetrotters not only were the funniest basketball team in the world, they also were the best basketball team in the world. They used to leave their funny balls under the bench and, at the end of the season, take on the Minneapolis Lakers (the NBA champions of that era) and whip them. Then they took out the funny balls.

The decline of the Globetrotters (at least as an athletic force) began when the Boston Celtics signed Chuck Cooper to a contract in 1950. Cooper was black. If he failed to attract the notoriety of Jackie Robinson, who integrated major league baseball four years earlier, it was only because few people cared about NBA basketball back in 1950. Today, two-thirds of the players in the NBA and ABA are black, and capacity audiences in New York, Chicago, and Los Angeles watch ball-handling tricks that once were the trademark of the Trotters performed by serious ballplayers like Earl Monroe, Connie Hawkins (who once played with the Globetrotters), Julius Erving, and Pete Maravich (who happens to be white). Meanwhile the Harlem Globetrotters still are doing one-night stands in Terre Haute, Lafayette, and Kalamazoo. But as Meadowlark says: "This is what the Globetrotters are all about."

What the Globetrotters also are all about are pregame and halftime acts including a tightrope walker, a juggler, two table tennis players, and an aerialist named Vino who ascends a ladder with knife in his mouth, sword balanced on the knife, tray balanced on that sword, four goblets on that tray, and four more goblets balanced on those goblets. Fantastic! But is it basketball? I posed that question to Meadowlark Lemon.

About 80 percent of what we do on the court is serious basketball; 20 percent is comedy. Most of the fellows do their own specialties, which depend on the particular positions they play. In the NBA and ABA, they have guards. We don't have them. We have running men. Our three running men would be considered guards, and we call their forwards corner men. We don't have a center. We have a pivot man, with me in that position when we're doing comedy.

At times when we play it straight, and there is a much bigger opponent on me, I won't play pivot. There would be another fellow in the pivot until we get a good enough lead, then I can go in and do my thing. This is the way it has been done when we have played people of a certain caliber long before my time, and we still have the same floor plan.

As far as the amount of serious basketball we play, I personally like to keep it at about 80 percent basketball whether we are playing the very best or only a church league team. We try to keep the format basketball with comedy and not comedy with basketball—and not a stage show. You see, there is a difference. You can take ten actors and put them on the floor and you would have yourself a stage show, but we play basketball.

We make the same moves. The people shoot the same jump shots. They try to place themselves in the same positions to get rebounds. We do not play the knock-down and drag-out type of basketball they do in the NBA and ABA. That's not our bag. We try to take something that may be a little hard and try to make it look easy. As an athlete you are supposed to make things as easy as possible, but with us you are doing two jobs, which means you can't take the short cut. You have to take the long cut because we are doing basketball with comedy. If you take the short cut, you have to eliminate one or the other, and that is not our thing. Our thing is to put both together and hopefully have it so a person can't tell where one ends and the other begins.

You have one thing in common with any winning team, and that is timing.

A team by the name of the Renaissance started that, the split-second passing of the basketball. As they were on their way out, I understand, the Globetrotters played against them. They began to pick up the same concept, and the Globies were able to exploit it to where it is today, which means taking basketball to many foreign countries where it wasn't seen before.

At one point I had to travel very long distances to be able to play on the same card as some of the NBA or ABA teams when they first began. They needed us to attract extra customers to hopefully have enough money at the gate to pay their ball players. I guess a lot of people have a tendency to forget that. There were occasions when we played on a double-header with one of the league teams. We would play first and by the time the other game was almost over there weren't many people in the stands. They had come to see us.

When I first came up to the Trotters we had like three or four units traveling. They would alternate. Today you can't do that. First of all, there aren't that many basketball players around willing to follow our traveling schedule. Then the economy is such that you can't carry many players with you. There aren't that many teams around the country that we can play because if they're not playing in a league, they have to disband. If we wanted to play a team for one week then cut them loose for a month, that team would have to disband. They would have to go out and get jobs, which would make it difficult for them to return and start playing basketball again. Now we play one or two teams during an entire season.

Maybe every now and then a city might have a semipro team that we might play. When we go abroad on occasion, the national team of some of the countries will challenge us. We can't play the college teams. At one point we used to play the senior college all-Americans in a 21-game tour: 21 games in 21 different cities. This was stopped for some reason which I'm not sure about. At one point before my time the Trotters used to play the Minneapolis Lakers.

Several decades ago the annual game between the Globetrotters and the Minneapolis Lakers used to be the highlight of the basketball season.

I think so. Yes. And for some unknown reason this was cut out also. Now we just barnstorm, entertaining more or less. But I must say that even for just the barnstorming type thing, we must have a certain caliber of ball player, or you will not be effective enough to bring out the crowd.

It's a steady grind. The barnstorming. The entertaining. It's a steady pace. We play approximately seven nights a week. Sometimes we play eight nights a week. Then again we

216

might play nine nights a week. I guess the most I've ever played was either 17 or 18 games in the span of two weeks. Each weekend we played four full games, which means, man, at night when it's all over, you go home and go to bed. You go to your hotel room and you get some food by room service and you go to sleep fast.

It's hard, but this was the way the Globetrotters were started and if you are going to keep the same format, this is what the Globetrotters are all about.

You have to show your basketball and you have to show your comedy. You could be a great college or professional coach, but not succeed here if you don't know our style. It's not easy to put it all together and make it happen in the end. It's like trying to put me in an algebra class and saying, now, what happens in this equation? That's not my bag. I'm not into that. This is what I'm into. This is what I feel I do best.

While I was sitting in the stands tonight the people behind me kept commenting, "They haven't done their funny ball routine yet," or, "They haven't done their baseball and football gags." And as the game got into the fourth quarter I began to worry that you actually might not do them.

See, you saw those routines when you were a kid, didn't you? I guess if you have kids now you carry them to our games. And if we continue, they probably will carry their kids. So you get to see it over and over, generation after generation, and the gags that we do have helped make this an institution. People will still come around and ask for the old routines. Over a period of time you might give your act kind of a face washing, but basically it's the same thing. It's like shooting a jump shot. You see variations. A certain player will shoot one way, a second player another way, but it's still called a jump shot. No matter what new we put in, fans in the stands still will be asking for the football and baseball bits and the water bucket routine. For us to leave them out would be like going onto the floor and not doing the "Sweet Georgia Brown" warmup.

Usually our routines follow time-outs. You call a time-out and you put it in. As far as some of the other things we do, some are ad-lib. They may be in our repertoire, but you still ad-lib them at different times. It's like a comedian onstage. He might tell some of the same jokes, but he will pick different times to tell them.

I saw the Globetrotters as a young kid in a newsreel at one of our local movie houses in Wilmington, North Carolina, and I said to myself, "This is what I want to do in life." Like many other youngsters I thought all I had to do was learn how to spin the ball on my finger and I would automatically become a Globetrotter. It goes a little deeper than that. You've first got to learn how to play basketball. You have to learn the fundamentals of the game.

Have you ever seen the Ice Capades? And you see these real great skaters come out and do their skating routine and after they get off, out comes this guy dressed up in a clown uniform, doing the identical moves but he's putting in comedy. Now if he didn't know the basics, there is no way he could do comedy. The same thing applies here. You try to learn basketball first.

We don't have Wilt Chamberlain anymore. We don't have Kareem Abdul-Jabbar. We don't have some of the strong 7-footers, but we do have some fine talent equivalent to other players in the league. Hopefully again in the future, we might be able to acquire that type of player that I just talked about.

Of course, today black ballplayers have other options besides the Globetrotters. When you joined in 1954, this wasn't entirely true. If Calvin Murphy and Kareem Abdul-Jabbar had been born a generation earlier, they would have played for the Trotters—or not played pro ball.

Yeah, when I came along you had 100 or 150 black ballplayers out to make maybe four or five positions in the NBA, and you had guys literally jumping over the basket, doing all kinds of tricks in midair, shooting real well, playing real well, and it was heartbreaking having to see them cut loose and told they would never play basketball again, because there was no room. This is why I have stuck by the Globetrotters so long. It's why I believe in the Globetrotters today, because I feel we have been pioneers in bringing professional basketball to the point where it is today.

When I'm out there, no matter how I feel, I go out and do that job. See, when you go to the other leagues of basketball, you have players who can shag and loaf until the time is right to go all out. Here you play before people who spend anywhere from $3 to $12 a ticket, who are the working man, who sometimes save a couple of months just to get enough money to buy that ticket. They don't care how you're feeling this particular night when they bring their family out to see you perform. A man may have had a fight with his wife. He doesn't care if you're up to it. He's trying to make up with his wife by taking her out of the house for a few hours. We can't get rid of his problems, but we can relieve him of some of the tension for two or three hours.

You come from Michigan City and you say we come through town every third or fourth year. We don't get a chance to come back ten or a dozen times a year like an NBA team might, so we've got to be ready that one time. You've got to put your thing together, whichever position you're playing. I'm a comedian, a showman, and when I'm in the pivot I don't care who is playing me. It doesn't matter how big he is. I'm out there to perform and the only way he's going to stop me from being funny is to beat me up and drag me out of the gym, and even if they beat me up I'm still going to be funny because I'm going to play off that. It doesn't matter if you're the greatest basketball player in the world, you can't let up because I'm going to sneak a few shots on you and some of them are going to fall. As far as my hook shots are concerned, I've been shooting them for a long time and in the position I get in, you have to jump to the ceiling to block them, and if I shoot them up a few might fall in, so I'm going to do my thing.

After I saw the Globetrotters the first time and found out

what they meant, I didn't want to do anything else. Later on in life one or two presidents called us ambassadors of good will in short pants. I think we have been able to create better relations in some of the countries we've gone into. No matter what's happening on the political surface, we are out there doing our thing and drawing people closer to each other. When people are laughing, they've got to be closer.

Some of the black NBA stars have criticized the Globe-trotters for being Uncle Toms.

I'm not into the controversial thing. That's not my bag. My bag is comedy. We had one player who was with us who had nowhere to go when we picked him up,* and when he was with us everything was cool. We weren't making, at that particular time, some of the best money in the world, but the minute he got away he began to put us down. If I put a piece of bread in your mouth today and you can do better tomorrow, you don't come around and slap my face. And some of the things this particular person says were true, and some of the things he says were lies just to make things seem more controversial and sell more books. The things he said about me were probably because I was the best known, and if it wasn't me it would have been someone else. These things you have to learn to live with. Like any professional athlete, when you're on top you've got a lot of people shooting at you. If you're doing so-so, everybody's shooting. No matter what field you are in, whether you are playing mumblety-peg, or spit to the line, you've got to live with it if you are the best.

---

*The player referred to is Connie Hawkins, whose biography *Foul!* was written by David Wolf. One of the chapters in that book was titled "Tomming for Abe." The Abe referred to was Abe Saperstein, now deceased, founder and owner of the Harlem Globetrotters. From 1963 to 1966 Hawkins traveled with the Globetrotters at a time when the NBA had blackballed him for being involved in a betting scandal. Hawkins sued the NBA, eventually won a $1 million settlement, joined the Phoenix Suns, and later was traded to the Los Angeles Lakers.

220

What about Meadowlark Lemon? You've been with the Globetrotters since 1954. Will you still be playing the game twenty years from now? Will you become the Satchel Paige of pro basketball?

I hope not. I guess I hope to be associated with the name of the Globetrotters, if we are still in existence, in some capacity. I hope to stay in show business because entertaining has been my life. Whether you're a football or baseball player, you have people out there watching you and cheering you, and you are entertaining them. I hope that I will never have to retire and go dig a hole for myself. When they take me out of here, I want it to be after I've played 18 holes of golf, or something like that. I just don't want to sit down in no rocking chair and pass away.

So, man, what can I say? This is the Globetrotters. And I think if we ever change what we are doing now, we will no longer be the Harlem Globetrotters. We will be something else, which would not be what the Harlem Globetrotters is all about.

33. *Steve Patterson*

"When I go out on the court it's time to do battle"

On a trip through Cleveland I called Steve Patterson center for the Cavaliers, and we agreed to meet at a restaurant near the Cleveland Arena. "You'll be able to recognize me," he said. "I'm growing a beard."

"You'll be able to recognize me too," I responded. "I'm 5 feet 10 inches tall."

Later when we sat down to talk and I had explained to Steve the purpose of this book, he said he thought it sounded interesting, then commented: "The thing that I'm sort of curious about is why you chose me? Why you think my opinion is going to be more valid than perhaps someone with a more established reputation?"

Patterson had a point. He finally had worked his way into a starting job with the Cleveland Cavaliers in his third season as a pro, but any ranking, statistical or imaginative, of NBA centers would find him well down on the list. I explained diplomatically that the ability to play basketball and talk about basketball were not necessarily interdependent. Besides, who knows how good Steve Patterson may become now that he has the opportunity to play regularly? He had been the starting center at UCLA in the two-year period between Kareem Abdul-Jabbar and Bill Walton, a time when that team continued its string of NCAA championships. I asked him to characterize the Cleveland style of basketball.

Part of the problem is we don't have a style. What we do is pretty much dictated by what the opposing team does. Our main emphasis is on defense and trying to take away the other team's strength. The tendency when you concentrate on the other team is you don't develop yourself from an offensive standpoint.

We are definitely a guard-oriented team because of Lenny Wilkens and Austin Carr. They score a lot of points because of their ability to take the ball one-on-one, but we are not a well-disciplined pattern offensive team nor are we a great running team either. We do one or the other well occasionally depending on the caliber of the opponent we play. We can run with Houston or Atlanta because they are not great defensive teams. Buffalo, same thing. When we play against New York or Boston and have to break down and grind it out, we have problems.

We haven't established our identity. This is partially because we don't know exactly what is expected of us as players because we're young and inexperienced. Do you understand what I'm saying? It's partly because the coaches have to find it for us and partly because we're not able to recognize it, yet.

222

This is my third year and it has taken me this long to get where I could do anything against the more experienced centers. The first couple of years I had no conception of what kind of shots I could take against them, or no conception of what I could do against them defensively. I didn't know what to begin to do to take away their strengths. A classic example is Nate Thurmond. It's only now that I'm beginning to know him, and I still haven't had a good game when we played the Warriors. I've had good rebounding games against him, but offensively I'm just beginning to get an idea of what I can do.

Now, I've had an advantage against Kareem, because I played so much against him in practice when we were at UCLA. I know I can shoot long jumpers, and occasionally when I'm hitting he'll come out and I can go around him. I know I can score against him inside using the backboard and basket for a shield. If you are underneath pivoting back and forth, that kind of thing. I'm able to score against Kareem, but I have problems with him defensively because of his size.

Each center I meet presents a different problem. Each one has a different strength offensively and defensively, and it's taken me a while to learn this. They say your first three years are the hardest, and I believe it. It's just now to the point where I'm comfortable out there on the court. There are still a couple of guys that I'm a little shaky against. Nate and Kareem are two of them.

I think I have a fairly realistic opinion of my ability, which may be unique in the NBA, or may even be unique even in all professional sports. Probably a lot of your journeyman players do. I know I'm limited. I'm an honest 6 feet 9 inches tall, which is a bit below average size for a pivot man. I've got a little better than average speed. I've got average jumping ability. I have to compensate for the averages by working harder day in and out. I've got to play at least 10 percent harder than my opponent on the court. Playing against guys like Lanier, or Jabbar, or Thurmond, I've got to play 50 percent harder just to stay even. The biggest problem with this is I have stamina problems. I'm not able to go 48 minutes a game, whereas they can play 48 minutes just because they can cruise a little more because of their physical abilities.

I went a 10- or 12-game stretch this season where I played 40–42 minutes a game, but it about killed me. At the end of that stretch, my performances really tapered off. For a while I was averaging 15 points and 15 boards a game, and against some fairly good teams, but I was unable to maintain it. I dropped off to where I had a couple of 6 points, 8 rebounds games, so we had to back off. Toward the end of the season I was playing 35–36 minutes a game and getting like 12 points and 12 rebounds, which is a more realistic projection of what I'm capable of doing, in addition to holding the opposing center to under his average.

There is a law of supply and demand in pro basketball, like in economics. There is a tremendous demand for 7-foot centers who can score 25 points a game and get you 15 boards. The teams are willing to pay big money for someone like that, but unfortunately there is a limited supply. Or fortunately for me. So that does create an opportunity for guys my size who have ability and the willingness to work hard. I have the potential to become a journeyman center and I have the ability to play on a winning team. You do not necessarily need a 7-footer to win.

Look at Boston with Dave Cowens. Look at Chicago with Clifford Ray. New York has been able to win with Willis Reed injured and Gianelli in the lineup. They are able to circumvent apparent weakness in the middle. We have the ability here in Cleveland to do the same. Everybody here says we need a Walton, a big dominating center. I don't think you need a dominating center if you have other strengths, if you're able to develop a team offense, becoming a running team, obtain great defensive play from all your players.

In a match between a journeyman center and a dominant center, what can the former hope to achieve?

It depends on what each guy's talents are. In my situation, the main thing I have to do is get them thinking about me,

224

establish myself out there in their minds. Part of that is being physical. I enjoy the contact. They call basketball a non-contact sport, but that's absurd, especially in the middle. I've got to go out there and start banging on guys immediately and just let them know that, though I may not be 7 feet, when they try to shoot or pass the ball they are not going to do it unmolested.

Part of that initially is to try and take away the spot that they want to establish themselves in. For example, Jabbar always wants to establish himself in the low post on the right hand side.* First of all, I've got to use my speed and get down court and get in that position first, and when he comes down and tries to establish himself I'll start bumping him all the way from the top of the key. I try to force him two or three feet further away from the basket than he wants to start.

Now Nate Thurmond, in guarding Kareem Abdul-Jabbar, will not try to play position on him. He will rely on his great size to be an inhibitor. But guys like Cowens, McAdoo, myself have to get in there and take position away from the big guy so that instead of his coming across and shooting that sky hook as a 6-footer, you make him hit a 6- or 10-footer, so you can drop his accuracy maybe 10 percent.

Of course, you've got to pay a price. If you saw that game on TV in Chicago, you know that Dennis Awtrey basically plays the same way. You take the risk of riling up the big guy when you do that.* You also take the risk of riling up Thurmond, Lanier, as well as the other tall men when you play that bump and run defense. You bump them and hold them, and they bump you back, and you just get into a shoving match out there. That's the only way I can survive on defense, because I'm not going to block their shots. I have to belly up to them. If you give them constant pressure you don't have to be up there in position to block a shot. At least that's what I found the last half of the season.

Now I've had guys score some points on me, but Dave

*As viewed from the center with his back to the basket, rather than from the offensive guard's point of view.

Cowens is shooting about 35 percent against Cleveland. Jabbar, the last time we played them, shot about 40 percent. I mean, the guy got 30 points, but he also took 36 or 38 shots. When a guy is averaging 54 percent from the floor and he has to work that hard to score, you feel like you're doing something right.

That's encouraging. Of course, when you play against someone like Thurmond who doesn't have to score too much to contribute to his team, then you can't be effective using those tactics. If he gets his 10 or 12 points, yet has 25 rebounds, you haven't done your job. Do you understand what I mean by that? So my criteria for success are different from what you read in the box score.

It's not always easy to establish position. Sometimes I try to play in back of the guy. Sometimes I try to play one side or the other. Occasionally I'll even try to front the guy. I don't do that to Jabbar anymore, just because of the lob. He's really the only center right now agile enough to handle a lob inside, since he's bigger enough than I am and they can throw it where I can't get it. Of course, Walton, when he comes into the league, will present tremendous problems as far as the lob goes. He is another one who you will just not be able to front, because you've seen what UCLA does to teams that front him. They just put the ball up around the basket and it's in. I already know ahead of time what I can't do against him.

What about that incident between Awtrey and Jabbar? I was at the game and to me it looked like unpremeditated murder on Awtrey's part. But when I got home my kids, who watched the game on television, said that a replay showed Jabbar elbowing Awtrey in the face a few seconds before.

*In a late season, nationally televised game from Chicago, Bulls reserve center Dennis Awtrey punched Kareem Abdul-Jabbar in the eye. Jabbar's response was to score 38 points as his team demolished the Bulls. I was at the game and Kareem must have missed a few shots after that incident—but I don't remember them.

If I was in the same situation I would have hit him too. Jabbar has a tendency to take a shot at Awtrey. See, his elbows are right at head level and when he comes in for a rebound it doesn't take much for him to swing that elbow around and stick it in your face. He popped Awtrey pretty good that one particular time, and I wouldn't be surprised if he popped Awtrey before that, because I know he's popped me several times.

What sort of relationships can opposing players have? You were Kareem's teammate at UCLA. When the final horn blows at the end of each game can you shake hands with the man you've been battling and forget what happened?

Yes, I definitely can do that. I don't know if everybody can. I don't know if Jabbar has the ability to do that. When I go out on the court it's time to battle. But once the game is through, I'm done with it. I have a good relationship with several of the guys. Neil Walk and I get along pretty well, but when we get on court it's tooth and nail. Another guy I get along well with is Rick Roberson, but I'll tell you: The game we had against Portland Tuesday night was one of the most physical games I had all year. He's a very physical guy. I have a friendly relationship with Jabbar, although I wouldn't say that we're friends. We've been acquainted for a long time.

We had a pretty strong rivalry in college. I've got a competitive spirit so that I'm not going to concede anything to anybody. Just because he's Jabbar and he's 7 feet 4 when he walks out on the court, I'm not going to say to him, you automatically can dominate the game. I'm going to challenge the guy. That's the way it is with everybody.

Bob Lanier is another example, although I will admit I had a pretty interesting experience with Lanier. I'm aware of his great strength, but I figured I was really playing the guy heads-up, and—[*Patterson paused.*] I don't know how he did it to tell you the truth. I was leaning on him, hammering him, practically hanging on him, and he just wrapped his arm around me and just: KRRRRRRCH! Threw me to the ground like I was a rag doll. It was like I wasn't even there. I mean, it was just the most—[*Patterson paused again, as though he couldn't find adequate words to describe the experience.*] I did a complete four-point landing, landed on both elbows, bruised them both, and they really swelled up on me. In fact, I've had trouble with the right elbow ever since. I've got bone chips in there.

Every once in a while one of the big guys will do that. Not trying to hurt you. In fact, Bob didn't appear to be angry, because as soon as he did it, he looked at me, offered his hand, and helped me up. But he gave a graphic illustration that, all right, you can play rough and you can play strong, but there is a line past which you cannot go.

I assume that everybody has to establish that line. Perhaps that was what Awtrey was doing with Jabbar, or vice versa.

I think so. It's going to be interesting to see what happens. I think a lot of it has to do with the respect that you generate. I'm not sure that Awtrey and Jabbar have mutual respect. If they don't this cheap shot is going to continue to have repercussions. But if someone respects you, once you've established that line you both respect that line. Can you follow what I mean by that? If someone doesn't respect you, then you're going to continue to battle for position on that line of respect, to determine how much you can get away with. I don't think I've established that line with everyone. Some guys I do; some guys I don't.

It's amazing that when you come into the league, people will battle you harder, individually trying to establish that line, and after you battle back and play so many times, then they begin to concede things to you. It's rather interesting. Once they know that you are going to fight them for this spot, or this position, and you're going to box them out every single time on defense once that ball hits the boards, then they will stop going to the offensive boards. Then you don't have to work as hard to accomplish certain things, which is really interesting. I find that happening now. Guys are beginning to concede certain things to me, so that I'm able to be more effective with less effort, which is an encouraging sign. That way I'm beginning to see that maybe in a couple of years I will be able to play 40-minutes-plus a game as I begin to get more things conceded to me.

When you first come in they don't concede anything. They try to take away everything. It's the law of the jungle. I always appreciated the things Bill Russell had to say about the psychology of the game. He did an article for *Sports Illustrated* several years ago about the "psych," about how it is such a big part of the game. It's astounding to me. Once you've established your "psych" against certain people, you know you can continue with it even though you sometimes don't have the ability to do certain things that they, in the back of their mind, think that you can.

Getting back to that one game between the Bulls and the Bucks, there were several other near fights. Robertson and Sloan squared off at one point. Another time Sloan kicked Fritz Williams while being held. Afterward, a member of the Bulls staff commented that he had thought the referees had allowed the game to get out of hand.

There are some officials who would not have allowed that to happen. Conceivably those fights wouldn't have happened if you had certain referees officiating that ball game. The quality of officiating varies from top to bottom. Officiating is a tough job. It really is. You need an incredibly strong personality to handle ten men at a time, and have them respect what you're doing, and accept judgments over a 48-minute game that is so heavily contested. I don't know if we need three officials. Two officials call as many fouls as need be called and three might hurt the game. But it's very interesting. We had one of the same officials that officiated the Bulls/Bucks game in our next game, which was a Tuesday night, and he was telling me: "Oh, man, what a boxing match." And I noticed that our game got very physical too. We happened to be playing Capital. Unseld and

Hayes are going to push you and grab you and knock you around as much as they can, and it's up to the officials to prevent this. It's a fine line also as far as officials are concerned when it comes to maintaining control. Some officials simply do not have the ability to either maintain that control, or they don't recognize where that fine line is. It was possibly the officials' fault that that game got so far out of control.

Of course, everybody involved with the game sees things from a biased point of view. I'm not certain that players on the court are in a position to judge how officials are doing their jobs.

I see some players complain about calls and I can't believe the stuff they're complaining about. It amazes me. I try not to bait the officials. I feel they are trying to do a job too. I'm trying to establish a rapport as much as possible with the officials, because I think if you respect them, they will respect you—although I have some difficulty with certain individuals. It really seems that certain referees have it out for you, or for certain teams. It just seems that way. Of course, I'm playing for an expansion team, a losing team, so it's hard to command the respect you want, because they see you night after night losing games that perhaps you should have won by making crucial mistakes that perhaps Boston, New York, or Los Angeles wouldn't make. I can understand why they might not have as much respect for you as you would like them to.

What about establishing yourself with your teammates?

That's difficult too, because on an expansion team you have guys coming in who figure that they single-handed are going to be the answer and that they are going to turn the situation around. You're dealing with very high draft picks and guys that are making unbelievable amounts of money, and they have been led by the press, and by the coaches, and by the fans to believe that they are going to be the most important part of our game.

But this isn't true. The team game is number one. The team game is the one you win with, and this is one thing that has been driven into my head. I had great coaching in high school and great coaching in college, and I always learned that, as a player, you have to give up the ball to get it. You've got to give up scoring opportunities to get better scoring opportunities. Some times a 15-foot open shot isn't always the best shot, because somebody might have an open layup. One of the problems, particularly with young teams, is that you settle for good shots when you could be getting better shots if you worked a little harder and took some more time on the 24-second clock.

The biggest problem I've had to deal with is the frustration of seeing us not get the shots that I know we can get. I have a tendency to give the ball up a lot quicker than most guys, because I'm used to having it come back—although I'm beginning to get it back now, because people are beginning to have more confidence in my game too. They are beginning to see the things I can do.

My first couple of years here I wasn't taking the open 15-foot shot because I figure we're going to be working for a better shot. But the difficult thing in starting with a new team is you have no mental framework with which to strive. You don't know what you are looking for in terms of offense. You don't have a team concept. Say you are Paul Westphal coming in with the Celtics, you know what's expected of yourself. Paul can look at the style of game his team has been playing and know he has to adapt himself to a certain degree. John Gianelli working with the Knicks. Basically he's learning by watching what the other centers do. You come in with an expansion team and one game you run, one game you walk, one game you do neither. It's extremely difficult to adapt to that situation, to learn how to get your shots, to learn who to give shots to, who to set picks for. It's a process of trial and error and it takes time. It really does. This is the thing we're beginning to work better at all the time. We began to work well together last year, then two starters were traded—Roberson and Johnson—so we had to start practically from scratch this year.

It takes years to develop a championship team where people begin to understand the subtleties of working together, of knowing in pressure situations who to give the ball to, what kind of shot to work for. This is part of the reason we had such success at UCLA because we all had great confidence in our teammates' abilities to deliver in certain situations, and in those situations we always went to those people, for those shots. With this team the only one we can really rely on is Lenny Wilkens. We know what he can do. But to win you've got to have more than one guy because you can't rely on him to win it for you day in day out.

34. *Jim Eakins*

"Round off the team with guys who are just very thankful to be there"

Perhaps no team in professional sports has had as troubled a history as the one that played the 1973–74 basketball season under the name of the Virginia Squires. In the first seven years of its existence, this franchise has had three locations (Oakland, Washington, and Virginia) and three names (Oaks, Capitals, and Squires), and in its most recent incarnation has played home games in three Virginia cities (Norfolk, Hampton, and Richmond). During this period an impressive array of all-star talent has come—and gone. Rick Barry, Charlie Scott, Julius Erving, Swen Nater, and George Gervin played for the Squires, then left to go elsewhere. The last two players had to be sold to the San Antonio Spurs during the 1973–74 season (when both played in the ABA All-Star game) to permit the team owner to pay his bills. Alas for the fans. Alas for the owner.

Standing at center, bravely weathering the winds around him, was one player who joined the Oaks-Caps-Squires in the franchise's second year and played six seasons, if not with brilliance, at least with honor. During that time Jim Eakins, tall and slender, missed only two games. He played in the ABA All-Star game in 1974 (although as a last minute substitute for ailing Billy Paultz). He has played some extremely fine games in the playoffs, particularly going heads-up with Kentucky's Artis Gilmore, against whom he averaged 24.8 points in five games. He leads his team in rebounds, blocked shots, and field goal percentage, is second in assists, and third in steals and scoring. "Jim does what he can do," says publicist Bobby Batson, "which means he plays hard every minute."

At Brigham Young University, Jim Eakins majored in political science and his experiences in surviving with the Oakland/Washington/Virginia franchise should offer him excellent experience for the political future he contemplates. He would like to run for Congress, and hopes he can remain in Virginia to use that state as a base. The only apparent blemish during a life of exemplary behavior occurred during a Squires-Pacers game in Indianapolis, when Eakins was arrested by the police (along with coach Al Bianchi and Charlie Scott) after an on-court fight. Actually the 6-foot 11-inch Eakins was trying to serve as a peacemaker, but the police mistook him for a teammate, who was 6 foot 2 inches tall.

Jim is married, has two children and, when forced by the ABA schedule to travel on Sundays, always wears a coat and tie because it is Sunday. Despite having just returned to Norfolk following a road trip, he drove downtown to the Scope arena to meet me during a freak early spring snowstorm, then insisted on driving me to the airport. I said, as we parted, that if he ever ran for national office, I'd vote for him. "Don't vote for me just because you like me," said Jim Eakins. "Wait until you see what stand I take on the issues."

My role as center has changed. It changed as the composition of the team changed. Of course, there are certain things that the big man has to do, no matter what team he plays with, especially on defense. He guards the basket and tries to keep the other team from scoring any easy layups. Make them work for everything they get.

When I broke into the league back in 1968 with the

Oakland Oaks, the championship team in the ABA that year, I was on the bench behind a center named Ira Harge. Ira was a 6-9 defensive center, and I was a 6-11 offensive center—and a rookie, a young player, at that. Consequently my role on that team was to provide the inside offensive punch whenever I got in there. So whenever I got the ball, I made a move toward the basket and shot it. Ira played the first and third quarters and I played the second and fourth. He was strictly defensive and would average only seven points a game.

The next year the team moved to Washington, D.C., and I played less time under our new coach, Al Bianchi. I was playing only three minutes a game and the coach was putting me in, like: "Go in and give Ira a blow." So I had to do some soul-searching and ask myself: "What does this team need in a center?" Although I started out as an offensive center, I looked at the composition of our team when we moved the next year to Virginia. The team had Ray Scott coming in. We had Charlie Scott. We had guys like Rick Barry and Mike Barrett around. They were tremendous offensive players who could put the ball in the basket, so I decided maybe I better turn my game around and go like Ira. So for my third, fourth, and part of my fifth year, I tried to be mostly a defensive player and passer. When I saw one guy controlling the ball too much, I tried to get into the center and pass it off, fuse it out from the middle.

Then with Charlie Scott jumping to the other league, Julius Erving being traded to New York, Rick Barry leaving, all of those superstars we did have going other ways, the pendulum, having swung from left to right, now has swung back to the middle. I've had to take up more of the offensive lead.

I attribute much of what I try to accomplish on the court now to that first year with Alex Hannum, him teaching me and showing me things. I can remember one afternoon when Ira and I were out shooting and he halted practice and called us over to the sidelines. He had a picture of Bill Russell blocking a shot, and he said: "Look at this form. Check

234

where his arms are, and where the arm he is not using to block the shot with is. Check how he is controlling his body. Check where his wrist is." Things like that as far as technique.

I had a problem blocking shots. I think I have learned to overcome it, but most young rookies, when they go to block a shot just go up and slap the ball. I had to learn that the referees in this league, whenever anybody slaps at a ball, call an automatic foul whether you hit the shooter or not. So you've got to go up and just flick your wrist to hit the ball away. Alex Hannum showed me things like that. He taught me when to try to block a shot and when not to. He realized, and I realized, with my jumping ability—which is about one-and-a-half sheets of paper off the floor in a great leap—I was not going to be a shot blocker. Even though I would get my share of blocked shots, my defense in that department would have to mainly be based on position and technique. So even though I was oriented offensively at the beginning, I didn't give up on the defensive end. I just wasn't experienced in that style of play.

How much actual coaching goes on at the professional levels? When I did a book on professional football several years ago, there was a story told by Jim Lee Howell, the old Giants coach. He said that with all the talent he had, he would just send his assistant coaches out to handle the team while he would stand on the sidelines blowing up footballs. When you have all stars of the caliber of Barry, or Scott, or Erving, does a basketball coach have to do anything more than hand them a basketball?'

I think he very definitely has to do more than that. In fact, instead of trying to load up your team with all stars, I remember Alex Hannum once saying that his idea of a perfect team would be to obtain one or two true all stars, such as Rick Barry, then surround them with guys who were merely very, very good players. Then have your one or two real good subs that come off the bench to help you. Then round off the team with guys who are just very thankful to be there. He didn't want people sitting on the bench, grumbling, and saying; "Boy if I could only get in there," causing attitude problems. That was his idea of a perfect team.

You have a hard time putting together a team like that. When you get to the pros, you have people who were supposedly the cream of the crop of some 600 colleges. You take a few dozen of the very top seniors every year and give them jobs in pro basketball. All those guys you draft were superstars in college, are used to being superstars, and when they come in and have to sit behind a veteran who has been out there for six years, they don't like it. They are itching to get out onto the court to prove themselves. They don't have the patience to wait anymore. It takes a tremendous amount of ability on the part of the coach not only to know the game, but to know how to handle the players, and how to keep those players from causing discontent, forming cliques, and disrupting the team.

But then a coach has to take a player like that and polish him. There are very, very few all-Americans who come right out of college and Bang! make it as a pro. In fact, I've only known two in the six years that I've been associated with the game: Charlie Scott and Julius Erving. They didn't have to wait on the bench and learn new techniques like I had to do.

So to get back to your original statement, I think there is a tremendous amount of coaching going on. I can remember when we were playing Kentucky my rookie year with Oakland and had a 13-point lead. The Colonels had a promotion that day and had about 14,000 fans in Freedom Hall. Kentucky started making a run at us and brought our lead down to 6 or 7 points. Boy that crowd of 14,000 fans in there were whooping it up, and the more they whooped, the more Kentucky rose up emotionally. So Alex jumped up and called a time out.

We dragged over to the bench and he simply said: "You guys are playing great ball out there. I have nothing to say to you at all. The crowd was starting to get behind them, so

236

during the time out I want the crowd to settle down and quit yelling and we'll go back out there and run them out."

During the 90 seconds time out, the crowd did sit back down. They relaxed, and by the time the ball was thrown back in they weren't yelling anymore. We clicked off 15 straight points and blew them out.

Strategy. Alex pulled a strategy move against us this year that almost worked. He's at Denver now and we had them down by 3 points. There was time out with 12 seconds left, and we figured he was going to go for a 3-point shot. So everybody gathered along the 3-point shot line to try and block the shot. If they didn't make it, we figured we could grab the ball and run out the clock. Instead, they set a screen for the center who took a long pass and went up to the hoop. He tried to stuff the ball and unfortunately for them, fortunately for us, missed the dunk.

But the idea behind it was sound. You get the lob pass by the basket and the clock doesn't start until the player touches the ball. So you get the dunk and only one second is gone on the clock and you're now only 1 point behind. You may intercept the ball when it is thrown in, or you can foul and hope we miss our free throws. Even if we make them you still have time to go for the 3-pointer. It was a gamble, but quite a strategic move that I never thought of. Coach Bianchi told us after the game that he should have figured Alex Hannum for that because it was an old Boston Celtics play.

I'm talking mostly about Alex Hannum because he was impressionable on me when I was young in the game, but I also think Al Bianchi is one of the great young coaches in the game now. He's quite a strategist too. He gambles a lot of times and the gambles don't always work, but I certainly can't say enough about him.

A lot of fans, myself included, probably wonder what secret strategies go on during those time-outs, when the television commentator says: "We'll be right back after the next message."

During our time-outs? Quite a bit of the time is spent in

telling us to get our butts moving or we're going to get kicked in the butt, and do something and do it right. But we will set up a play and the coach will diagram how he wants it run, or how he wants an ad-lib off a play. We developed one play recently that is simply just an ad-lib off an old play. We used to have one forward pop up to the top of the key, receive the ball from the guard, then pop it to the other guard going back door. The other teams started to recognize what we were doing so they would overplay the forward popping up so we couldn't get the ball in to him. But as our second guard kept going down and never getting the ball the defensive guard became very lax with him. So lately we just ad-libbed off that and instead of passing it to the forward first and having him pass it to the cutting guard, we began to bypass the forward and lob it over everybody's head to the guard cutting down. Well, I'll be doggoned if we haven't gotten ten or eleven hoops off that in the last few games, so things like this go on.

During the time out the coach may try to settle us down if something happens. I got into an argument with one ref the other night, and probably most of the next time out was spent by Al trying to cool me off so that I wouldn't go out there and do something drastic.

Many things get talked about. If you are going great, like that one time with Alex, there is not much your coach can tell you. If you are going so-so then you get berated and told to get the lead out. If you are behind, you really get berated. You talk about strategy and new plays and what to try. If a certain forward is in foul trouble, we will flash one of our forwards in and try to get that fifth or sixth foul called on him.

In looking over your career record, I've noticed that you haven't missed too many games.

I've missed two games in my pro career, and that's including preseason and playoffs. They were both in my bad year in Washington, my second year in the league. I missed

238

one regular season game toward the end of the year and I missed one playoff game. I was there and able to play, but I wasn't inserted in the game. Since moving to Virginia, and I'm finishing my fourth season here, I haven't missed a single game. I've been fortunate in not being forced out of any games because of injuries. Disabling injuries are something that all basketball players worry about, but I've been lucky.

It does take luck as well as durability. Nate Archibald missed most of this season merely because somebody accidentally stepped on him in the first game of the year.

Of course, the more you play the more the probability of your getting hurt is there. Luck can be a factor. You can attribute it to anything you want. I can't say I've been staying away from contact, because I take my lumps out there as much as anybody else. And I do get tired, especially this season. I've played more this year than any other year, and coming down in the stretch during February we had 18 games in 28 days. Then in March we have 17 games in 31 days. Those are a lot of games. Then when you string them down the road you might get six games in seven days, which all adds up to a very fatigued center. Since we wrapped up our playoff berth, Al has done more platooning to try and give his starters more rest, and that has been helpful.

You've had success in playing against Artis Gilmore. Is it because you get up when you play him?

Yes and no. I think it's more than that. It's the type of basketball different players play. But certainly, just like every center in the "other league" will get up for Kareem Abdul-Jabbar, or Dave Cowens, or Nate Thurmond, we do the same in the ABA. Artis Gilmore is the dominant all-star center in this league, so I do try extra hard to produce against him. But I've got a good outside jump shot which I hit right from the top of the key, or 15 feet out. Artis just loves to stand underneath the basket and check everything, so he had not been coming out on me. I just stand out there and pop in 10-, 12-, or 15-footers until he does. Then when he does get out there, he's 15 feet away from the basket in a position he's not used to, so I would drive him and rely on quickness to get around him, hoping he will either foul me or let me go. This is the basic reason I've had really good games against someone like Artis Gilmore.

Now I've had some very terrible games against a player like Zelmo Beaty, who though not being a big center under the bucket will come out with you and beat on you the whole way in, or whatever you're going. He's out there 15 feet away pushing you to 18 feet away. So it's a matter of different styles of play by different people. I try and get Zelmo in as far underneath the bucket as I can, whereas I try to take Artis outside.

If there's one player I haven't found out what tactic to use against it's Billy Paultz, the center for the New York Nets. When Swen Nater was here earlier in the year, he used to start our games against New York. Paultz must weigh 290 pounds at least, he's 6 feet 11, and he has very, very long arms. I have had a couple of good games against him, but the bad games very much overshadow the good ones. He uses his weight very well against somebody like me. With 290 against 215 pounds, you are talking about a 75-pound difference in there, and that's quite a bit of weight to use when you want to. When I try to push on him, it's like trying to push this building down. I don't budge him an inch. I've tried driving the man, but he is surprisingly agile. He recovers quite well, and he jumps well, so that if he does come out with me, he blocks my outside shot. I don't know what the answer is for Paultz. I'm still working on that.

Before you go into each game do you think about the player you'll be matched up against?

Very much so. I mentally go over who I'm playing against, what he likes to do, what I've had success doing against him previously, and if I do get around him who his backup man

240

will be. You take New York: If I do drive around Paultz then I've got Larry Kenon to face since he'll be sagging in there. If I get by Kenon, then Julius Erving is the last blockade to the bucket. You have three shot blockers in there, so it's very difficult for me to drive. Against New York I won't force myself to the basket, but will concentrate more on establishing shots for others on my team.

Certainly against Kentucky I have done well, and since my team recognizes this, they will go to me a little more. Against New York I try to uphold my average and we will go to one of the forwards. George Carter usually has a pretty good game against New York. Or we will go to the hot man. It might not be George. It might be one of the guards. We will find out who is hot, and go to that man, and work on the weak spots of the other team.

What was it like playing with superstars like Barry, or Scott, who like to have the ball a lot so they can score. Maybe you might want to deny that.

Well, I don't deny it. They did it. I can remember when Rick felt he wasn't getting the ball enough when he was hot. I'm not bad-mouthing Rick or anything like that. Rick is a tremendous basketball player. He's got all the talent in the world, and he's already proved it. But I will say that players with the most talent think they can do it all, that when the team got behind, they thought they were the only ones who could bring the team back, so that's the way they worked their game.

During my second year, in that transition period, I would see players come down and hog the ball and try to do everything one-on-one. I don't know how many times Rick Barry scored 50 points for Washington but it was numerous. Sitting there on the bench and being in on the huddles I could see what we were attempting to do and what was developing. Rick would go down and get the ball, dribble up half court, call a play, go to the hoop, and either score or get fouled. After he's done that about five times, the other four players are just standing there watching what Rick's going to do. This is a problem we have had with the superstars. We had it with Charlie Scott. We had it very much with Julius Erving.

Julius Erving used to work one-on-one, go to the hoop, look great, fantastic move, score half the time, but the other four players were standing around. It was five against one. The defensive players didn't have to worry about their men. It all centered on Julius or Charlie or Rick or whoever it was, and they would score 50 points, but we would lose by 30. And I could see this happening and that's where I decided that when I got my chance in there I would try to even things up when the ball came into the center. If the forward had been predominating I would try to get my guard to cut and give him a jump shot, try to get more of a team pattern. I would look for the pass before looking for my shot.

Only a few days ago I was in Atlanta watching the Hawks play the Capital Bullets. Atlanta failed to make the playoffs despite two of the league's top scorers in Pete Maravich and Lou Hudson. One difference I noticed between the two teams was that when Capital went back on defense everybody was talking, particularly center Wes Unseld. When Atlanta was on defense, there was almost total silence.

We had a team meeting one year. We had some problems. We had lost something like four or five in a row, and we were too good a team to be losing that way. The players got together and started throwing ideas out, and one of our problems was that we hadn't been talking on screens, or switches, or blocking men out, or relaying calls. The guard would call the play and only half the team would hear it. Just a matter of poor communications. As far as communications on defense, since the center is under the basket and able to look and scope the whole situation, he should be the leader in talking and saying what's going on. So I try to remind my forwards that we need rebounds, "Let's get on the boards!" Or the switch is coming. The screen is coming. I try to do this

242

because I'm right there in the key on defense and only moving a few feet from one side to the other. I stand there and yell to the guard: "Screen right!" or "Screen left!" or "Watch out! Something's coming up."

Last night we played in Memphis, and they ran a "five" play and scored on it. I was watching, and the next time they ran a "five" play, I knew what was coming. My guard hadn't recognized it, but it was a simple play where everybody cleared out and isolated their guard on my guard one-on-one. I yelled to him: "You're isolated! Get up on him and don't let him take the outside shot. If he drives on you, you've got help under the basket."

It helps when we communicate, not only the center, but everybody talking. I'll be fronting my man and my forward is yelling to me: "You've got help. I'm right here, Jim. I'm right behind you." Now I don't have to worry about them lobbing the ball behind me. And I know if I can hear him, that guard out there can hear him too. So he's not going to throw the ball. The best games that Virginia has played this year—and they have been few—were games where everybody talked and communicated. A vital ingredient in any team sport is to communicate. Even more so in basketball.

That's a part of the game that is so interesting, but you can only hear it if you're sitting courtside. It's too bad that the players couldn't be equipped with microphones.

You wouldn't want to do that. Some of the language that comes out down there is terrible.

I've always watched games emotionally, cheering one team as a fan, watching the ball. It's only been since I started doing this book that I began to realize some of the subtle things that do occur on a basketball court.

Well, I can certainly understand that. I don't know how I'm really going to put this, but I have taken people as guests to games, and driving home they would ask me questions:

"How come the guard put two fingers up at this time, or put five fingers!" I would say, "He's calling a play." They would say, "What do you mean, a play?" (I'm not talking about women; I'm talking about men too.) I would say, "Well, we have certain plays that we run out there to try and score. They are set, and we have numbers for them, so we call them out: one, two, three, four, five."

My friends would be shocked. They didn't realize. They thought we just got out there and threw the basketball in and just sandlotted, just played free-lance the whole way. They didn't realize there was any strategy to the game, any playmaking, or defense,. It was amusing to me, because these were sports-oriented people, not people who were going to their first basketball game. The average fan doesn't realize the strategy that goes on, the plays you try and run at certain times for certain situations, and the things you try to do out there.

"We buy season tickets to the high school games in Michigan City every year. And I always considered myself a fairly sophisticated fan even though I never played basketball competitively. But doing this book has been a revelation. We attended the sectional championship this season and watched our team play LaPorte, a nearby city. Whenever one of the LaPorte players would go up to the free throw line, his teammates would gather around him. It dawned on me while I was sitting there, that out of 7,000 spectators in that auditorium, there were probably not more than a few dozen who had any idea what that huddle was all about.

Yeah, probably there were two things they could have been doing. They were calling either what defense they were going to drop back into—zone press, full court, half court, basic zone, man-for-man—or maybe what play they were going to use the next time back down the floor.* Very often

---

*Later, while editing this interview I telephoned Skip Collins, the LaPorte basketball coach, and asked him the reason for the huddle. He said it was first, to offer the shooter a word of encouragement, and second, to call the

we'll come down and run two plays in a row, and the first play is just to set the man up for the second play that's coming. The first play will pop the man out one way and probably give him a good screen so he gets a nice jump shot, then we run the second play when his man's overplaying and waiting for him to pop, reverse it, and pop him the other way, give him the screen for a layup underneath. Several times plays we run are setting things up for one, two, or three plays in the future.

It's a fascinating game.

I find it that way, very much so. I haven't studied it as much as some players. When I was playing with Larry Brown, who is now head coach of the Carolina Cougars, everything he did he had to have a reason for. He wanted to know why it was done, when, and how? Of course, he was preparing to become a coach, so he was trying to learn as much about the strategy of the game as he could. I haven't taken that deep an interest in it, because I don't plan to become a coach, otherwise I would. But it is a fascinating game and the principles you learn in sports can carry over into any facet of life that you take.

35. *K. C. Jones*

"You can see things that they don't see"

K. C. Jones was a member of two NCAA championship teams at the University of San Francisco, won a gold medal with the USA

defense. LaPorte used five basic defenses. Sitting in the stands, I had been only partially right, since I guessed they probably were calling the next offensive play.

squad at the Olympics in 1956, and during the nine years he spent with the Boston Celtics that team won NBA titles eight of those years. The Capital Bullets program describes the former guard as "probably the most well-known NBA player of all time who never averaged double figures. . . . He became an accomplished player by mastering defense and developing the 'intangibles' that make a player with ordinary ability extraordinary." Since retiring as a player he has served as assistant coach at Harvard, head coach at Brandeis, assistant coach at the Los Angeles Lakers (that team's championship year), and head coach of the San Diego Conquistadores of the ABA before becoming head coach of the Bullets at the start of the 1973–74 season. I spoke to him in the locker room before a Bullets home game against K. C.'s former team, the Boston Celtics. It was the last game of the regular season. "How do you prepare a team before a game?" I asked.

You try to put down some of the other team's patterns, get your players familiar with what they like to use a lot, and give them some idea of what they can do on defense. That's one thing. Then we talk about what we want to do on offense. We talk about individual personnel, matchups, their weaknesses and strengths. It takes ten or 15 minutes just to go through that. They've seen the other club before, but we want to remind them what to expect.

You've already made the playoffs. Another win or loss doesn't mean anything to you at this stage in the season. Do you have trouble motivating your team to go out and play?

They're motivated for this game already. For one thing, Boston is one of the top teams in the league. When you play Milwaukee, or New York, or Los Angeles, you really don't have to get them up in the air. It's there, the competition. But you take a team like Cleveland, or Philly, one of the teams that haven't done well. Then you have difficulty. Those type clubs are not really up to us in personnel, and the players know it, so you just hope that things go right. More times than not, when you go in against one of those teams you find them up to play you, so you wind up in the third

246

quarter 10 or 12 points behind before you realize it's time to get down to business. Then your team will start playing, but sometimes it's too late, because the other team is not through with its momentum.

What affects your decision on sending in substitutes, both who and when?

It depends on how things are going out there, and more times than not it winds up with the same men going in at about the same time. If the starters are doing well, they are going to stay in the whole first quarter, and maybe into the second quarter. If things are not going well, substitutions will come midway into the quarter, for one position or maybe two. Somebody may be hurting us so you might substitute early. You call a time out and tell your team to get on him because he's hurting us. It may be that we are in trouble rebounding. You may see a lot of things out there that make you decide you need a change.

What do you say during time-outs?

If things are going good, you compliment your team, say they're doing a great job. You let them know what they are doing, how the defense is working. Maybe the ball is not going in so you let them know it, if that's the only thing wrong with the offense. If things are really going bad out there and we are being hurt in two or three departments— the defensive boards or them running fast breaks—you try to turn things around.

You should be familiar with Boston, having played your entire NBA career with the Celtics. Have they changed much since then?

Not basically. They have the best running game in the league, and have had it for years. Their basic pattern is to work to their shooters: Jo Jo (White), Havlicek, Nelson. That's the same thing we were doing with the old Celtics:

Russell and I and Satch. And they try to wear you out. They are a very smart club. The whole team will focus on your weakness as a team, or individually. They are so grooved to the game that they can pick out small things like that and take advantage of it.

I like the Boston style, and it has been successful. Eight championships, 10, 13, whatever it is. It's just basic basketball, and we would like to get our break running to the point where theirs is: *Zap!* You know, fluid. The other thing is taking advantage of the weaknesses that the other team has. You try to pattern after something that has been good for you. The Celtics style was very good for me as far as being a player, but that might not always be true for me as a coach. Your personnel might be different, so you adjust to your personnel. If you don't have the personnel to run, you don't run. But they will be able to do something else, so you do it. I'm one to adapt myself to the personnel rather than the other way.

This is a young club. Phil Chenier and Kevin Porter are third- and second-year men. You have Tom Kozelko who is a first-year man and so is Nick Weatherspoon, and you can see things that they don't see because they are out there playing. The role of the coach is to add to their game. The players are usually very open to this. If they were sitting up there coaching, they would do the same with their players. You teach too. You try to get into their minds as to what their game is. A guy like Elvin, who is 6 feet 9, plays both ends of the court, dives after loose balls, blocks shots, gets on the offensive boards, and he scores too. Yet there are things that I can pick out and add to his game to make him a still better player.

This is my first year here, and it takes you about a half year to get to know your players as to what they like on court and off court. Then during the season you make changes as to what will help them and their game.

You coached the previous season in the ABA. Is there a difference between that league's style and that of the NBA?

The difference is personnel. They're a younger league, one thing, which means they are not that professional yet. They'll get better and better. This is only their seventh year and basically that's the difference. Another difference might be that you have better players here. You might have a Jerry West, an Oscar Robertson, and those guys have been around the pros for years. They are making new stars like McGinnis at Indiana, Erving, Gilmore. These are all good, young players, but over there you may have one star on each club, while over here you may have two or three.

You'll be starting the playoffs next week. Is it a different atmosphere?

Completely different. Everything is condensed, and you know there is no tomorrow. The edge is with the team that has been champion before, opposed to the team that hasn't been champion. The one that has been champion goes out there confident and operates that way, and the team that hasn't been champion are a little leery. Psychology is with the championship club. They know what they're doing out there, hustle, and come on even stronger.*

36. *Dave Cowens*

"You have to be enthusiastic to succeed"

During the third quarter of a late-season game between the Capital Bullets and Boston Celtics, the ball flew out of bounds near the Celtics' basket. Flying behind the ball came David W. Cowens.

*Two weeks after this interview, the defending champion New York Knicks eliminated the Capital Bullets four games to three in the first round of the playoffs.

He seemed 10 yards out of bounds when he reached the ball to bat it back; he was another 10 yards further out when he arrested his momentum. Unfortunately, Dave only had succeeded in batting the ball back into the arms of Elvin Hayes, who immediately initiated a Bullets' fast break going the other way. Cowens was so far off the court that he practically could have reached over one shoulder and turned on the water in the shower. He would have been pardoned had he decided to await the inevitable conclusion of Capital's break where he stood, particularly when you considered that Boston was down two dozen points in a game they didn't need to win to make the playoffs. Nevertheless, Cowens launched himself full speed in pursuit of the play, arriving just in time to see the Bullets' basket. An exercise in futility? Perhaps, but it is an example of the desire that has allowed Dave Cowens to be ranked as one of the dominant NBA centers despite having only average size for his position. He is 6 feet 9 inches tall and weighs 230 pounds.

Because desire is difficult to measure, Dave Cowens attracted few scouts while attending high school in Newport, Kentucky. "I wasn't one of the guys everyone wanted," he recalls. "I had a few offers to attend college on scholarships but not many. I had none from the Big Ten. None from the West. None from the East. Just a few from around the Kentucky area and down South." He finally decided to attend Florida State.

"Yet five years later you were rookie of the year in the NBA," I commented. "And two years after that, the NBA's most valuable player."

"Anybody can be," said Dave Cowens. "Just because you aren't very good in high school doesn't mean you can't improve as you grow older. A lot of players reach their peak early. I've seen it. They become the big cheese, get satisfied, and never reach their full potential."

You try to capitalize on your strengths as a player, within a team concept, and try to put the other player at a disadvantage. That's the game of basketball—creating mismatches. If a player is strong but not quick, you force him into situations where he has to use quickness. That way he can't use his strength. If he is quick but not exceptionally strong, you want to take him closer to the basket.

In professional basketball it's better to be very mobile than exceedingly strong. You can be more of a threat if you're mobile, because you can avoid confrontations with big, strong fellows by moving around them. A strong player has to corner you before he can start muscling you.

You use more strength on defense than you do on offense. There's less finesse and more bulling involved. Since you don't have the ball, you have both hands free. You don't have to worry about traveling violations, so you can concentrate on trying to keep the other person from getting to a position from where he can hurt you. You can use your hands, your feet, your elbows, as long as xou don't do it excessively.

To play against the big fellows, you need endurance and stamina, because they constantly are maneuvering you into an area where you don't have a lot of room. Forwards and guards can flit around on the circumference moving to open areas where they can get the ball and take an open shot, but a center doesn't do that as much. He has to get as close to the basket as possible, and the closer he gets to the basket, the more his movements are restricted.

If a center's talents are well balanced, however, he won't have to limit himself to certain areas of the court. I try to combine quickness with strength. I'm a fast center, but I've always played inside and consider myself a fairly strong person. Ideally a center should be strong enough to compete close to the basket, yet mobile enough to move effectively into the outside areas. Then he has the best of both worlds. He can adapt his style of play to take advantage of the style of the center he's matched up against.

For example, Tom Boerwinkle of the Chicago Bulls. Tom hasn't played much lately because of injuries, but he's big and heavy. He's not as mobile as Steve Patterson, Elvin Hayes, or myself, so you want to take him away from the basket and make him cover a larger area. This puts him at a disadvantage. But if you go inside with him, then he has the advantage, because he can lean on you and throw his weight around.

It becomes an isometric exercise close to the basket. You have to both establish position and maintain it. If you are quick enough to get to the position first, but not strong enough to stay there, then you've wasted energy. By being able to work inside or outside, you can put others at disadvantages.

Kareem Abdul-Jabbar of the Milwaukee Bucks and Nate Thurmond of the Golden State Warriors are very mobile for 7-foot-tall men, but they hesitate to move too far away from the basket. They feel one of their strong points is to be intimidating shot blockers. So when we play Milwaukee or Golden State I try to lure them away from the basket. You can only succeed in doing this, however, if you can consistently take and hit open shots given to you from 15 and 20 feet out. If you can't score from outside, there's no reason for them to come out and guard you. When you do begin scoring they have to move out with you to take away that open shot, and this opens up the middle and allows our forwards to work underneath their forwards.

I can't rebound with Jabbar and Thurmond standing next to me. They are taller, can jump better, so they can reach the ball at a higher altitude than I can. I don't stand a chance in that type of situation. So I try to get a better rebounding position by beating them to a spot and keeping myself between them and the basket. That way they're effectively screened off.

On defense, you always want to stay between your man and the basket. You want to maintain contact with him, keep your hands on him, so you don't always have to look at him. That way you can watch what's going on in other places on the court. If a man breaks loose you can react fast enough to go over and help out. That's the team concept. On offense you try to negate contact. The less contact you have on offense the better, because you want to be free to move.

Basketball is a game of action versus reaction. If you are always back on your heels reacting to what someone else is doing, you are behind from the beginning. You want to take charge: Be the aggressor on both defense and offense. It's a cat and mouse game. That's where fakes come in. You look one way and go the other. You fake here, do a quick reverse, and set the man up. Quickness and agility are more important than strength. You need good condition and stamina as well.

The real heavyweight is at a disadvantage, because the game moves so fast now. The more weight a player carries the more of a chore it is for him to run up and down the court. It's more strenuous on his leg joints. Some of the heavier centers come downcourt late. I can run upcourt, take my position, and for a while it's a four-on-five game: their four against our five. If the other team holds the ball while their center is walking up court, I can stand there and rest, because I got into position quicker than he did.

That's the way I've always played. You don't run up the court with your man and say, "Well, he's not going to get the ball." You run up the court, turn around, and be prepared to do something other than guard your man, help your teammates. That way you are always ready.

One question you must get asked often is, how you would compare yourself with your predecessor at Boston, Bill Russell? Your styles of play seem so completely different. [Russell provided the prototype for the classic, shotblocking, defensive center, who didn't need to score to help his team. Cowens is more aggressive on offense, averaging nearly 20 points per game, operating out near the top of the key, facing the basket rather than functioning with his back to it.]

A basketball player's value is measured by how he succeeds in contributing to his team's success. Using this criterion I can't see how anyone could be ranked higher than Bill Russell, because the Celtics won over and over again in pressure situations with him at center. The fans in Boston became complacent in victory. They expected the Celtics to win all the time. They expected complete domination. Eventually Russell and the others on the team grew older. The youthful incentive wasn't there. They began to lose more games. They got bumped out of first place during the regular season. Yet when it came down to the playoffs they just blasted, because they knew how to perform as a unit.

Our present team plays basically the same game as the old Celtics. We probably don't have the discipline they used to have. We do more free-lancing than the old Celtics—or at least that's what I'm told. I never really saw the old Celtics much, but from what I understand they were more pattern-oriented. They didn't do fancy things. They just executed very well. They had very heady ball players who were willing to make sacrifices so that the team would succeed. They never made excuses, but just went out and did their job. That, coupled with a lot of breaks and good luck, allowed them to attain a level of success that probably never will be surpassed in pro basketball, or in any professional sport.

People often talk about your present squad as being a running team rather than a pattern team, but don't you still run patterns—only at a faster pace?

Oh sure, we have patterns. When you fast-break it's organized, not free-lance. Actually, it's disciplined free-lance ball, because a lot of timing goes into executing a fast break properly. You just can't run downcourt as fast as you can. You have to get there at the right time, so that when the ball handler gets ready to pass the basketball, you are in position to receive it. If he can't shoot, he needs somebody else to take a shot. It takes discipline, and you have to practice for hours and hours.

We have the potential to run fast breaks extremely well. It's an exciting brand of basketball because it's so fast and you score a lot of points. It's not the come-down, set-it-up, work-off-a-pick, get-your-jump-shot, and come-back-to-the-other-end-and-play-defense style of ball. But you have to be able to do that too.

The old Celtics were a good running team, because they got a lot of defensive rebounds. You need good rebounding to trigger your fast breaks. Of course, Bill Russell didn't

254

really want to chip in on offense perhaps as much as I do now. I don't say that to be critical of him. It depends on your team strategy for winning. I'm more of a factor on offense with this team than Bill Russell was, so I throw the ball out and run downcourt without waiting. I'm down there as a trailer, playing like a forward, shooting jump shots. With Bill if they didn't get the fast layup, they would wait for him to come down, set up and run a play.

It was not that he couldn't run. Bill Russell filled a lot of breaks, but he figured his most important job was defense. And I agree with him: Defense for centers is the most important role. You have to be the clog. You can't just allow people to sift through the key without noticing you. You have to make them aware of your presence, and he was able to do that far more successfully than I ever will, because physically he was made for that role. I'm not. He was the great intimidator. When the smaller players came close to the basket, he intimidated them by blocking shots. I intimidate them by not letting them get started. I try to keep them outside and use my quickness against their quickness. We also switch a lot of defense. I may wind up guarding a 6-foot guard even quicker than I am, but I still should be able to keep him from penetrating.

Bill Russell's style was definitely more effective in that sort of situation because he had to worry less about mistakes. If one of the guards' men broke loose, he would wait until he shot the ball then go up and block the shot. I have to move to pick up the man before he shoots, and I'm more likely to foul him in that sort of a situation. Also, when I switch on him, the center who I have been guarding now is guarded by one of our smaller players. The other team has a mismatch inside and they have me outside. That's the kind of situation that teams try to create, and if they capitalize on it they'll score an easy basket, but that's the nature of our defense.

There weren't many guys who could block shots like Bill Russell could, but many times you have to know when to block a shot. You can't just leave your man. Only a few players have been able to wait until the ball is shot before they block it. Chamberlain could. Kareem. Thurmond. The great big guys. Elmore Smith has the timing and jumping ability required. Elvin Hayes can do it fairly well, but I don't know of too many other ones. Those are the ones who can block shots, but Russell could do it more consistently. That was his forte. That was his thing.

Sure you do, and conversation helps. The court is 50 feet wide, so the guards can yell for the ball if the crowd isn't too noisy. Once you're running downcourt, assuming that you're running down the left side, you can yell, "Left lane!" Or if you're coming up behind the player dribbling the ball, who normally is supposed to be in the middle of the court, you can yell, "Trailer!" He'll hear you and won't have to look to know where you are.

You have to follow certain rules while running the fast break. When the player dribbling the ball reaches half court, he always should hold just a second and look behind him to determine where everybody is. Then he can see how many defensive players are moving downcourt, how many offensive players are going with him, and decide what the avenues are and the potential for this fast break working. If you look downcourt and see five defensive players in front of you, you are not going to have a fast break. You don't have a fast break until you have the other team at a disadvantage.

It's all reaction. It's something you've been over and over and you know what to do, but making it succeed is very difficult. You may get to the right place and still miss the shot. You can fumble the ball. You might think, "Oh well, I'm really tired. I won't bust my humps to get down there." All those human things come into play.

Or it may look like the other team is beaten without you, so you don't bother to cover.

256

That's right. But your man might miss an easy layup. That happens maybe once in 50 times. If that one time you do hustle down there, get the rebound, and score anyway it's a great thrill. You have to be enthusiastic to succeed. Little things like that count. Basketball games in the pros normally are won by no more than 10 points. Usually less. If you are shooting 100 times a game and scoring 100 points, 10 points don't seem like much. But games are won by picking up the loose balls and converting the other team's mistakes and your own mistakes into points.

It is astounding to me how sometimes a team, that may be playing exceptionally well, suddenly hits a cold spell and the other team runs off 20 unanswered points and either comes from way behind or blows open the game.

It happens all the time. I really don't understand what happens to a team as a unit, although momentum plays a large part in it. Momentum seems to affect nearly everybody at one time or another, and it even affects the substitutes. They come in when your team is running well, and you still don't lose any ground. There's a building feeling of confidence. It's a very positive wave length between all the people playing on that team. They practice together a lot of hours, and when something is going good, it's just like electricity. It's like static flowing through their bodies. Positive things start happening. The other team tries to retaliate, but nothing seems to work right for them.

When the other team starts running a lot of points off against your team, you have to be steady. You can't say, let's change. You just keep playing your game and working the percentages, because they are still there. You play steady so that when a time out comes, or someone gets hurt, or something happens to break the other team's momentum, your steadiness will permit you to take control once again, get back into your game, shift the scoring around, and go back to winning.

This happens a lot of times in the game of basketball. If it's a close game it probably doesn't happen very long. One team will get a head of steam and make two or three quick buckets, and the other team will come right back. If you play steady, your fundamentals come through.

One question that I haven't had a chance to ask anybody yet: Are there any tactics involved at the center jump which might permit one team to gain possession of the ball over another?

It depends on how high a fellow can jump, and his ability to time the ball at its peak and tip it to one of his teammates. You don't have too many plays for this situation. There is a defensive tap and an offensive tap. I try to tip the ball into an area either where there are no players from the other team or one of our taller players. But a lot depends on luck unless you have a center who just dominates every tap like Jabbar. The referee throws the ball, and he goes way up there, and you can't jump as high as he can. Sometimes you are fortunate enough to get up there and maybe hit his arm or time your jump so that as he's hitting the ball down you deflect it.

The players outside the circle are important, since they have to be alert and ready to step in front of somebody else to get possession. Before each center jump I'll tell my teammates I'm going to try and tip the ball either forward or backward. We have one play where I tip the ball to the side and one of our men takes off for the basket for an easy layup. You do that when you think you have a sure tap, but usually it doesn't work because if the other team knows you have a sure tap, they will have a man back prepared to stop you. Usually you don't see quick baskets on the jump unless you get lucky.

When the action stops during a basketball game, the players often do a lot of talking. What do you say?

A number of things. I don't know. It's all about the game. Whatever happens. You recognize something, so you try to help your teammates out. You might tell them, "I'll take your

258

man to mix them up." They might be calling a play and you recognize it, so you go over and tell your teammate what it is so he can pick it up when it happens. You might say: "You've got to screen this man out, because he's great on the boards." Your man may already know that, but you remind him. You're out to help everyone. I get help from other players, and they get help from me. That's the way it's got to be.

You play 82 games during the year, more if you count preseason and the playoffs. Can you be up for each game?

There are nights when you don't have the incentive. There are nights when you really don't care, but you have to be there and you have to play. Really, on those nights you shouldn't show up. It's like an office worker who has to go to work each day whether he wants to or not. On certain days he's not going to be very productive, but he has to be at work in order to earn his money. It's the same way in basketball, because there are days when you do not feel like playing and you can't motivate yourself. You don't want to put out and sacrifice. Sometimes you rationalize and think that it's best you not go out and kill yourself this night because it's not going to be good for you in the long run.

When you make your niche in the league, your reputation, you can afford to relax on occasions. Not very often, but just every now and then. Once or twice a year you can get away with it and your team can still win. It depends on who you are playing against.

Yet it's getting harder to relax. The poor teams are getting tougher. None of the top teams won 60 games this year, because the balance in the league was so much better. Teams are on a more even keel. With trades made, additional players coming through the draft, one more year of getting good players to the below .500 teams, it built the league to a point where you had to play every game positively, and with enthusiasm, otherwise you were going to get beat.

You look forward to the end of the season and the playoffs and when they happen, you say, time really flew. You can't believe this year is over and there is a big void to fill, with nothing to do for four months basketballwise. It's nice though, because you gain complete independence and you can go and do whatever motivates you.

37. *Ralph Simpson*

"Just play every day"

I rode with one of the ABA referees on the limousine from La Guardia Airport. The New York Nets were playing at home that night. When we arrived at the motel, about a mile from the Nassau Coliseum, he suddenly looked worried and asked the desk clerk if the Denver Rockets also were staying here. She didn't even know, so I told him, yes. I knew because I had come to do an interview with Rockets player Ralph Simpson, a perennial all-star game participant, consistently one of the highest scoring guards in the ABA.

"We usually don't like to stay in the same place with the teams," admitted the referee. "I had forgotten: Denver is the only team in the league that stays here."

Perhaps that says something about the Denver Rockets. It was what might most charitably be described as a Ma and Pa motel. Not yet seedy, but old. Lumpy mattresses. One of those motels where if you want to make a phone call after 11:00 P. M. you're in trouble. Where there's nothing down the road but more road.

I called Ralph Simpson on the room phone and told him I had checked into the motel. "Come on over," he said. Ralph Simpson grew up in Detroit, attended Michigan State University, but left after two years to join the Denver Rockets. When his college class graduated, the Chicago Bulls selected him in the NBA draft, but the Rockets offered him enough money to remain in Denver.

260

*What do you do if you're a professional basketball player the day
of the game? A lot of times you just lay around in bed and hope
there's a decent movie on television. A Randolph Scott Western was
on the screen when Ralph greeted me. His monotone TV set was
flickering badly. I asked about his position and how he plays it.*

A guard has to do more than a forward or center. He has
to have a wide-open view of the game and be in control of
himself at all times.. He has to see the whole floor. He has to
know what players haven't touched the ball so he can give it
to them. He has to shoot. He has to know what plays you run
from center, what plays you run for forwards, therefore he
has to know all the plays, all the players, what shot they can
shoot best, how fast they can run. Maybe on a fast break
some forwards can't run as fast as the guard so you can't lead
them as much. He has to know what the coach wants, because
the guard has control of the ball all the time. He has to know
how much time is on the clock. He has to know the coach, the
players, the opponents, so therefore he has to know
everything. Then he has to play himself.

A guard has to prepare himself before the game and know
that certain plays work better against certain defenses. For
instance, Utah plays a zone-type defense, so we have plays
that work real well against their type of zone. We're playing
New York tonight and they're one of the fastest teams in pro
basketball, so you want to try and take them out of their
tempo. We'll try to slow the game up. They run because they
have the personnel to run. The running team has an
advantage in today's game of basketball against a slower
team. We haven't been able to run well the past three or four
years because we don't have the personnel. We don't have a
real forward on our team. We have four centers. It really
makes it tough.

I hope that someday I'll probably play with another team,
because the personnel on our team just don't have it. Our
owners are from the old school, where they don't like to pay
the money. If you look at our team, there is nobody making a
big salary but me. I get the feeling at times that Alex

Hannum, our coach and general manager, doesn't want to pay me what they're paying. It's just that I was at the right place at the right time. Chicago had drafted me number one, and maybe I should have gone to Chicago.

I think the only reason the Rockets kept me was because the papers were saying that Denver was going to fold. Then it came out that Chicago was going to sign me. I was the best player on the Denver team, and they had to sign me or it would have looked bad for the team, and the fans would have lost interest. They couldn't have sold any season tickets. So they signed me and I'm still in Denver. I will say that they have great fans. I love the city, but I also like to play basketball. The money doesn't mean that much. I'd like to play with a winning team.

When you were growing up in Detroit, did you think you might someday earn that kind of money for playing basketball?

No, I never did. It just got to a point one day, when I was a freshman in college and I found out I could play with these guys. I was playing on the playgrounds with Dave Bing, Chet Walker, Bob Lanier, and one day I realized I could play. Brewster Center is where everybody got together, then they changed over to a place called St. Cecilia's, and that's where all the pros go now. They have a league there and the turnout is fantastic. I haven't been home for a couple of summers, but I'm going home this summer.

Did you refine your game playing against the pro players? Was it a matter of instruction?

It was a matter of playing. You go out there and play. I played more than they did. The pros would play certain hours. I was at other playgrounds, other recreation areas, playing all day, then on and off with the pros, and I would pick up stuff they would do. But there was never any instruction. The pros just came and played. Now they go out and put on clinics. I put on free clinics all over Denver and this summer I'm going to have a basketball camp.

262

When you hold a clinic what do you teach? If you had met Ralph Simpson of ten years ago what would you have taught him?

Fundamentals. Anything you do has to be based on fundamentals. Then play all the time to develop the talent. Develop your own style based on fundamentals. Each player has a unique style of play. The only way you can develop your own style and talent commensurate with your body, your build, is just play every day. Somebody else is out there playing every day getting better than you are. If you don't play every day, somebody else is going to be better. Simple as that. Then learn to play defense, how to keep your feet spread, how to dribble the ball low, the correct way to shoot the basketball, the correct way to drive, things like that.

Walt Frazier commented to me that a lot of kids seem to think that he suddenly grew up and suddenly, like Shazam!, he was Walt Frazier with all of his basketball talents developed. But obviously that didn't happen to you.

No, I just played a lot. I still play all the time. That could be detrimental because before going into the season I'm liable to have played three months. Take a little time off, but still work on my game all summer. I watch Walt Frazier play quite a bit. He plays with a team that plays great defense. They're a smart team. Over the past couple of years I don't think he's been as good a defensive player as he was, because he's playing more offense. It's hard to work as hard on both defense and offense, but it can be done. John Havlicek does it, but he has the stamina. I don't think Walt Frazier has the stamina, but he runs the team flawlessly. It was just like I was talking about in the beginning. He knows who to give the ball to, and when. He knows who hasn't had a shot. He knows other teams, what kind of tempo they like to run, who scores the points for that team, and where he scores the points at. He goes and gets rebounds.

That's important. He does a lot of things that people don't see out there. He very seldom throws the ball away. He has developed to be a pretty good offensive player where at one time he wasn't. I don't think he has the offensive potential of Oscar or Jerry West, but he's developed. Probably if he wanted to score more he could, but he's into the game more, running plays, getting the ball to the shooters up front. That's why the Knicks win, because play together. Everybody plays defense. Everybody rebounds. They've got great players, and they're paying those great players too. Everybody on the team probably makes over $150,000. On our team I don't know anybody who makes over $50,000 but me.

One of the strong points of your game has been your ability to score—or have you been forced into that role?

I think I've been forced into that role the last couple of seasons, because when I came into the league I was a raw player. I didn't know the game that well, but I always was good offensively. But scoring is a small part of the game. When I was growing up I wanted to be like Oscar Robertson. He could do everything. I patterned myself after him when I was younger, then realized I had to develop my own style. I was a good play maker for a while, then I got here.

My first year I was really playing good ball. The first 20 games I was really happy. I wasn't starting the first few games, but I came off the bench and was ready to play. Joe Belmont was our coach, then he got fired. Stan Albeck came in and he didn't want to play rookies. I was still a junior in college, so he put me on the bench. I worked on my game, came back the next year, and took off like a bat out of hell that season. Alex Hannum was the new coach and general manager. I was averaging 31 points a game until the all-star break. I hadn't signed a contract with Denver at the time, and before the game I was talking with Al Ross. Alex walked in and you know how he feels about Al Ross. He doesn't like him, because he's the one that took Spencer Haywood from Denver. Alex figured I was getting ready to jump leagues, so he stopped playing me. I had been playing about 38 minutes

264

a game and I went down to about 26 minutes a game. We didn't have that good a team, but we hustled and it was exciting to watch us play. We were a running team that year. And Alex stops playing me for about 10 games, and my scoring average starts dropping. I asked him: "How come you're not playing me?" and he says, "You're jumping leagues." Well, I didn't jump leagues so he started playing me again.

What about shooting? How do you put the ball up in the air?

Shooting is reflexes, but I know what makes a good shooter. Shooting is practice mostly. I practice a lot. I shoot some every day. Shoot while you are playing. Shoot sometimes on your own. Practice, practice. All the time practice. I shot so many shots a day when I was younger, it just became a habit. If you get in a game and you miss, something is wrong. But in the pros you play so many games that if you miss one night there's another game coming up.

We've got so many games in so many small cities. Three or four games straight. Cities like Norfolk, Hampton. It's hard to get into those places. You're always changing airplanes. By the time you get in there, you're worn out. You're playing half what you really are.

It gets down to economics again. We're the only team in this league that stays in this motel. Everybody else when they play the Nets stays at the Holiday Inn. My roommate left. Steve Jones. He said he's not staying here. He went down and checked into the Holiday Inn. It's all economics. Try and save a buck.

We talked maybe for another half hour, the TV screen still flickering in one corner. Ralph Simpson had questions of his own to ask, many of them about the Chicago Bulls. "Why did Chicago draft me?" he asked at one point. "I know why. I just wondered if you knew."

I said I didn't.

"Because I'm going to be a great player," he said. "Because they felt I could come in and play right away. They didn't want to play anybody unproven. Motta's assistant Phil Johnson came to quite a few of our games. I'm just thinking about what might have been."

Later that night, although Ralph Simpson and his team played well, they lost a close game to the New York Nets and failed to qualify for the playoffs. Alex Hannum got fired. There are 10 teams in the ABA and eight of them qualify for the playoffs. They play 84 regular-season games to eliminate two teams. When you're a player with one of those two teams, you're really at the bottom.

38. Brian Taylor

"Defense is always having someone who will help out"

I visited the Nassau Coliseum on Long Island in late March to see the New York Nets play their last game of the season against the Denver Rockets. New York won, simultaneously assuring themselves first place in the ABA's eastern division and knocking the Rockets out of the playoffs. Before the game I spoke with Brian Taylor, formerly of Princeton, the ABA's rookie of the year the previous year. "How do you play the position of guard?" I asked.

It all depends on what type of ball players you have around you. Last year we had forward George Carter as an offensive scorer, but he can't be compared to Dr. J.* We also have Larry Kenon and Billy Paultz, so up front we have three guys who can score for us. My job this year was more or less keeping them happy, getting the ball inside, getting the ball out on the fast break, laying the ball off, doing the job defensively, stopping the guard out front, and also helping out.

*Dr. J is Julius Erving, ABA scoring leader two seasons in succession.

266

I felt this year was a good year for us in so many different ways, because in the beginning we lost nine games in a row and everyone couldn't understand that. We had Dr. J, and Dr. J is the top name today in pro basketball, but what it boiled down to is that it took a team effort. That means everybody has to be involved both offensively and defensively. You can't just watch one guy do his thing, because you have guys standing around, and it's easy to defend against one-man teams. But if Doc makes a move and has two or three guys trying to stop him, there must be somebody open.

With my speed I can penetrate and somebody is going to pick me up, so I just lay it off to someone else for the shot. That's the way the game has to be played. The ball has to be kept moving. Then you have to play that helping-out defense.

It takes quickness and a knowledge of the game, because once they find out how quick you are, they play you a certain way where they won't allow you to penetrate. They force you to take the outside shot, but I feel I have so much quickness that it's almost impossible to try and cut it off. And if they do, then they can't help out on the other ball players. If Dr. J does something, my man can't help out because he's too busy trying to guard me.

That's one good thing about having a guy like Dr. J on the team, because they more or less base their defense on stopping Dr. J, not stopping Brian Taylor, which is good. When people who guard me tough, hang all over me, I give them one fake and go around them. The guards that give me the most trouble are the ones who are just as quick as I am. Roland Taylor of Virginia is built close to the ground. He's a good defensive player. You find the stronger guys try to bump you, but I don't like to come in contact with them. I try to face them and go one way or the other.

They're always bumping you around, because the officials are most of the time looking toward where the ball is, and there is a lot of bumping going on where the ball isn't. It's definitely a physical game. I'm just happy to be able to play 75 games, which I did this year.

People say they really can't understand how we could put it

together in only one season. We finished fourth in the east last year. It boils down to the type of individuals we have on our team. We are young in age, but we are mature even though we still have a long way to go. I feel as we get older, our communications will improve. We'll get to know one another much more. Finishing first is something we really worked hard to achieve. You've got to give us credit for that.

How do you communicate?

On offense, being able to communicate is very important for a guard. He has to be the leader out there, someone who calls the plays, someone who has the other four ball players' respect, and that takes years of experience. This is only my second year and I feel in time I'll become one of the finer leaders in all pro basketball. But it takes time. It takes respect. And I think the best way to get respect is by helping your teammates get off. I think I've proven that I can help them get easier shots.

We've won a lot of games over the past month just by knowing where the other ball player is going to be. Of course, that's highly unusual for a ball club that's only been together for one year. There are only three players left from last year's team: Paultz, Billy Melchionni, and myself, That's quite a changeover. When we lost nine games in a row, a few people said that we were going to get it together, that it would just be a matter of time. A lot of others felt we shouldn't be losing with the type of talent we had here. Those were the ignorant people who didn't know what it takes to put a championship team together. It takes time. Time is a key factor. It's certainly a key factor in professional basketball, because if you don't show you can play as soon as you get in, they don't wait around to see.

You played at Princeton. Was it much of a jump moving from the Ivy League to the ABA?

I don't think so. My style of ball was such that I played

against great competition all my life. The Ivy League wasn't that bad. It was better than it had been in the past because the Ivy League had recruited some top blue-chip ball players, a lot of them being black. It was much more competitive than people thought it to be, so the transition from Princeton to professional ball wasn't really that difficult because of my style of play and the background I had.

I was a scorer in high school. I was a scorer in college. But at Princeton the coach taught me the meaning of defense. You can't win without it. Pete Karouse, Princeton's coach, firmly believed that the best type of defensive play was man-to-man. Knowing that I wanted to play as a professional, that really helped out.

How do you defense somebody man-for-man?

Studying is the key. You watch and study the guy you guard during the course of the season and you know him like a book. You know the things he can't do and the things he can do. You try to force him to his weaknesses. That's the key. And like I said before, you communicate. Communication with your teammates, forcing your man a certain way, forcing him toward your teammate so you can have help. Defense is always having someone who will help out, because everybody in professional basketball is so good offensively you need help. Individual defense is one thing, but team defense is another.

What you try to do on defense is try to stay between your man and the ball, keep your eye on the ball, and keep your eye on the man, and cheat over closer to the ball a little bit. We play somewhat of a zone anyhow. I think most professional teams do, so you just keep an eye on the ball, keep an eye on your man, and zone him. But if you guard a man who is very dangerous offensively, you stick to him. You don't turn your back. You face-guard him. You stay close to him and also keep an eye on the ball.

You talked about playing a zone, but technically that's

Well, everybody is playing a zone. There's a fine line. That was the key part of our season after we lost nine straight. We decided we weren't going to play the pressing defense we had been playing in the beginning, but would fall back and help one another, or play somewhat of a zone, It's very difficult to detect sometimes. Other times it's obvious. It's not being called, but the way we look at it, if they are going to call us playing a zone, they are going to have to call the other team too, because that's the only way they can stop us, especially with Dr. J.

Your coach Kevin Loughery last year coached the last place team in the NBA, and now he's coach of the first place team in the ABA. How much does team success depend on the coach?

If you don't have good ball players, even if you are a good coach, nobody will notice it. There are some coaches who do well with mediocre talent and they are recognized for their ability, but very few. I think Kevin has done an outstanding job. He inspired me to give it all I have. He's gotten along well with the team. It was like a rookie year for him as well as for everybody else. Just to be in this position tonight, where we can clinch the division, is an outstanding thing.

The difference between this year and last year, of course, is winning. This year it's a pleasure to come to the Coliseum to play. Last year when we were losing, it seemed that everybody just didn't want to show up. I'm really ready to go out there and do my thing now.

270

39. *Lucius Allen*

"I'm getting my mental game together"

Standing tall on the edge of the basketball court, resplendent in brown trousers and shirt spangled with gold buttons, Lucius Allen looked the picture of health. But he wasn't playing. His teammates on the Milwaukee Bucks were warming up for their playoff game with the Chicago Bulls, but instead of starting at guard, Lucius, microphone in hand, was doing the commentary for the telecast being beamed back to Milwaukee. When he lowered the mike and moved off court you saw why. He reached for a pair of crutches leaning against the press table.

Several weeks previously he had gone after a ball out of bounds in a game at Detroit and skidded on a warmup jacket left carelessly by the side of the court. Something in his knee snapped. He needed an operation to repair torn ligaments. The former UCLA all-American was done for the season.

Curiously, the Bulls' starting guard Jerry Sloan also was at the playoff game in civilian clothes, having injured his foot in the first round of the playoffs, also in Detroit. Milwaukee and Chicago, it might be said, were playing their important match, each minus a pawn. But Lucius Allen, who plays chess as a respite from his basketball duties, might disagree with the comparison. In chess parlance Allen (and Sloan) might better be compared to knights. When I had spoken with Lucius Allen in Milwaukee during one of their practice sessions I had asked him, knowing his interest in chess, if there weren't certain parallels with that game and the sport of basketball.

You can describe parallels between basketball and chess, but the game of basketball is basically a game of defense, whereas chess is a game of offense. Your offense is usually your best defense in chess. One move on a chessboard can kill you, or make you. It can go either way. The same thing is true in basketball, even though the move may happen in a split second. One situation on the floor can be the difference between winning and losing the basketball game.

In chess, position is practically everything. In basketball you try to get to favorable positions, but even though you get to those positions, you may not be able to exploit them. In chess it's the same thing. You may get into a favorable position yet not be able to see the move that's going to win the game for you. In basketball you might get into good position to get the layup, then blow the shot. Or other intangibles may defeat you: a big center blocks the shot, a quick guard you didn't see comes from behind you. In chess, everything is in front of you on the board, and if you don't win the game it's your own fault. In basketball there are five guys working together, and sometimes you can shift the blame to other people.

Another way that basketball and chess are alike is in the mental discipline that's involved. Me, I use chess the day of the game, because it helps my concentration. It gets me in a frame of mind more conducive to concentrating. It gives me the discipline that you need in order to play basketball on the professional level.

You definitely need discipline in basketball. It's more a mental game than a physical game, because even though it is physical you have to train yourself to get into a frame of mind where you can make the plays, where if you have a 15-foot jump shot you can make it eight out of ten times. It's a thinking game, knowing what shots to take.

In chess I'll sit there and think about what's happening to all the pieces on the board. The objective, of course, is to capture the king, whereas in basketball the objective is to score the basket. You have to harmonize the actions, put them all together to get the desired end. Chess helps my basketball in the sense that after seeing the harmony on the board, I can come out and see things happening on the floor.

For instance, if I see that Bobby Dandridge has a hot hand and I have the ball, I'm going to try to get it to Bobby. If Kareem hasn't touched the ball for half a quarter, I'll get it to him. Basketball players are funny—especially the big men—because if they aren't getting the ball, touching the

272

ball, shooting the ball, then they tend not to rebound. You need the big man involved in rebounding or else you are not going to have the ball to score on the other end. It helps me as far as picking out the things it takes to win the game, organizing and coordinating the players together, all the pieces on the board.

Mack Calvin also mentioned the necessity of keeping the big men happy.

Certain forwards are more rebound-oriented. Say a Paul Silas with Boston. Cornell Warner on our team. Not having the ball doesn't affect their game nearly as much as it would one of the scoring forwards, say a Bob Dandridge or a Dave DeBusschere. They have to put the ball up, feel as though they are part of the game, and if they don't feel they are being a part of it, then it's very easy for a basketball player to say, "Well, forget this game. This is just one of those days where I'm not going to be playing my game like I know I can." It tends to make them not work nearly as hard getting the job done from a team concept.

It's very important to keep everybody involved, especially the big men, because we guards initially have the ball and it's very easy for us to get involved in the flow of the game. For instance, I noticed last night Chicago was down and Norm Van Lier was shooting the ball most of the time. That can happen very easily to a guard, because we have the ball and it's easy to say, "I'm going to bring us back myself." It's very hard not to get that idea in your mind. On the other hand, when we get behind, a lot of times we'll just go into Kareem every time, then the other team knows what we're doing as well as we do, and we can be defensed. So it has to work both ways. You can go to him too much and go to him not enough. It's tricky to get a balance in there: keep everybody happy, keep everybody involved, and keep everybody playing hard.

I try to improve every year.* The year I was in Seattle I

*In his first five seasons in the NBA, Lucius Allen's scoring average, with one exception, improved each year: 9.8, 7.1, 13.5, 15.5, 17.6. His was a reserve, and I didn't get that much of a chance to play. I came here and I was still a reserve, but I got more playing time and, consequently, with more time your statistics go up. The past two and a half years my playing time has leveled off, but because I'm getting so much playing time I'm consequently getting better. In the future I don't think I'm going to improve as much as far as fundamentals go—in terms of shooting, passing, and playing defense—but I'm getting my mental game together, which is helping me statistically to do better.

Things are becoming more easy for me, because first of all, I know what I'm capable of doing out there on the floor. Secondly, I'm getting a chance to do what I know I can do, and I'm not being held back in any way by the coaches. A lot of times coaches can help psych ballplayers out. I don't have that pressure. I can go out and just do my thing: play my game. And if I have a bad game, if I have a bad three games, I still know I can snap out of it, and I will snap out of it. This helps me relax out there on the floor, so consequently it helps my game as far as the aspects involved in making statistics.

I think I will continue to improve for the next two or three years, then I probably will reach a plateau and level off for a few years. Possibly in the waning years, I'll start on the downward decline. But there is a lot of room for improvement with me. I know the areas where I have to improve. They may not be visible statistically, but I'll know personally that I'm improving in those areas as far as leadership, as far as taking control in pressure situations, when the game is tied and there's two minutes left. I know that this is what is going to be expected of me in the future. And I know that I will rise to the occasion and be able to do the job.

And yet the Lucius Allen that I remember playing at

respective field goal shooting percentages were: .442, .447, .505, .484, .495. His statistics in rebounds and assists exhibited a similar upward trend, almost as though his progress as a player had been preordained by a computer.

UCLA was an exceptional player, as was your teammate, the former Lew Alcindor. You are going to rise to still higher levels?

That is certainly true. In order to play professional basketball, you have to learn a new game. You have to become so much better, so much more a pressure ball player, so much better in the fundamentals area. A guy who is not fundamentally sound is not going to make it in the pros, but fortunately myself and Abdul-Jabbar, then known as Lew, had a great teacher in John Wooden. He taught us the fundamentals. We just had to learn a new game, because we already had the fundamentals. And I think Abdul-Jabbar, even as awesome and great as he is, is improving.

For instance, one of his big statistical improvements is rebounding. He's blocking more shots. He's still scoring. He's much stronger in getting the outlet pass, because in college he would get the rebound, and it was so easy in college for us to run by guys that we didn't need an advantage. You can't trick these guys in the pros. You have to get the outlet pass out quickly in order to gain an advantage at the other end, get three-guys-on-two, four-guys-on-three, whatever.

I have improved in creating situations on the floor. When I was with Seattle, and my first years here, I would try and create a situation on the floor off the dribble, and the guys were a little too smart for me. I would turn the ball over. Now I've become more possession-conscious. I tend to make fewer errors, although I'm still far from where I should be.

It's a whole new ball game on this level. A coach can make you a great college player, but here in the pros, it's you and the other guy. You are going to have to beat him every night, 82 nights out of the season, then hopefully get into the playoffs, and have to beat him again in a series which is even tougher because they have a chance to prepare for you.

It's so much easier in college, because you only play two games a week. You have five days to practice and get it all together. On the pro level you are meeting great players night in and night out, smart players night in and night out, and it definitely places a premium on your mental capacity. It puts a premium on your ball playing ability. It definitely is a whole new ball game on this level.

This is the third in a series of books I'm doing on sports. Previously I've interviewed football players and auto racers. And I've interviewed athletes from a number of other sports for various magazine articles. I've come away with the impression that maybe professional basketball players have a higher native intelligence than most other athletes. It's just a gut feeling; I haven't gone around measuring IQ's.

I think on the whole, basketball players are forced to express themselves earlier. A basketball player gets exposed to pressures much earlier, because basketball games have between an 0 and 7 point spread, so we are exposed to more pressure situations which make us grow emotionally a lot faster than, say, football players. A football player is into the same emotional stress, but he's just not into it as many times. A tennis player doesn't have to worry about five other guys, therefore his emotional thing isn't on the same level. The fact that basketball is a team game, that it's a tough game, and the fact that there is so much publicity involved with the sport has forced players to get into the public eye and express themselves more than other ball players.

I think the fact that basketball players walk around with half their body exposed also makes them a lot more comfortable around people. People are seeing you with hardly anything on and you are just expected to be cool under social circumstances. I don't think we have a higher IQ. I think that we are forced to deal with people and because we are forced to deal with people, it helps us be more relaxed and express ourselves a lot better.

Usually when I've attended a pro basketball game in the past, I've sat up in the cheap seats. It costs money to bring a wife and three children to the game. But while doing this book I've had a chance to sit down courtside, and it has given me a

*different perspective, a greater appreciation of how physical
the game is—*

Up there you can't hear the dialogue, can't hear the calls
and why a certain call is made, and can't see it as well. When
you are up high you have to guess at what's happening. It's
like being up in the Goodyear blimp. You can't see what guys
do with their hands, their bodies, and the little things that go
into making a basketball game.

*—and yet in some respects you also can't see the game as well
from down below. You can't see the flow of the game. It's like
watching a football game from the sidelines: You can see the
blood, but you can't locate the ball. At courtside I'll watch ten
bodies come together in a blob of flesh and elbows, and suddenly
Dandridge will come flying out to an open area, and somehow
the ball will get to him. I wonder how you can see Dandridge
in time to get him the ball?*

Ballplayers on this level have to have an instinct for the
ball. Some players have an instinct for being around the ball
all the time. For instance, Jerry Sloan. He has a knack for
knowing where the ball is, whether it's on a rebound,
whether it's on the floor, whether it's in a position where he
can get the steal. All professional ball players have these
instincts. Some, of course, have instincts sharper than others.
But everybody has to have the instinct of a basketball player
to know how the play is going to go, where the ball is going to
be, and what you are going to do in that situation. After
you've been exposed to it time and time again, then you
react. Of course, when we're on offense I know what's
happening because we have called the play and I know our
ball players and where we like to be.

Say it's a quick action play, and Bobby Dandridge is cutting
under the basket, and at the point when I pass the ball he
isn't free. People behind me say, "Ahhhh—" They suck in
their breath thinking I'm going to throw the ball away. Then
they see where Bobby may not have a step, but he has three

277

or four inches on the guy, and suddenly he's in good position. This comes with play and practice and knowing each other and knowing what's happening on the floor.

It's very important to know how your teammates play and react to situations: where they are most comfortable and where they are uncomfortable. This is the hardest task for any guard, to make the play, to be able to gamble that he is going to get there and catch the pass. It doesn't work all the time. A lot of people say: "Booooo! Terrible pass, Allen. What are you thinking about? Why didn't you shoot it?" But they don't see what's really happening on the floor.

A lot of times people will criticize Oscar for not taking a jump shot when he's "open". But what he's doing is drawing people toward him to free somebody else. A lot of times it doesn't work. The defender might say, "Well, he's not going to shoot. I'll fake, retreat." He might get a hand on the ball, might steal it, so it's an instinct for basketball that everybody has got to have to play on this level.

Basketball definitely is a game of inches, and I would say it's probably a game of half inches. It's a game of half steps, not whole steps. It's a game of luck. All of these things go toward making a team a good team, a player a good player. You have to have a knack of knowing where the ball is going to be. You have to have a knack of anticipating what is a fake and what isn't a fake.

For instance, when I'm guarding a guy I won't look at his eyes, because I found that I get faked out too easily that way. So I just watch his midsection, because I know wherever the midsection goes, the rest has got to follow because that's the main part of his body. Little things like that go toward making things happen on the floor.

You operate in the backcourt with Oscar Robertson, and perhaps unfortunately anyone who does that automatically becomes known as the "Other Guard." Tom Van Arsdale was the "Other Guard" with Oscar at Cincinnati and said it was a great learning experience.

That's true. Oscar has made me aware of many things, yet

278

Oscar isn't a guy that goes and says, "Hey, Lucius, you should do this, that, and the other." He doesn't teach that way. He teaches you by what he does on the floor. For instance, there was a game in last year's playoffs against Golden State where Nate Thurmond had five fouls on him. Me, I didn't know that when Nate Thurmond has five fouls and the game is close you go in to Kareem, and you penetrate, and you try to get another foul on Nate. But I see Oscar with the ball and I'm hammering, hollering, and yelling, saying: "I'm open! Let me have it! Let me have it! Let me have this shot!" Instead, he drives in and creates a situation to try and force Nate Thurmond to make an error.

He knows. It's amazing how he knows the number of fouls everybody has on the floor, even the substitutes. He knows what the guy likes to do. Certain ballplayers prefer to go right. Certain ballplayers prefer to go left. Personally, I prefer to go right, and in practice I wonder: How does Oscar always manage to get in my way? Well, he has observed me play, and he knows what I like to do, so he anticipates that, and forces me to do something I don't want to do. So now I know that I must do that to others.

These things I never thought about as a basketball player myself until I was forced to think about them with Oscar. In practice, he does so many things. He is just such a great leader that you don't have to go and ask questions to learn. You can become the "Other Guard," and rightly so, because there is so much that he knows about the game and other ball players that I would never even think about.

He definitely has helped me in many areas as far as consistent shooting. In my "Before Oscar" years, when I was with Seattle and part of my first year here with Milwaukee, I used to watch Oscar play, and I would say: "Well dang! How does he make that shot every time?" I found out what he does. He dribbles before he shoots. He never catches the ball and just shoots it right up. And I say: "Wow, let me try that." So I go out and I'm shooting about 45 percent from the field when I was with Seattle, and I come here and observe Oscar and I find out now that I've become a 50 percent shooter. I've become known around the league as a good shooting guard, and I know I can hit an open shot eight or nine times out of ten because I have a chance to take a dribble. Even though I may have a hand in my face I know they'll have to foul me to block my shot.

Before I used to rush things. I used to say, "Dang! Here he comes. Let me hurry and get it off so he won't block it—"

Didn't care if you made it. Just had to get it off.

Right! Right! Because growing up, the worst thing in the world that can happen to you in the school grounds is to get your shot blocked. All the other guys go, "Hey! Hey!" Booing, cheering, yelling, the whole thing. So you tend to not want to get your shot blocked. You don't care if you make it. You just want to get it off as pretty as you can.

The art of good shooting is really just concentrating on the basket and putting the ball in the air. And I've started to do this. I observed Oscar. And he told me one day. We were in practice and I shot wide open and missed, and he said: "Take a dribble." That was it; "take a dribble," and I haven't heard him tell me anything else about shooting since then, but I watch him warming up on the floor and he might not miss three shots in an entire warmup because he's sitting there, and he's concentrating so hard about it going in, like a machine.

Watching our local high school games I've always thought that one of the flaws of certain players is that they would get the ball under the basket and dribble before they shot. Wilt would do the same thing. Doesn't it often simply permit the defense to collapse around you?

There are times on the floor when you don't have time to take the dribble. But the consistent shooters—Jerry West, Walt Frazier, Earl Monroe, Pete Maravich—take a dribble and then they let loose. Now forward is a different position. Forward is a position where you are always on the move, always doing something, so you are only going to be open for

280

a fraction of a second. Dave DeBusschere never takes a dribble. Bobby Dandridge never takes a dribble. They just catch it and shoot it and consequently they aren't as good shooters as say an Oscar Robertson or a Walt Frazier, because they don't have the time to sit there and set and take the good one, go into their machine bit.

Now you get them in a one-on-one game and you could never tell, because they actually can shoot better than anybody. But statistically you'll find the Walt Fraziers and Oscar Robertsons are going to take the dribble and get their shot off.

A number of the interviews I've done for this book have been with former UCLA players: Gail Goodrich, Sidney Wicks, Swen Nater, Steve Patterson, yourself. If you had taken all those former UCLA players and funneled them into a single professional club, would you be able to clean everybody out?

I don't know if we could clean everybody out, but we would have an exceptionally good team. In fact, it was tried last summer. There is a guy in the ABA who felt he should get all the new UCLA ball players together, all the old UCLA ball players together, and make one great professional team. It wouldn't be a minor league operation at all, because in the past decade the UCLA players have dominated the basketball scene—not on the professional level as much as on the college level, but still more than any other institution.

We thought that it would be a great idea. We thought we would win every game. It would be impossible for us to lose. However, last summer at the Ralph Bunche memorial game—which is to provide scholarships for blacks to attend UCLA—we got our team together. We had Gail Goodrich, Abdul-Rahman, myself, Sidney Wicks, Curtis Rowe, Kareem, Swen Nater, Henry Bibby. The other team had Connie Hawkins, Julius Erving, Mack Calvin, Curtis Perry, a number of others. They had a pretty good team and they just ran us off the floor. So we found we wouldn't win *every* game, but we felt we would win most of them. It may be an ego thing for UCLA graduates, but we tend to think that as ball players *we* are sort of the cream of the crop. We like to think that even though it might not be true.

A lot of people have the opinion that you could take Kareem Abdul-Jabbar and put him on the court with four people off the street and still win ball games.

Uh, yes. I think another ball player by the name of Bob Love made a statement like that and Bobby Dandridge showed him that you can't throw just any ball player out here and win. I think Abdul-Jabbar is an awesome force in basketball; however, I *know* that he can be defensed, and if he doesn't have the correct supporting cast, his team wouldn't win 50 percent of their games. I don't think you can take people off the street and make a championship caliber team. You aren't going to win the championship every year anyway, especially in this league, but to have a team that's going to be up there year in, year out, you need balance.

Abdul-Jabbar is the main man as far as basketball is concerned, but he can't beat five guys. When a team is sagging on Kareem, it tends to stop his team from getting layups because everybody is in the middle. So first of all, you have to have guys that are going to be able to penetrate, change the tempo of the game. You also are going to need guys who take perimeter jump shots without the dribble. You need guys who know when to shoot and when to get it in to the big fellow. You must have guys who are complete ballplayers in every aspect of the game, because if they can't execute the fundamentals then Kareem would never get the ball. You can throw four guys out there and win some games, but not 50 percent.

I think it was proven here in Milwaukee. We needed a guy like Oscar Robertson, who was a legend in basketball, to come here in order for us to win a championship. And after Oscar leaves, it's going to put a premium on myself and the others to see if we can win without him. As good ball players as we are, we can't go out and do it unless all five are

282

involved, participating, and contributing. Basketball is a team game, and anyone who thinks you can put any four guys out there with Abdul-Jabbar and still win hasn't played with him and doesn't realize the problems involved in playing with such an awesome force in basketball.

What are the problems?

There is the problem that everybody knows what you are going to do, therefore we can be defensed. Teams come up and tell their center: "Well, we're going to give you a little help from this guy because his man doesn't shoot too well, then you are going to force Kareem out, beat him down the floor, and when you get there take away his position." It's awfully tough to maneuver to get Kareem into position to score, because he can't do it himself. He has to have guys cutting. We have to have movement to get him open. If guys don't respect my potential to hit the 15- or 20-foot jump shots, or respect Bobby Dandridge's ability to hit 15- or 20-foot jump shots, Kareem would never get the ball. The players on the other team have to respect us in order for Kareem to be as awesome as he is.

There is also the problem of defense. He is such a great force on defense that it tends to make you not want to work as hard, but then he has his games where he doesn't want to work as hard. In fact, this happens lots of times. You have to know what he's going to do in certain situations and it's a lot of hard work. Any team with an Abdul-Jabbar can be defensed, and it's going to take exceptional ability on the other guys' parts to pick holes in that defense. There are problems when it's not working. If Bobby and I aren't hitting the same night, then we are going to lose simply because Abdul-Jabbar cannot do it by himself.

Of course, Abdul-Jabbar is going to get his any night: his rebounds, his scoring. His statistics are always going to be a foot above everybody else's even if it doesn't look like he's doing anything, because I've seen him get 25 points in a half and it didn't look like he even scored. It was all layups and stuff. Those are the things that the other teams want to guard against. They don't want him to get the easy close shots, therefore they have to give up something elsewhere. It's then a matter of the other ball players realizing what it is. The coaches have to recognize what's not working, what the other team is doing, and consequently make changes to stop that defense. Yes, he can be contained, but I don't think that by containing him you contain the Bucks. To beat any team you have to exploit its weaknesses. This team doesn't have that many weaknesses, therefore we don't lose as many times as the weaker teams. However, we do have weaknesses, and I know what they are, and I would tell you, but I don't really want them to come out in a book. If I were a coach I know how I would go about beating us.

You destroyed my image of the combativeness of basketball players last night. When Milwaukee played in Chicago in March, it turned into a Pier 5 brawl. Yet, yesterday you were sitting on the bench near where the Bulls were warming up. Norm Van Lier came over and was joking and laughing with you. Bobby Weiss stopped by apparently to ask about your leg. It was like a reunion of the VFW. What happened to all the hatred that's supposed to be flowing between these two teams?

Norm Van Lier and I are intense competitors on the floor, but off the floor if we ever get a chance to get together we are the best of friends. The reason is that he played with Oscar, I played with Oscar. We came into the league at the same time and we have a lot of respect for each other's ability. Consequently we were friends when he wasn't a starter and I wasn't a starter. However, on this level of basketball, a guy has a job to do. For instance, against Norm Van Lier my job is to stop him from penetrating *any way that I can!* You know? I mean, I'm not going to go out and hurt Norman. I'm not going to go out and hurt anybody. And I don't think any of the Bulls would go out and purposely hurt somebody, simply because it could end that person's career, and basketball is

284

our livelihood, and we ball players have a lot of respect for the other ball player's livelihood. We know what it would be like for him not to have his job.

Now, in the heat of battle, everybody gets emotionally involved, and when your team is losing by a lot, or a little, you tend to be more emotionally involved than the other guy, therefore fights will break out. However, after it's all over you'll find that most basketball players who have a fight will go out and drink beer together and laugh and say, "What got into me?" For instance, Fritzie Williams and I had one of the biggest fights in the playoffs a couple of years ago, but we were best of friends before and we're best of friends now.

In basketball you have a job to do. For instance, I know what Norman Van Lier's strengths are. He knows what my strengths are, and he's going to try to take those strengths away on the floor any way he can. If that means getting emotionally upset on the floor, he's going to do that because that's his job. Consequently, it's going to be my job to do the same thing. If we don't live up to that, then first, we're not going to get the money we think we deserve, and second, there is the matter of pride. Yet I enjoy his company. In the summer I go to Chicago to visit him and he comes to visit me, but on the floor it's: "I don't like Norman Van Lier! I'm going to stop him! I'm not going to let him do what he wants to do!" He is the same way with me.

There's another parallel with chess. Even though you want to go out and kill this guy on the chess board and use any trick possible, you still can be friends. For instance, you may be losing, but you aren't going to give up because you possibly might get a stalemate out of the game even though he has so much more material than you. After the game you're shaking hands: "That was a great game. I enjoyed it. Let's talk about it." Basketball players do the same thing.

I don't know if Kareem would be too eager to shake hands with Dennis Awtrey. When they lined up against each other in last night's game, you could almost see the electricity. On the next play Kareem led the fast break down the floor.

Kareem is the type person who is off to himself. Because of maybe some emotional things that might have happened to him in his childhood, he tends to think people are always trying to abuse him, always trying to misuse him one way or another. Consequently, I think something possibly will still happen with him and Awtrey, because he has that intense desire to get even. If he saw Dennis Awtrey on the street, he probably wouldn't speak to him, but he certainly wouldn't run over and jump on him. The time for him to do that would be on the basketball floor, in front of the people who saw Dennis Awtrey hit him. I'm still apprehensive about that situation because I think it's explosive. Knowing the type of person Abdul-Jabbar is, something definitely still can happen, but I don't think he will be out there to hurt anybody maliciously. He's not plotting how to get him.

[Lucius Allen and I were talking at the Milwaukee Arena on a Wednesday afternoon, a day between playoff games. On the court the Bucks were involved in an intensive practice session with Coach Larry Costello shouting instructions to the players.]

What about the level of coaching in the NBA? You've played for some pretty fair coaches: Johnny Wooden, now Larry Costello. But the players are so accomplished when they become pros, how much coaching do they actually need to do?

At other levels of basketball—Johnny Wooden in college and Walt Shublon who was my high school coach—they were more like teachers. Some guys had the fundamentals, but most had to be taught, whereas on the professional level Larry Costello doesn't have time to teach the ball players. If the player doesn't have it by the time he's old enough for the pros, then he isn't going to be a pro. So Costello doesn't attempt to teach you; he directs his attention to preparation. *(Lucius pointed toward the court where the Bucks stood motionless while Costello talked with Ron Williams.)* Now, what he's doing out here is he's giving instructions as to what is necessary for us to do in the playoffs. He's telling Fritzie what Van Lier

286

likes to do: He likes to go left. He likes to penetrate, and if you want to stop him, you're going to have to play him tight. You're going to have to play him physically. You're going to have to keep a hand on him.

Those are the things that coaches tell you on the professional level. Even if they tell you to do it, you may not get it done on the floor. In college, if you don't do what the coach is teaching, he'll take you out of the game. Here the coach can't afford to do that simply because the ball players are used to playing with Oscar, Fritzie, Bobby, Cornell, and Kareem. That's our best team out there and it has been proved over the season. If he yanks a man and puts someone else in, the team suffers. The man taken out also suffers. Egos are on such a level here that it could ruin him for a series, and a professional coach cannot afford that. So you try to get them to do the things you feel will make you win, and if they do them and you win, the coach is right. If you lose, it's up to the coach to make adjustments. If he tells you to go out and do something and you don't do it, they have films at this level and they'll show you: "We told you to do this and you did that." This is where the coaching is different than it was in college.

Coaching on the professional level depends more on getting along with the ball players and giving them confidence in your way. Convince them that your way is the way to get it down. This is how the professional coach gets the job done, whereas in college it's more a dictatorship. You are going to do it, or else. It's definitely on a different level, and it places more of a premium on the professional coach's personality and what he thinks is important, whether the team should lose a few to get something accomplished, or should they risk ruining somebody's ego by sitting him on the bench for three weeks. There are tougher decisions to make on this level than on the collegiate level.

Well, it's certainly a fascinating game.

Yes, it is. Yes, it is. And the more I get into it, the more I find that there is to learn. Right now I love to have rookies coming into the league on me. I know how Oscar Robertson felt the first time I came in and tried to guard him when I was with the Seattle Supersonics. Yet I can't tell how he feels now, even though I've gotten the years in. He still knows so much more than me that it's ridiculous. He has so many more tricks than I have so far as getting done what he wants gotten done. It is amazing, and I mope that when I reach his level I have as much knowledge about the game. Or Larry Costello, who is not even playing. He knows and sees so many things on the floor more than what I see. I can't even comprehend all the things that might be running through his mind in the course of a game.

Glossary

ABA   Founded in 1967, the American Basketball Association is the second and smaller of the two major professional leagues. It contained ten teams in mostly medium-sized cities at the beginning of the 1973–74 season.

AD-LIB   In the theater an actor who ad-libs adds words not in the script. In basketball ad-lib refers to the act of moving the ball without using a set play. In other words, the players try to score by improvising.

AREA   Any portion of the court. In a set play a player may move to an "area" of the court either to get open for a shot or to draw his man with him so someone else can get open. Some defenses are predicated on keeping men from getting to areas from where they can score.

BACKBOARD   The backboard is the rectangular barrier behind the basket, measuring 6 feet by 4 feet. Originally all backboards were made out of wood and painted white, but most large arenas now use glass backboards to allow people sitting behind them to see the action.

BACKUP   The person who plays in reserve behind a starting player. A second-string center is more often referred to as a backup center.

BASE LINE   The out-of-bounds line beneath, and parallel with, each basket.

BASKET   The circular rim of metal, or "hoop," through which the basketball must be thrown to score. A net is attached to this rim. A team scores a "basket" (worth 2 points, or 3 for ABA long shots) when the ball goes through the rim.

BENCH   Football players sit on slablike, wooden benches at their games. Basketball players usually sit on more comfortable chairs, but those chairs collectively are still referred to by the term bench. *The* bench often is used to refer to a team's reserve strength, as in: "The Bulls have a good bench."

BIG GUY   Centers on NBA teams frequently are referred to as big guys. When anyone talks about *the* Big Guy, however, he means Kareem Abdul-Jabbar of the Milwaukee Bucks.

BLOCK   The act of knocking a shot down after it leaves a player's fingers.

BLOCKING The NBA Guide defines blocking as "personal contact which impedes the progress of an opponent." This is illegal in basketball and the opposite of charging.

BOARDS Short for backboards. It is also a slang expression for rebounds, as in: "Elmore had 17 boards in the game."

BOX, BOX OUT When a player positions his body between the basket and another player, he boxes him out. This should permit him to rebound a missed shot.

CENTER One of the three basic positions in basketball. Centers generally play toward the middle of the court, near the basket on both offense and defense. Usually this position is played by the tallest player on the team.

CENTER JUMP At the beginning of each period, the referee throws the ball up in the air above two players at center court to start play. They attempt to tip it to one of their teammates.

CHARGING When the player with the ball runs into a defensive man who has established position, it is called charging. The foul called is known as a charging violation. See: Blocking.

COLLAPSE A team in basketball that collapses does not necessarily start losing the game. It's a term used to describe a form of defense where the defending players sag back toward the inside giving the other team open long shots but prohibiting them from getting the ball inside for high percentage inside shots.

CORNER There are four corners on each court, the points where the side lines and base lines intersect. More specifically, *the* corner is the area near each actual corner. The forwards usually play in the corners.

COURT The field on which the game of basketball is played is known as a court. The equivalent expression for other sports would be field for football, track for auto racing, rink for ice hockey.

DOWNCOURT The other end of the court from where the basketball currently is. A player who begins to run toward the opponent's basket on a fast break is said to start downcourt.

DRIBBLE The act of bouncing the basketball with one hand. A player cannot advance the basketball more than one step unless he dribbles the ball.

DRIVE To dribble toward the basket with the ball.

DUNK A crowd-pleasing shot where a player able to reach above the basket literally crams the ball down through the net with one or two hands. This maneuver is illegal in college and high school basketball.

EXPANSION   What happens when a reasonably well-balanced professional league decides to become an unbalanced, but wealthier, league by adding a new team, or teams, in different cities. The league thus expands as the NBA did when it granted a franchise for a team in New Orleans in 1974. An "expansion draft" is held permitting the new franchise to pick players, usually second-string ones, from the established teams. Several million dollars will exchange hands. It usually takes an expansion team several years before it can compete on equal terms with the older and more experienced teams.

FAN   A breed of citizen who complains about any calls made against his team by referees, who boos all opposing players regardless of their race, religion, or national origin, and who pays $3 and up for this privilege.

FAST BREAK   The act of moving the ball down court before the other team can get back on defense. Usually a fast break results in the breaking team getting an easy shot near the basket.

FILLING THE LANE   There usually are three lanes, or running paths, on any well-disciplined fast break. The center lane is usually occupied by the player with the ball, probably a guard. The two outside lanes, or wings, are filled by two other players who run down court with the guard to spread the defense and perhaps receive a pass if the ball handler is covered. A player who takes part in the fast break on the wing is doing his job in "filling the lane." The final offensive participant in a fast break is the trailer, who runs down court behind the ball handler to rebound in case the shot is missed.

FINESSE   A bridge term where a player wins a trick by skillfully playing a low card. In basketball the term refers to the use of guile and skill, rather than brute physical ability, to get an open shot.

FLARE   In football a flare pattern is one where a running back angles quickly out of the backfield, usually moving at a 45-degree angle. Basketball players have borrowed this expression to describe the motion of a player who cuts at an angle for the sideline to take part in a fast break.

FORCING THE BALL   Taking a low percentage shot, one where

you either are heavily guarded or are too far from the basket. When one player tells another he is "forcing the ball," it is his diplomatic way of saying he is shooting too much.

FORWARD   One of the three basic positions in basketball. Forwards usually play in the corners of the court. They usually are taller than guards, but not quite as tall as the centers.

FREE-LANCE   A free-lance writer is one who is self-employed, like the author of this book. In basketball the term means the same as ad-lib: moving the basketball without a set pattern.

FREE THROW   When a player is fouled by another player, he usually is awarded one or more free throws depending on the rules which vary from year to year and league to league. The NBA Guide defines free throw as: "the privilege given to a player to score one point by an unhindered throw for goal from a position directly behind the free throw line."

FREE THROW LINE   The line from which free throws are shot. The free throw line is 19 feet from the base line, or 15 feet from the backboard.

FUNDAMENTALS   The basic unwritten rules by which you are able to play basketball skillfully and with a minimum of error. For instance: Dribble with your fingers, not your palms; shoot one-handed shots with back spin; don't pass cross court. You do not get penalized if you ignore "fundamentals," but you probably will not be as successful a basketball player without at least a knowledge of them.

GOALTENDING   A player who blocks a shot after it has begun its descent toward the basket, or who knocks the ball out while it is still on or above the rim, will be called for defensive goaltending. The offense gets credit for scoring a basket. This rule limits the abilities of big men to literally prevent the other team from scoring by simply batting away every ball shot near the basket. Most goaltending calls are made against the defense, but offensive goaltending can be called if an offensive player knocks the basketball into the basket while it is still on the rim. No basket is scored and the defense gets possession of the ball.

GUARD   One of the three basic positions in basketball. Guards usually play nearest mid-court on both offense and defense. They are the shortest men on the field since they do not have to play near the basket where height is essential. A guard's main duty on offense is to bring the ball down court and set the play in motion.

HAND CHECKING   In professional basketball, players often

place a hand on the man they're guarding so they can check his position without necessarily looking at him. At other levels of the game this would be called a foul, particularly if the player being checked had possession of the ball.

HIGH PERCENTAGE SHOT Any shot that you make more often than you miss. Layups and dunks are high percentage shots, because they should be made every time. Any open shot from within 15 or 20 feet is considered a high percentage shot since NBA players are so skilled they rarely miss those shots. The purpose of the offense is to see that the team gets a high, rather than low, percentage shot during the 24 seconds it has possession of the ball. See: low percentage shot, offense.

HIGH POST A position taken by an offensive player with his back to the basket and about 15–20 feet from that basket, usually up near the top of the free throw circle. See: post, low post.

HOLE Slang expression for the area immediately under the basket, the no-man's-land where the big men battle for rebounds once the ball is shot toward the basket.

HOME COURT The arena where a team plays in its home town. The Chicago Bulls play in the Chicago Stadium. The New York Knickerbockers play in Madison Square Garden.

HOME COURT ADVANTAGE For various intangible reasons, a team that plays on its home court is thought to have an advantage over a visiting team. It may partly be because of the support from its fans, who buoy their heroes to victory and perhaps even intimidate referees. Other factors involve a player's ability to eat regularly and sleep at home every night rather than climb on another airplane for a trip to another city. A home court advantage may be real or imagined.

HOOK A shot usually taken by centers near the basket. With their back to the basket they rotate their body and bring the basketball up with their arm in a long sweeping motion that sends the ball arching smoothly into the basket. It is a beautiful shot to watch when executed properly and is nearly impossible for the defender to block. Several decades ago centers used hook shots as practically their only weapon, but double-teaming and sagging defenses make this shot more difficult to get off today. Another variation of the term is when a defensive player grabs an offensive player going past him. He is sometimes said to have hooked him, as a fisherman might hook a fish.

HOOP Another name for the basket, also for the 2 points scored when a basket is made.

INSIDE   The area closest to the basket.

JUMP SHOT   A shot where a player jumps and shoots while hanging in mid-air. One reason for taking a jump shot is to get it off high enough so the defender cannot block it. When taken on the run, the purpose of the jump often is to allow the player to gather himself briefly before letting the shot go.

KEY   The arch-shaped area immediately in front of the basket at each end. While on offense, players can remain in this area for periods of only three seconds at a time. (See: three-second violation.) During free throw attempts players stand on each side of the key while the fouled player takes his shot.

LAYUP   A shot made from almost under the basket. The player usually bounces the ball off the backboard and into the basket. It is a shot that never should be missed.

LEAGUE   A group of individuals or organizations who gather together to promote activities of mutual interest. The NBA and ABA are professional basketball leagues.

LOOSE BALL FOUL   A foul committed while neither team has possession of the ball, usually while players are battling to get position for a rebound.

LOW PERCENTAGE SHOT   Any shot you miss more often than you make. See: high percentage shot, offense.

LOW POST   A position taken by an offensive player with his back to the basket near the base line on either side of the key. See: high post, post.

MAN-FOR-MAN   A style of defense where each defensive player is responsible for guarding an offensive player. The opposite of zone.

MATCHUP The relationship between two players as they guard each other, and also the relationship between one five-man team and another five-man team that permits one to have an edge over another. How players or teams match up against each other may determine their success. For example, a 6-foot 2-inch player may guard a 6-foot 6-inch player. In such a matchup, the tall player should have an easier time shooting over the smaller player. Or a fast breaking team may have difficulty when matched up against a slower team that rebounds very well. Often when one team appears to have a "jinx" on another team there is no magic involved, but only the way in which their players or styles of play match up to give one team an intangible edge.

MISMATCH A mismatch occurs when a small player finds himself guarding a taller player, as above. But often mismatches are created during games when an offensive team moves the ball and sets picks to force the defense to switch assignments. A short guard may suddenly find himself matched up with a tall forward or center. When that occurs, the offensive team tries to take advantage of the mismatch by passing the ball to their player so he can shoot over his smaller defender.

MOVES Anything a player does to get himself an open shot. He may fake with his head, his body, or the ball in order to make the defensive player believe he is going one way, then turn and go the opposite direction. Any ballplayer who is able to quickly get open for shot is said to have "moves."

NBA Founded in 1946 after several attempts to establish a professional basketball league, the National Basketball Association is the largest of the two major professional leagues. It contained 18 teams in the largest cities at the beginning of the 1974–75 season.

NET The open-ended meshed fabric hanging from each basket that deflects and delays the basketball's drop through the basket to make it easier for the referees to judge that a basket has been scored.

OFFENSE The team that has the ball is on offense. *The* offense refers to the art of moving the ball around to get an open shot, as in: "We have to rely on our offense to score."

ONE-ON-ONE One player with the ball attempting to maneuver for a shot while being guarded by one other player. Teams often have specific plays designed to clear out a side of the court so one of their players can go one-on-one. The advantage usually goes to the player attempting to score. When ABC Sports televised pro basketball during the 1971–72 and 1972–73 seasons, they produced a one-on-one tournament featuring NBA stars as a half-time diversion.

OPEN MAN An offensive player who temporarily has freed himself of his defender. Teams use pattern plays and set picks to get someone in the open. Dave DeBusschere of the New York Knicks helped popularize the expression in 1970 when he wrote a book (with Dick Schaap) following the Knicks championship season entitled *The Open Man.*

OPTION A choice. In offensive basketball most plays have options, so that if the defense overplays one man to stop the play the ball can go to another man, or the first man can cut in another direction to get open.

OUTLET PASS   A pass usually thrown by the center, who rebounds the ball, to a guard starting downcourt to start the fast break.

OUTSIDE   Any area of the court away from the basket.

OVERPLAY   To guard a player extremely tight. Or to guard him by playing to his strength, for instance guarding him on the right if he normally likes to dribble with that hand.

OVERTIME   If a game remains tied at the end of four quarters, the teams continue to play 5-minute overtime periods until one emerges a winner.

PASS   To throw the basketball to another player.

PASSING LANE   The path—or direct line between one player and another—in which a pass is made.

PATTERN OFFENSE   A system where a team brings the ball downcourt, pauses, calls a play, then runs that play with all five players knowing exactly what move they must make to maneuver the defense so that one of their teammates gets an open shot. The opposite of ad-lib and free-lance.

PENETRATE   A player, usually a guard, penetrates when he moves around the person guarding him and drives with the ball to a point near the basket where he either has an easy inside shot or can pass off to an open man.

PERIMETER   The outer area of the offensive court, in the NBA a more or less imaginary line beyond which most players probably won't shoot the ball even if they are open. In the ABA there is an actual semicircular line painted on the court 25 feet from the basket. Any shots made from beyond this line score 3 points instead of only 2.

PERSONAL FOUL   According to the ABA *Guide:* "a personal foul is a foul which involves contact with an opponent."

PHYSICAL   Being "physical" means pushing, shoving, holding, playing right on the edge of committing a foul. A physical ballplayer in the pros is not necessarily a dirty ballplayer.

PICK   An offensive player sets a pick when he positions himself on the court in such a way that a player trying to guard one of the other offensive players must bump into him. The defensive player then is said to have been picked. The player who sets the pick must remain stationary, otherwise he may get called for a blocking foul. The same as "screen," for which the NBA Guide

296

definition is: "A legal action of a player who, without causing undue contact, delays or prevents an opponent from reaching a desired position."

PICK AND ROLL   A basic basketball maneuver involving the pick (see above). If the defensive player decides to switch with a teammate instead of fighting his way through the pick and following his man cross court, he may find himself guarding a much taller player. The result is a mismatch. That taller player then can run (or roll) toward the basket to receive a pass for an easy layup.

PIVOT   According to the ABA Guide, "A pivot takes place when a player who is holding the ball steps once or more than once in any direction with the same foot, the other foot being kept at its point of contact with the floor. *The* pivot usually refers to the center position since most plays rotate (or pivot) around the center.

PLAY   As in football, a pattern of movements by the offensive team designed to result in a score.

PLAYMAKER   Any member of the team who sets an offensive play into motion. Ordinarily one player on the team, the guard who brings the ball downcourt, has the responsibility for calling, and starting, the play.

POSITION   The place where a player stands on the floor. Also the job that the player has on the team, as: guard, forward, center. But more often the term is used to describe a condition where one player has an advantage over the other, as: "He has position on him."

POST   To take an offensive position near the basket with your back to it. An offensive player is said to "post" his man when he takes such a position. See: high post, low post.

PRESSURE   Anything you can do defensively without drawing a foul is known as "pressure." Usually it refers to the act of a defender in very firmly shoving his opponent away from the basket. See: physical.

QUARTER   Each professional basketball game is divided into four 12-minute periods, known as quarters. Two quarters make a half. Two halves make a complete game, unless the score is tied and an overtime results.

RANGE   The effective distance from which a player can hit a basket more often than he misses it.

REBOUND   A basketball that bounces back into play after failing to go through the basket rebounds. The player who leaps and gathers in that basketball is said to have gotten a rebound.

REFEREE   The individual in the gray or striped shirt who makes all those incredibly bad calls against your team when they're losing.

RELEASE   What happens when a team goes from defense to offense, particularly when it involves a fast break. The players are, in effect, "released" from their defensive responsibilities and start (or release) downcourt, hopefully to receive a quick outlet pass that will enable them to score an easy basket. Release also refers to the act of shooting the ball, as in: "He has a fast release on his shot."

ROOKIE   A first-year player.

SCREEN   See: pick.

SET PLAY   A play in which the patterns of the offensive players are established in advance. See: pattern offense.

SIDELINE   The line that establishes out-of-bounds at the side of the court.

SKY HOOK   Specifically a hook shot by Kareem Abdul-Jabbar of the Milwaukee Bucks. It is an expression coined originally by Bucks' broadcaster Eddie Doucette, referring to the altitude from which Jabbar (being 7 feet 4) releases his hook.

STAT SHEET   The list of field goals, free throws, rebounds, assists, and other numerical data (statistics) that are mimeographed immediately after the game for circulation to the press.

STATISTICS   The numerical data related to the game (see above) that you use to prove that your team should have won that game.

STEAL   To take the ball away from another player.

STEPS   A player with the ball cannot move more than one foot without bouncing (dribbling) the ball. If he does so and the referee notices, he is called for steps, also known as traveling or walking.

STRONG SIDE   The side of the court on which the player with the ball happens to be standing. The opposite side is known as the weak side. If the player moves with the ball to that side, then it becomes the strong side.

STUFF   The act of shooting a dunk shot, where the player, usually a tall center, stuffs the ball through the basket instead of shooting it. See: dunk.

298

SWING GUARD   A guard who moves without the ball and thus functions on offense much like a third forward.

SWITCH   Two defensive players guarding their men man-to-man often will switch and take the other's man if they happen to cross. A switching defense is one in which the players do a lot of switching rather than staying on their men.

TECHNICAL FOUL   A foul that usually is called on someone for arguing too vehemently with the referee. According to the ABA *Guide:* "A technical foul is a foul which doesn't involve contact with an opponent and can be assessed against a nonplayer as well as a player. The other team gets to shoot one free throw and retains possession of the ball. Anyone who receives a technical call is fined $50 and if he receives a second technical call, he has to leave the arena."

TEMPO   The rate of speed or pace at which a team plays the game.

TEN-SECOND LINE   The same as the mid-court line. Once the team throws the ball in bounds from their defensive court, they have 10 seconds to cross that line into their offensive court, or they lose possession.

THREE-POINT LINE   The ABA credits a player with 3 points for a basket shot from more than 25 feet. A semicircular line is painted on the court to identify this scoring zone.

THREE-POINT PLAY   A play in which a player hits a basket, is fouled, and makes the following free throw resulting in 3 points being scored for his team.

THREE-SECOND VIOLATION   Offensive players are permitted to remain in the key-shaped area in front of the basket for three seconds at a time before their team shoots. If they remain in longer, their team loses possession of the ball. See: key.

TIP   The act of rebounding the ball one-handed up into the basket.

TRAILER   A player who follows his teammate, or teammates, driving down court on a fast break.

TRAVELING   See steps.

TURN-AROUND JUMPER   A jump shot in which the player shooting it begins with his back to the basket.

UPCOURT   For all practical purposes, the same as downcourt. The other court from the one you're in.

WEAK SIDE   The side of the offensive court opposite where the ball is. See: strong side.

WHIRLPOOL BATH What players climb into after playing a game against a physical opponent. Actually it is a hot water tub fitted with a high-pressure water circulating device used to soothe sore muscles and treat injuries.

WING The position of the player or players filling the outside lanes on the fast break.

ZONE A form of defense where each defensive player is responsible for a certain area of the floor rather than one man. Zone is the opposite of man-for-man. It is a style of defense that (at least in theory) is illegal in pro basketball for a simple, practical reason: It forces teams to take long shots, eliminating the rough, inside play that seems most popular with the crowds. According to the ABA *Guide:* "A team is considered in a zone when one or more defensive players protect or defends an area and does not guard an individual player." In actual practice most teams with large centers (Milwaukee with Kareem Abdul-Jabbar, Kentucky with Artis Gilmore) violate the letter, if not the spirit, of that rule.